CONCURRENT PROGRAMMING IN ML

Concurrent Programming in ML presents the language Concurrent ML (CML), which supports the union of two important programming models: concurrent programming and functional programming. CML is an extension of the functional language Standard ML (SML) and is included as part of the Standard ML of New Jersey (SML/NJ) distribution. CML supports the programming of process communication and synchronization using a unique higher-order concurrent programming mechanism which allows programmers to define their own communication and synchronization abstractions.

The main focus of the book is on the practical use of concurrency to implement naturally concurrent applications. In addition to a tutorial introduction to programming in CML, this book presents three extended examples of using CML for systems programming: a parallel software build system, a simple concurrent window manager, and an implementation of distributed tuple spaces.

This book includes a chapter on the implementation of concurrency using features provided by the SML/NJ system and provides many examples of advanced SML programming techniques. The appendices include the CML reference manual and a formal semantics of CML.

This book is aimed at programmers and professional developers who want to use CML, as well as students, faculty, and other researchers.

CONCURRENT PROGRAMMING IN ML

JOHN H. REPPY

Bell Labs, Lucent Technologies, Murray Hill, New Jersey

CAMBRIDGE
UNIVERSITY PRESS

CAMBRIDGE
UNIVERSITY PRESS

32 Avenue of the Americas, New York NY 10013-2473, USA

Cambridge University Press is part of the University of Cambridge.

It furthers the University's mission by disseminating knowledge in the pursuit of education, learning and research at the highest international levels of excellence.

www.cambridge.org
Information on this title: www.cambridge.org/9780521480895

First published 1999

A catalogue record for this publication is available from the British Library

Library of Congress Cataloguing in Publication data
Reppy, John H.
Concurrent programming in ML John H. Reppy.
p.   cm.
Includes bibliographical references.
ISBN 0 521 48089 2 hardback
1. ML (Computer program language)   2. Parallel processing
(Electronic computers)   I. Title.
QA76.73.M6R47   1999
005.2'752 – dc21   99-20465
                                                            CIP

ISBN 978-0-521-48089-5 Hardback
ISBN 978-0-521-71472-3 Paperback

Contents

Preface

This book is about the union of two important paradigms in programming languages, namely, *higher-order* languages and *concurrent* languages. Higher-order programming languages, often referred to as *"functional programming"* languages,[1] are languages that support functions as first-class values. The language used here is the popular higher-order language *Standard ML* (**SML**) [MTH90, MTHM97], which is the most prominent member of the **ML** family of languages. In particular, the bulk of this book focuses on concurrent programming using the language *Concurrent ML* (**CML**), which extends **SML** with independent processes and higher-order communication and synchronization primitives. The power of **CML** is that a wide range of communication and synchronization abstractions can be programmed using a small collection of primitives.

A concurrent program is composed from two or more sequential programs, called *processes*, that execute (at least conceptually) in parallel. The sequential part of the execution of these processes is independent, but they also must interact via shared resources in order to collaborate on achieving their common purpose. In this book, we are concerned with the situation in which the concurrency and process interaction are explicit. This is in contrast with implicitly parallel languages, such as parallel functional languages [Hud89, Nik91, PvE93] and concurrent logic programming languages [Sha89]. The choice of language mechanisms used for process interaction is the key issue in concurrent programming language design. In this aspect, **CML** takes the unique approach of supporting *higher-order concurrent programming*, in which the communication and synchronization operations are first-class values, in much the same way that functions are first-class values in higher-order languages.

Concurrent programming is an especially important technique in the construction of systems software. Such software must deal with the unpredictable sequencing of external events, often from multiple sources, which is difficult to manage in sequential languages.

---

[1] I choose the term "higher-order" to avoid confusion with "pure" (*i.e.*, referentially transparent) functional languages.

Structuring a program as multiple threads of control, one for each external agent or event, greatly improves the modularity and manageability of the program. Concurrent programming replaces the artificial total ordering of execution imposed by sequential languages by a more natural partial ordering. The resulting program is nondeterministic, but this is necessary to deal with a nondeterministic external world efficiently.

This book differs from most books on concurrent programming in that the underlying sequential language, **SML**, is a higher-order language. The use of **SML** as the sequential sub-language has a number of advantages. **SML** programs tend to be "mostly-functional" and typically do not rely on heavy use of global state; this reduces the effort needed to migrate from a sequential to a concurrent programming style. The high-level features of **SML**, such as datatypes, pattern matching, the module system, and garbage collection, provide a more concise programming notation. Recent advances in implementation technology allow us to take advantage of the benefits of **SML**, without sacrificing good performance [SA94, Sha94, TMC$^+$96]. One of the theses of this book is that efficient system software can be written in a language such as **SML**.

History

The language design ideas presented in this book date back to the language **PML** [Rep88], an **ML** dialect developed at AT&T Bell Laboratories as part of the **Pegasus** system [RG86, GR92]. The purpose of the **Pegasus** project was to provide a better foundation for building interactive systems than that provided by the C/UNIX world circa 1985. We believed then, and still do, that interactive applications are inherently concurrent, and that they should be programmed in a concurrent language. This was the motivation for designing a concurrent programming language. We finished an implementation of the **Pegasus** run-time system before the design of **PML** was complete. We tested our ideas on this run-time system by writing prototype applications in **C** with calls to our concurrency library. Our experience with these applications convinced us that the concurrency features of **PML** should be designed to support abstraction. It was this design goal that led me to develop "first-class synchronous operations" [Rep88].

Shortly thereafter, I began a graduate program at Cornell University, and started working with early versions of Standard ML of New Jersey (**SML/NJ**) [AM87, AM91]. In the spring of 1989, Appel and Jim developed a new back-end for **SML/NJ**, based on a *continuation-passing style* representation [AJ89, App92]. A key feature of this back-end is that the program stack was replaced by heap-allocated return closures. In the fall of 1989, this led to the addition of first-class continuations as a language extension in **SML/NJ** [DHM91], which made it possible to implement concurrency primitives directly in **SML**. Exploiting this feature, I implemented a coroutine version of the **PML** primitives on top of **SML/NJ** [Rep89]. Others also exploited the first-class continuations provided by **SML/NJ**: Ramsey, at Princeton, implemented **PML**-like primitives [Ram90], and Cooper and Morrisett, at Carnegie-Mellon, implemented **Modula 2+** style shared-memory primitives [CM90]. Morrisett and Tolmach later implemented a multiprocessor version of low-level shared-memory primitives [MT93].

While first-class continuations provided an important mechanism for implementing concurrency primitives, they did not provide a mechanism for preemptive scheduling, which is key to supporting modular concurrent programming. To address this problem, I added support for UNIX style signal handling to the **SML/NJ** run-time system [Rep90]. With this support, I modified my coroutine version of the **PML** primitives to include preemptive scheduling, and the first version of **CML** was born. It was released in November of 1990. This implementation evolved into the version of **CML** that was described in the first published paper about **CML** [Rep91a], and was the subject of my doctoral dissertation [Rep92]. In February of 1993, version 0.9.8 of **CML** was released as part of the **SML/NJ** distribution. After that release, a major effort was undertaken to redesign the Basis Library provided by **SML** implementations [GR04]. This effort grew into what is now known as *Standard ML 1997* (**SML**'97), which includes the new basis library, as well as a number of language improvements and simplifications. From the programmer's perspective, the most notable of these changes is the elimination of imperative type variables and the introduction of new primitive types for characters and machine words [MTHM97]. **CML** has also been overhauled to be compatible with **SML**'97 and the new Basis Library, and to use more uniform naming conventions. Although some of the names have changed since version 0.9.8, the core features and concepts are the same. Most recently, Riccardo Pucella has ported **CML** to run on Microsoft's Windows NT operating system.

Since its introduction, **CML** has been used by many people around the world. Uses include experimental telephony software [FO93], as a target language for a concurrent constraint programming language [Pel92], as a basis for distributed programming [Kru93], and for programming dataflow networks [Čub94b, Čub94a]. My own use of **CML** has focused on the original motivation of the **Pegasus** work: providing a foundation for user interface construction. Emden Gansner and I have constructed a multithreaded **X Window System** toolkit, called **eXene**, which is implemented entirely in **CML** [GR91, GR93].

CML has also been the focus of a fair bit of theoretical work. The semantics of the **PML** subset of the language has been formalized in several different ways [BMT92, MM94, FHJ96]. My dissertation also presents a full semantics of the **CML** concurrency mechanisms [Rep91b, Rep92] (Appendix B presents this semantics, but without the proofs). Nielson and Nielson have worked on analyzing the communication patterns (or *topology*) of **CML** programs [NN93, NN94] as well as on control-flow analysis for **CML** [GNN97]. Such analysis can be used to specialize communication operations to provide better performance.

While **CML** is not likely to change, there will continue to be improvements and enhancements to its implementation. The most important improvement is to provide the benefits of kernel-level threads to **CML** applications (*e.g.*, to mask the latency of system calls). To provide these benefits requires a new run-time system, which is under construction as of this writing. This new run-time system should also make a multiprocessor implementation of **CML** possible. The other major effort is to build useful libraries, particularly in the area of distributed programming and network applications. The **CML** home page (see below) will provide information about these, and other, improvements as they become available.

Getting the software

The **SML/NJ** system, **CML**, **eXene**, and other related software are all available, free of charge, on the internet.

Information about the latest and greatest version of **CML**, as well as user documentation, technical papers, and the sample code from this book can be found at the *Concurrent ML* home page:

> `http://cml.cs.uchicago.edu/index.html`

CML is also available as part of the **SML/NJ** distribution, which can be found at the **SML/NJ** home page:

> `http://smlnj.org/index.html`

This page also provides links to the **SML/NJ** Library documentation and to the online version of the *Standard ML Basis Library* manual.

Overview of the book

This book was written with several purposes in mind. The primary purpose of this book is to promote the use of **CML** as a concurrent language; it provides not only a tutorial introduction to the language, but also examples of more advanced uses. Although it is not designed as a teaching text, this book does provide an introduction to Concurrent Programming, and drafts of it have been used in courses at various universities. Because of the strong typing of **SML** and the choice of concurrency primitives, **CML** provides a friendlier introduction to concurrent programming than in many other languages. **CML** also provides a good example of systems programming using **SML/NJ**, and I hope that this book will inspire other non-traditional uses of the language. This book does not make an attempt to introduce or describe **SML**, as there are a number of books and technical reports that already fill that purpose; a list of these can be found in the Chapter 1 notes (and on the **SML/NJ** home page).

The book is loosely organized into three parts: an introduction to concurrent programming, an expository description of **CML** (essentially a **CML** tutorial), and finally, a practicum consisting of example applications.

The first chapter motivates the rest of the book by arguing the merits of concurrent programming. Chapter 2 introduces various concepts and issues in concurrent programming and concurrent programming languages.

The next four chapters focus on the design and use of **CML**. First, Chapters 3 and 4 give a tutorial introduction to the basic **CML** features and programming techniques. Chapter 5 expands on this discussion by exploring various synchronization and communication abstractions. Finally, Chapter 6 describes the rationale for the design of **CML**; this chapter is mainly intended for those interested in language design issues, and may be skipped by the casual reader.

The subsequent three chapters present extended examples of **CML** programs. While space restrictions constrain the scope of these examples, each is a representative of a natural application area for concurrent programming. Furthermore, they provide examples of complete **CML** programs, rather than just program fragments. Chapter 7 describes a controller for a simple parallel software-build system. This illustrates the use of concurrency to manage parallel system-level processes. The next example, in Chapter 8, is a toy concurrent window manager, which illustrates the use of concurrency in user interface software. Chapter 9 describes an implementation of distributed tuple spaces. This provides both an illustration of how a distributed systems interface might fit into the **CML** framework, and how systems programming can be done in **SML** and **CML**.

The book concludes with a chapter on the implementation of concurrency in **SML/NJ** using its *first-class continuations*. **SML/NJ** provides a fairly unique test-bed for experimenting in concurrent language design, and this chapter provides a "how-to" guide for such experimentation.

There are two appendices, which provide a more concise description of **CML**. Appendix A is an abridged version of the *CML Reference Manual*; the complete manual is available from the **CML** home page. Appendix B gives an operational semantics for the concurrency features of **CML**, along with statements of some of its properties (proofs can be found in my dissertation [Rep92]).

Citations and a discussion of related work are collected in "**Notes**" sections at the end of each chapter. These notes also provide some historical context. The text is illustrated with numerous examples; the source code for most of these is available from the **CML** home page.

Acknowledgements

This book has taken a long time for me to write, and many people have helped along the way. Foremost, I would like to thank my wife, book coach, and primary proofreader, Anne Rogers. Without her encouragement, I doubt this book would have been finished. My graduate advisor at Cornell University, Tim Teitelbaum, provided support for the research that produced **CML**.[2] Andrew Appel and Dave MacQueen encouraged me to start this project, and have helped with implementation issues.

In addition to Anne, a number of other people provided feedback on portions of the text. Emden Gansner and Lorenz Huelsbergen performed the second pass of proofreading on many of the chapters. Greg Morrisett provided detailed feedback about Chapter 10, and Jon Riecke helped with the semantics in Appendix B. Nick Afshartous, Lal George, Prakash Panangaden, and Chris Stone also provided feedback on various parts of the book. Riccardo Pucella has helped with recent versions of the **CML** implementation, including the Windows NT port. I would also like to thank my editor at Cambridge University Press, Lauren Cowles, for her patience with this book — I hope the final result was worth the wait. I would also like to thank the many users of **CML**, who found those pesky bugs and used the language in ways that I never envisioned.

John H. Reppy
Murray Hill, NJ

---

[2]While a graduate student at Cornell, I was supported, in part, by the NSF and ONR under NSF grant CCR-85-14862, and by the NSF under NSF grant CCR-89-18233.

Legend

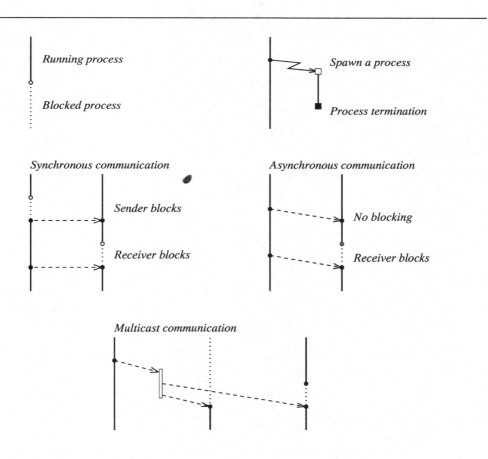

Running process

Blocked process

Spawn a process

Process termination

Synchronous communication

Sender blocks

Receiver blocks

Asynchronous communication

No blocking

Receiver blocks

Multicast communication

1

Introduction

Concurrent programming is the task of writing programs consisting of multiple independent threads of control, called processes. Conceptually, we view these processes as executing in parallel, but in practice their execution may be interleaved on a single processor. For this reason, we distinguish between concurrency in a programming language, and parallelism in hardware. We say that operations in a program are *concurrent* if they can be executed in parallel, and we say that operations in hardware are *parallel* if they overlap in time.

Operating systems, where there is a need to allow useful computation to be done in parallel with relatively slow input/output (I/O) operations, provide one of the earliest examples of concurrency. For example, during its execution, a program P might write a line of text to a printer by calling the operating system. Since this operation takes a relatively long time, the operating system initiates it, suspends P, and starts running another program Q. Eventually, the output operation completes and an *interrupt* is received by the operating system, at which point it can resume executing P. In addition to introducing parallelism and hiding latency, as in the case of slow I/O devices, there are other important uses of concurrency in operating systems. Using interrupts from a hardware interval timer, the operating system can multiplex the processor among a collection of user programs, which is called *time-sharing*. Most time-sharing operating systems allow user programs to interact, which provides a form of user-level concurrency. On multiprocessors, the operating systems are, by necessity, concurrent programs; furthermore, application programs may use concurrent programming to exploit the parallelism provided by the hardware.

One important motivation for concurrent programming is that processes are a useful abstraction mechanism: they provide encapsulation of state and control with well-defined interfaces. Unfortunately, if the mechanisms for concurrent programming are too expensive, then programmers will break the natural abstraction boundaries in order to ensure acceptable performance. The concurrency provided by operating system processes is the most widespread mechanism for concurrent programming. But, there are several disadvantages with using system-level processes for concurrent programming: they are expensive to create and require substantial memory resources, and the mechanisms for interprocess communication are cumbersome and expensive.[1] As a result, even when faced with a naturally concurrent task, application programmers often choose complex sequential solutions to avoid the high costs of system-level processes.

Concurrent programming languages, on the other hand, provide notational support for concurrent programming, and generally provide lighter-weight concurrency, often inside a single system-level process. Thus, just as efficient subroutine linkages make procedural abstraction more acceptable, efficient implementations of concurrent programming languages make process abstraction more acceptable.

1.1   Concurrency as a structuring tool

This book focuses on the use of concurrent programming for applications with naturally concurrent structure. These applications share the property that flexibility in the scheduling of computation is required. Whereas sequential languages force a total order on computation, concurrent languages permit a partial order, which provides the needed flexibility.

For example, consider the **xrn** program, which is a popular UNIX program that provides a graphical user interface for reading network news. It is both an example of an interactive application and of a distributed-systems application, since it maintains a connection to a remote news server. This program has a rather annoying "feature" that is a result of its being programmed in a sequential language.[2] If **xrn** loses its connection to the remote news server (because the server goes down, or the connection times out), it displays a message window (or "*dialog box*") on the screen to inform the user of the lost connection. Unfortunately, after putting up the window, but before writing the message, **xrn** attempts to reestablish the connection, which causes it to hang until the server comes back on line. Thus, you have the phenomenon of a blank message window appearing on the user's screen, followed by a long pause, followed by the simultaneous display of two messages: the first saying that the connection has been lost, and a second saying that the connection has been restored. Besides being an example of poor interface design, this illustrates the kind of sequential orderings that concurrent programming easily avoids.

---

[1] It should be noted that most recent operating systems provide support for multiple threads of control inside a single protection domain.

[2] This anecdote refers to version 6.17 of **xrn**.

1.1.1 Interactive systems

Interactive systems, such as graphical user interfaces and window managers, are the primary motivation of much of the work described in this book, and the author believes that they are one of the most important application areas for concurrent programming. Interactive systems are typically programmed in sequential languages, which results in awkward program structures, since these programs are naturally concurrent. They must deal with multiple asynchronous input streams and support multiple contexts, while maintaining responsiveness. In the following discussion, we present a number of scenarios that demonstrate the naturally concurrent structure of interactive software.

User interaction

Handling user input is the most complex aspect of an interactive program. An application may be sensitive to multiple input devices, such as a mouse and keyboard, and may multiplex these among multiple input contexts (*e.g.*, different windows). Managing this many-to-many mapping is usually the province of *User Interface Management System* (UIMS) toolkits. Since most UIMS toolkits are implemented in sequential languages, they must resort to various techniques to emulate the necessary concurrency. Typically, these toolkits use an *event-loop* that monitors the stream of input events and maps the events to *call-back* functions (or *event handlers*) provided by the application programmer. In effect, this structure is a poor-man's concurrency: the event-handlers are coroutines, and the event-loop is the scheduler.

The call-back approach to managing user input leads to an unnatural program structure, known as the *"inverted program structure,"* where the application program hands over control to the library's event-loop. While event-driven code is sometimes appropriate for an application, this choice should be up to the application programmer, and not be dictated by the library.

Multiple services

Interactive applications often provide multiple services; for example, a spreadsheet might provide an editor for composing macros, and a window for viewing graphical displays of the data, in addition to the actual spreadsheet. Each service is largely independent, having its own internal state and control-flow, so it is natural to view them as independent processes.

An additional benefit of using process abstraction to structure such services is that it makes replication of services fairly easy. This is because processes are reentrant by their very nature (*i.e.*, they typically encapsulate their own state). In our spreadsheet example, supporting multiple data sets or graphical views should be as easy as spawning an additional process.

This is a situation where an "object-oriented" language might also claim benefits, since each service could be encapsulated as an object. In many respects, processes and objects provide the same kind of abstraction: hiding state and providing well-defined interfaces. The obvious difference is that concurrent languages provide the additional benefit of interleaved execution of services, whereas in a sequential object-oriented language the execution of services must be serialized.[3]

Interleaving computation

Even on a uniprocessor, it is possible to gain performance benefits from concurrency. An event driven interactive system has large amounts of "dead-time" between input events. If an application receives a hundred input events per second (which is quite a lot), then it has millions of instructions it can execute between events. Since most events can be handled in a few thousand instructions (*e.g.*, add a character to an input buffer, and echo it), there is an opportunity to execute other useful computation between input events. While multi-tasking operating systems support this kind of interleaving between processes, it is difficult to interleave computation with I/O inside a single sequential program. Applications that are programmed in a concurrent language, however, can exploit this interleaving for "free." Furthermore, as processors become faster, the amount of useful work that can be done between input events increases.

In addition to the performance benefits, interleaving computation is very important to the responsiveness of an application. For example, a user of a document preparation system may want to edit one part of a document while another part is being formatted. Since formatting may take a significant amount of time, providing a responsive interface requires interleaving formatting and editing. A traditional UIMS toolkit makes it difficult to write applications that provide responsive interactive interfaces and do substantial computation, since the application cannot handle events while computing. Typically, the computation must be broken into short-duration chunks that will not affect responsiveness. This structure has the added disadvantage of destroying the separation between the application and the interface. Concurrent programs, in contrast, avoid this problem without any additional complexity.

Output-driven interfaces

The inverted program structure required by traditional UIMS toolkits has the disadvantage of biasing a program's structure towards input. The application is quiescent until the user prods it, at which time it reacts in some way, and then waits for the next event. This is fine for many applications, such as text editors, which do not have much to do when the user's attention is elsewhere, but it is a hindrance for applications with *output-driven* interfaces.

---

[3]Of course, this restriction does not apply to concurrent object-oriented languages.

Consider, for example, a computationally intensive simulation that maintains a graphical display of its current state. The interface to this application is output-driven, since under normal circumstances the display is updated only when a new state is computed. But this application must also monitor window events, such as refresh and resize notifications, so that it can redraw itself when necessary. In a sequential implementation, the handling of these events must be postponed until the simulation is ready to update the displayed information. Separating the display code and simulation code into separate processes simplifies the handling of asynchronous redrawing.

Discussion

While the use of heavy-weight operating-system processes provides some support for multiple services and interleaved computation, it does not address the other two sources of concurrent program structure. Similarly, although event-loops and call-back functions provide flexibility in reacting to user input, they bias the application towards an *input-driven* model and do not provide much support for interleaved computation. A concurrent language, on the other hand, addresses all of these concerns.

1.1.2 Distributed systems

Distributed programs are, by their very nature, concurrent; each processor, or node, in a distributed system has its own state and control flow. But, in addition to the obvious concurrency that results from executing on multiple processors, there are natural uses of concurrency in the individual node programs.

As the story about **xrn** illustrated, synchronous communication over a network can block a program for unacceptable periods of time. This phenomenon is called *remote delay*, where the execution on one machine is delayed while waiting for a response from another. Using multiple threads to manage such communications allows other tasks to be interleaved with remote interactions.

Another performance problem that should be avoided in distributed programs is *local delay*, where execution is blocked because some resource is unavailable. For example, a file server might have to wait for a disk operation to complete before completing a file operation. In a server that allows multiple outstanding requests, local delay can be a serious bottleneck, since the delay associated with one request affects the servicing of other requests. A solution to this is to use a separate local process for each outstanding request; when one process experiences local delay, the others can still proceed. This is essentially the same as using concurrency to hide I/O latency in operating systems.

1.1.3   Other uses of concurrency

Reactive systems are another class of naturally concurrent programs. A reactive system is one that reacts to its environment at a speed determined by its environment. Examples of reactive systems include call processing, process control, and signal processing. User interfaces and, to some extent, the node programs in distributed systems might be considered reactive systems, although they do not have the hard real-time requirements of "pure" reactive systems.

Many other kinds of programs also have a naturally concurrent structure. Discrete event simulations, for example, can be structured as a collection of processes representing the objects being simulated. Concurrency can also be used to provide a different look at a sequential algorithm. For example, power series can be programmed elegantly as dataflow networks. And, of course, concurrency is important in expressing parallel algorithms.

1.2   High-level languages

Writing correct concurrent programs is a difficult task. In addition to the bugs that may arise in sequential programming, concurrent programs suffer from their own particular kinds of problems, such as races, deadlock, and starvation. What makes this even more difficult is that concurrent programs execute nondeterministically, which means that a program may work one time and fail the next. A common suggestion to address this problem is to use formal methods and logical reasoning to verify that one's program satisfies various properties. While this is a useful pedagogical tool, it does not scale well to large programs.

For large systems, one has to mostly rely on good design and careful implementation, which is where the choice of programming language makes an important difference. A high-level language with well-designed primitives is the most important ingredient in helping the programmer write correct and robust software.

The question of which programming notation to use is often the subject of religious debate. The trade-offs are fairly obvious: higher-level languages help programmer productivity and improve the robustness of software, while lower-level languages allow more programmer control over performance details. As implementation technology improves (and computer time becomes cheaper), the trend has been to migrate towards higher-level languages. While most people would agree that the performance lost when switching from assembly language to **C** is well worth the improved programmer productivity, there is no such consensus about the next step.

It is the view of the author that the higher-order language *Standard ML* (**SML**), which provides the sequential substrate for the programming examples in this book, is a good candidate for the next step. **SML** provides a number of important benefits for programmers:

- A strong type system, which guarantees that programs will not have run-time type errors (or "dump core").

- A garbage collector, which improves modularity and prevents many kinds of memory management errors.

- An expressive module system, which supports large-scale software construction and code reuse.

- Higher-order functions and polymorphism, which further support code reuse.

- A datatype mechanism and pattern matching facility, which provide a concise notation for many data structures and algorithms.

- A well-defined semantics and independence from architectural details, which makes code truly portable.

SML also provides a level of performance that is becoming competitive with lower-level languages, such as **C**. In particular, there is a widely used and freely distributed **SML** system, called *Standard ML of New Jersey* (**SML/NJ**), which provides quite good performance.[4] It is the author's view that the notational advantages of programming in **SML** outweigh the slight loss of performance, when compared to **C**. A thesis of this book is that efficient system software can be written in a language such as **SML**.

1.3   Concurrent ML

This book uses a concurrent extension to **SML**, called *Concurrent ML* (**CML**), as its primary programming notation. **CML** can either be viewed as a library, since it compiles directly on top of **SML/NJ**, or as a language in its own right, since it defines a different programming discipline.

Following the tradition of **SML**, **CML** is designed to provide high-level, but efficient, mechanisms for concurrent programming. Its basic model of communication and synchronization is synchronous message-passing (or *rendezvous*) on typed channels. Creation of both threads and channels is dynamic. Most importantly, **CML** provides a mechanism for users to define new communication and synchronization abstractions. This allows proper isolation of the implementation details, improving the robustness of

---

[4]Of course, this is application specific. **SML** beats **C** on many symbolic applications, but does not compete as well on array-based numerical applications.

the system. **CML** also addresses performance issues by providing efficient concurrency primitives. **CML** has a number of features that make it a good programming notation for building large-scale systems software:

- **CML** is a *higher-order* concurrent language. Just as **SML** supports functions as first-class values, **CML** supports synchronous operations as first-class values. These values, called *events*, provide the tools for building new synchronization abstractions.

- It provides integrated support for I/O operations. Potentially blocking I/O operations, such as reading from an input stream, are full-fledged synchronous operations. Low-level support is also provided, from which distributed communication abstractions can be constructed.

- It provides automatic reclamation of threads and channels, once they become inaccessible. This permits a technique of speculative communication, which is not possible in other concurrent languages and libraries.

- Scheduling is preemptive, which ensures that a single thread cannot monopolize the processor. This allows "off-the-shelf" code to be incorporated in a concurrent thread without destroying interactive responsiveness.

- It has an efficient implementation. Concurrency operations, such as thread creation, context switching, and message passing are very fast, often faster than lower-level **C**-based libraries.

- **CML** is implemented on top of **SML/NJ** and is written completely in **SML**. It runs on every hardware and operating system combination supported by **SML/NJ** (although we have not had a chance to test all combinations).

CML, and the multithreaded user-interface toolkit **eXene**, which is built on top of **CML**, have been used for a number of substantial applications (*i.e.*, applications consisting of at least 10,000 lines of **SML/CML** code).

Notes

The importance of using concurrency in the construction of user-interface software has been argued by a number of people. Most notably by Pike [Pik89a, Pik94], and by Gansner and the author [RG86, GR92]. A recent paper by Hauser et al. describes the various paradigms of thread use in two large interactive software systems [HJT+93].

Liskov, Herlihy, and Gilbert give arguments as to why the node programs in distributed systems should either have dynamic thread creation or use one-way message passing (which they call asynchronous communication) for communicating with other nodes [LHG86]. The basic argument is that without one of these features, avoiding performance problems with local and remote delays requires too much complexity. These arguments are also motivation for using a concurrent language, instead of a sequential one, to program the nodes. Many languages and toolkits for distributed programming provide some form of light-weight concurrency for use in the node programs. Examples include the language **Argus** [LS83], the language **SR** [AOCE88, AO93], and the **Isis** toolkit [BCJ$^+$90].

In addition to the examples found in later chapters of this book, there are a number of examples of the application of concurrency in the literature. McIlroy describes the implementation of various power series computations using the language **newsqueak** [McI90]. Andrews and Olsson illustrate the use of **SR** with a number of small application examples, including parallel numerical computation and simulation [AO93]. A book by Armstrong, et al. gives examples of the use of the concurrent language **Erlang** for a number of applications, including database servers, real-time control, and telephony [AVWW96]. **CML** has also been used for experimental telephony applications [FO93].

It is expected that the reader is familiar with the 1997 revision of **SML**, since it is the primary notation used in this book. A number of books give good introductions to **SML**. The second edition of Paulson's book [Pau96] gives a comprehensive description of the language, concentrating mostly on "functional programming" using **SML**, but it also discusses the module system and imperative features. A book by Ullman provides an introduction to **SML** aimed at people with experience programming in traditional imperative languages, and has been recently revised for **SML**'97 [Ull98]. Other books include Reade's book on functional programming using **SML** [Rea89], Stansifer's primer on **ML** [Sta92], and a book on abstract data types in **SML** by Harrison [Har93]. A recent book by Okasaki describes many purely functional data structures [Oka98]; these can be particularly useful for concurrent programming since there is no danger of shared state. In addition, there are tutorials written by Harper [Har86] and Tofte [Tof89]. The formal definition of **SML** and commentary on the definition were published as a pair of books [MTH90, MT91]; a revised definition, which covers **SML**'97, has also been published [MTHM97]. In addition, the **SML** Basis Library Manual is available electronically from

```
http://standardml.org/Basis/index.html
```

and also as a book [GR04].

This book also uses libraries and features that are specific to the **SML/NJ** system; these are described as they are encountered. More detailed documentation is included in the **SML/NJ** distribution, and is also available from the **SML/NJ** home page. An abridged

version of the *CML Reference Manual* is provided in Appendix A. As described in the
preface, both **SML/NJ** and **CML** are distributed electronically free of charge.

2

Concepts in Concurrent Programming

Concurrent programming differs from sequential programming in several significant ways. Conceptually, we can view the execution of a concurrent program as an *interleaving* of the sequential execution of its constituent processes. Since there are many possible interleavings, the execution of a concurrent program is *nondeterministic*; *i.e.*, different interleavings may produce different results. In effect, a concurrent program defines a *partial* order on its actions, whereas a sequential program defines a total order. This nondeterminism is both the bane and boon of concurrent programming: on the one hand, it creates additional correctness problems, while on the other hand, it provides flexibility and a more natural program structure. As argued in Chapter 1, the choice of programming notation can help the programmer control the complexity of concurrency, while reaping its benefits.

A concurrent language typically consists of a sequential core (or sub-language), extended with support for concurrency. The concurrency support can be divided into three different kinds of mechanism:

- A mechanism for introducing independent sequential *threads* of control, called *processes*. The process creation mechanism can be either *static*, restricting the program to a fixed number of processes, or *dynamic*, allowing new processes to be created "on-the-fly."

- A mechanism for processes to *communicate*. Communication involves exchanging data, either through shared memory locations (*e.g.*, variables) or by explicit message passing.

- And a mechanism for processes to *synchronize*. Synchronization restricts the ordering of execution in otherwise independent threads, and is used to limit the program's nondeterminism where necessary.

The choice of language features used to provide these mechanisms, along with the sequential sub-language, characterize a concurrent programming language. In particular, the choice of synchronization and communication mechanisms are the most important aspects of concurrent language design. Most concurrent languages can be classified as either *shared-memory* languages or *message-passing* languages (sometimes called *distributed-memory* languages). Shared-memory languages rely on the imperative features of the sequential sub-language for interprocess communication, and provide separate synchronization primitives to control access to the shared state. Message-passing languages provide a single unified mechanism for both synchronization and communication. Note that the distinction between shared-memory and message-passing languages has to do with the style of process interaction; many message-passing languages, including **CML**, are implemented in shared address spaces.

In this chapter, we survey the important issues in concurrent programming, and examine some of the better known language features for supporting concurrency. This discussion is partially to give the reader a feeling for some of the design choices, as well as a way of highlighting some of the important issues in concurrent programming. It also provides definitions of various abstractions that are implemented later in the book using **CML**.

2.1 Processes

A process consists of a thread of control (*i.e.*, an instruction stream and program counter), and a local state (*i.e.*, local variables, program stack, *etc.*). A process is essentially a sequential program that shares some of its state with other sequential programs. A concurrent programming language must provide a mechanism for defining the processes that comprise a program; in the remainder of this section, we examine some of the ways in which this mechanism is provided.

Perhaps the simplest notation for process creation is the static concurrent composition of statements, which has the form:

$$stmt_1 \ \| \ stmt_2 \ \| \ \cdots \ \| \ stmt_n$$

and is executed by executing each of the $stmt_i$ in parallel; the whole statement terminates when each of the individual statements has terminated. This construct is often called a *cobegin* statement, since it was first introduced as a way to compose concurrent *begin-blocks*. If combined with recursive procedures, the cobegin statement can support the creation of arbitrary numbers of processes, but it is an awkward programming notation.

Another approach to process creation is to provide a declarative notation for processes, similar to procedure or module declarations. The **Ada** task declaration provides one example of this. In **Ada**, task implementations are defined in task type declarations and instances of a task are created by declaring variables of the corresponding task type.

While this approach provides more flexibility than the cobegin statement, it is still rather heavyweight and cumbersome.

Most recent concurrent languages provide process creation via a *spawn* (or *fork*) primitive that dynamically creates a new thread of control to run concurrently with its creator. While there are widely used concurrent languages that only provide static process creation, there do not seem to be very strong arguments in favor of it. On the other hand, there are strong arguments in favor of providing dynamic process creation, many of which are presented in this book.

2.2   Interference

Most concurrent programs require some sharing of data between different processes, but if independent processes are accessing and modifying shared state, the order of accesses can affect the result of the program. Sequential programs do not suffer from this problem, since the order of execution is deterministic. To illustrate this point, consider the following program:

```
let val x = ref 0
in
  x := !x + 1;   x := !x + 2;
  print (!x)
end
```

Simple examination is sufficient to determine that this program will print the integer 3 every time it is executed. But consider a version where the assignment statements are composed in parallel, instead of sequentially:

```
let val x = ref 0
in
  (x := !x + 1) || (x := !x + 2);
  print (!x)
end
```

The execution of each assignment statement consists of three individual steps: read x, add a constant to it, and store the result. We assume that the individual steps are *atomic*; *i.e.*, that they are executed as indivisible operations. Since the statements are composed in parallel, the steps can be interleaved in different ways, resulting in either 1, 2, or 3 being printed. This is the canonical example of *interference* between processes. The two assignment statements are examples of *critical regions*; *i.e.*, regions of code that are potential sources of interference in the absence of proper concurrency control. Synchronization provides the mechanism for avoiding this interference.

While the above example is expressed in terms of shared-memory primitives, it is important to realize that interference also occurs in message-passing concurrent programs. For example, memory could be an independent process and the memory operations could be implemented using messages.

2.3 Correctness issues in concurrent programming

Because concurrent programs consist of multiple processes and have nondeterministic behavior, they give rise to a number of correctness issues not found in sequential programs.

A common problem suffered by concurrent programs is *deadlock*, which is a situation in which a set of processes are blocked waiting for some event that cannot occur. Deadlock is caused by cyclic dependencies among processes. For example, consider the following program, where two processes P and Q share two resources A and B:

```
P: acquire A; acquire B; compute; release B; release A
Q: acquire B; acquire A; compute; release A; release B
```

Assuming that only one process can hold a resource at a time, the following program can deadlock with P holding A and Q holding B. The problem is that there is a cyclic dependency between P's acquiring of resource B and Q's acquiring of resource A.

A problem that is similar to deadlock is *livelock*, where processes are not making progress, even though they are not blocked. For example, suppose that we modified the above program so that P and Q release the first resource that they acquire when the second is held, and then try again:

```
              P                              Q
  1: acquire A;                  1: acquire B;
     if  (B is held)               if  (A is held)
        then (release A; goto 1)      then (release B; goto 1)
        else acquire B                else acquire A
     compute                        compute
     release B; release A          release A; release B
```

One possible execution of this program is a strict interleaving of P and Q, which results in an infinite execution:

```
P: acquire A
Q: acquire B
P: if (B is held)
Q: if (A is held)
P:    then release A
Q:    then release B
P: acquire A
Q: acquire B
...
```

Neither process is blocked, but neither makes progress.

When reasoning about concurrent programs, it is necessary to consider all possible execution sequences (or *process histories*). We define a *property* of a concurrent program to be a statement about the program's behavior that is *true* in all possible executions of the program. There are two classes of properties that are of interest:

- *Safety* properties assert that a program never enters a bad state. Or more formally, that for any program execution, every state satisfies the statement. Mutual exclusion is an example of a safety property, since it asserts that the program is never in a state where two processes are executing in a critical region. Another important safety property is the absence of deadlock.

- *Liveness* properties assert that a program eventually reaches a desirable state — for every execution there is some state in which the statement is true. Termination is an example of a liveness property, since it asserts that a program will eventually terminate.

Fairness is a particular form of liveness property that is important to concurrent programming. The most general concept of fairness is that a system component that is enabled *sufficiently often* should not be delayed indefinitely. For example, in a time-sharing system, is a process guaranteed to make progress if it is ready? If the scheduler is priority based, and there are always higher priority processes that are also ready to run, then the process will be delayed (this is called *starvation*). There are different *strengths* of fairness based on how the phrase "sufficiently often" is interpreted. Under *strong fairness*, any component that is enabled infinitely often is never delayed indefinitely. While under *weak fairness*, any component that is enabled "almost always" is never delayed indefinitely.[1] For example, if we have a component that alternates being enabled for a second then not enabled for a second *ad infinitum*, then under strong fairness it will not be starved (because it is enabled infinitely often), whereas under weak fairness it can be starved (because it is not enabled infinitely often).

We can also distinguish different notions of fairness by the kind of system component that they refer to: *process fairness* says that a process will get to make progress, while *event fairness* says that an enabled event will get to occur. The scheduling example in the previous paragraph is an example of a process fairness concern. An example of event fairness can be found in selective communication. Consider a process that repeatedly synchronizes on the choice of reading from two channels, where there is always input available on both channels. If the process always reads from the same channel, then the "event" of reading from the other channel is delayed indefinitely, which is unfair.

In the implementation of concurrent programming languages, fairness concerns are closely coupled with scheduling policies. For example, consider a process scheduling policy for a uniprocessor that lets the currently running process have sole access to the processor until it either blocks or terminates. Such a policy allows an infinitely looping process to starve other processes, and thus is unfair. While a strongly fair scheduling

---

[1]This terminology is a bit confusing. The statement that a component is *enabled almost always* means that it is not enabled only finitely often.

policy is impractical to implement in general, it is possible to implement strongly fair policies for many higher-level concurrency primitives.

2.4 Shared-memory languages

As seen in Section 2.2, correct execution of shared-memory programs requires synchronization to control the access to shared state. In general, there are two kinds of situations in which synchronization is required between processes: to avoid interference when accessing shared variables, and to ensure that operations are only performed under certain conditions.

As we saw above, when the operations on a shared value consist of a sequence of statements, concurrent execution of the operations by two or more threads can result in indeterminate results. To avoid this, the operations must be executed atomically. For example, if the assignment statements in the above example are atomic, then the answer will always be 3. *Mutual exclusion* synchronization is used to ensure that processes execute the critical regions atomically.

The other situation arises when the state of the shared object determines which operations are enabled. For example, a shared object might allow multiple readers to access it concurrently, but require exclusive access for writers. In this case, both the read and write operations are disabled when another process is writing, and the write operation is disabled when processes are performing reads. A process uses *condition synchronization* to wait until some condition holds before executing an operation.

To illustrate the different forms of shared-memory synchronization primitives, we use the classic example of a producer/consumer buffer. This is an abstraction of a common situation in which one, or more, processes, called *producers* are generating data that are being fed to one, or more, *consumer* processes. Figure 2.1 gives the basic structure of the system. The interesting part is the finite buffer used to connect the producer and consumer processes. A natural way to implement the buffer is as an abstract data type with the following interface:

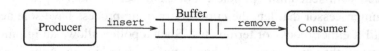

Figure 2.1: Producer/consumer system

```
type 'a buffer
val buffer : unit -> 'a buffer
val insert : ('a * 'a buffer) -> unit
val remove : 'a buffer -> 'a
```

The buffer is the shared state in the system, and access to its internal representation must be controlled, which requires mutual exclusion synchronization. There is additional condition synchronization required to keep the producer from inserting items into a full buffer, and to keep the consumer from attempting to remove items from an empty buffer. To simplify the presentation, we use a buffer size of one.

2.4.1 Semaphores

One of the most basic synchronization mechanisms is the *semaphore*, which is a special integer variable with two operations: **P** and **V**. Given a semaphore s, the execution of $\mathbf{P}(s)$ by a process p forces it to delay until $s > 0$, at which point p executes $s := s - 1$ and proceeds; the test and update of s are performed together as an atomic operation. Execution of $\mathbf{V}(s)$ results in the atomic execution of $s := s + 1$.

A semaphore s can be used to implement mutual exclusion for a critical region by initializing s to 1, and by bracketing the critical region with $\mathbf{P}(s) \dots \mathbf{V}(s)$. When a process P enters the critical region, s goes to 0, which prevents any other process from entering until P exits. Such a semaphore is called a *binary semaphore*, since it only has two values. Semaphores can also be used to implement condition synchronization. In this case, the semaphore is initialized to 0. When a process wants to wait for a condition to become true, it executes $\mathbf{P}(s)$, causing it to block. When another process makes the condition true, it executes $\mathbf{V}(s)$, which signals to the waiting process that it may proceed.

The code in Listing 2.1 gives a possible implementation of the one-element producer/consumer buffer using semaphores, which illustrates both styles of semaphore use. We assume that the function `semaphore` creates a new semaphore initialized to the given value, and that the functions P and V are as described above. The semaphore `lockSem` is used for mutual exclusion synchronization to ensure that only one process can access the buffer's state at a time, while the auxiliary counter `waiting` and the semaphore `waitSem` are used to provide condition synchronization on the state of the buffer (*i.e.*, empty or full). The actual condition synchronization scheduling is performed by the functions `wait` and `signal`. This implementation allows multiple producers and consumers to share the buffer. The key to making this sharing work is that `signal` wakes up all the waiting processes, which means that when a producer puts a value into the buffer it is guaranteed that if there is a blocked consumer, then the value will be consumed (and vice versa).

There is a more concise implementation of the one-element producer/consumer buffer that uses one semaphore to mark the empty state, and another to mark the full state. In

```
datatype 'a buffer = BUF of {
    data    : 'a option ref,
    waiting : int ref,
    lockSem : semaphore,
    waitSem : semaphore
  }

fun buffer () = BUF{
    data    = ref NONE,
    waiting = ref 0,
    lockSem = semaphore 1,
    waitSem = semaphore 0
  }

fun wait (BUF{waiting, lockSem, waitSem, ...}) = (
    waiting := !waiting+1; V lockSem; P waitSem)

fun signal (buf as BUF{waiting, waitSem, ...}) =
    if (!waiting > 0)
      then (
        waiting := !waiting-1; V waitSem;
        signal buf)
      else ()

fun insert (buf as BUF{data, lockSem, ...}, v) = (
    P lockSem;
    case !data
     of NONE => (data := SOME v; signal buf; V lockSem)
      | (SOME _) => (wait buf; insert (buf, v))
    (* end case *))

fun remove (buf as BUF{data, lockSem, ...}) = (
    P lockSem;
    case !data
     of (SOME v) => (data := NONE; signal buf; V lockSem; v)
      | NONE => (wait buf; remove buf)
    (* end case *))
```

Listing 2.1: Producer/consumer buffer implemented with lock and wait semaphores

effect, this scheme implements both the mutual exclusion and condition synchronization using the same semaphores. Listing 2.2 gives the code for this version. While this version is more compact, the alternating use of the two semaphores is subtle and makes its harder to extend.

A major problem with semaphores is that there is no linguistic support for their correct use. For example, the code in Figures 2.1 and 2.2 have P and V operations scattered throughout; insuring that they are properly matched and that all accesses to shared state

```
datatype 'a buffer = BUF of {
    data     : 'a option ref,
    emptySem : semaphore,
    fullSem  : semaphore
  }

fun buffer () = BUF{
      data     = ref NONE,
      emptySem = semaphore 1,
      fullSem  = semaphore 0
    }

fun insert (BUF{data, emptySem, fullSem}, v) = (
      P emptySem;
      data := SOME v;
      V fullSem)

fun remove (BUF{data, emptySem, fullSem}) = let
      val _ = P fullSem
      val (SOME v) = !data
    in
      data := NONE;
      V emptySem;
      v
    end
```

Listing 2.2: Producer/consumer buffer implemented with condition semaphores

are protected requires close examination. Furthermore, implementing patterns of synchronization that are more complicated than mutual exclusion can be tricky.

2.4.2 Mutex locks and condition variables

The term *mutex lock* is essentially another name for a binary semaphore (it is a contraction of "mutual exclusion"). A mutex lock has two states: *locked* or *unlocked*. One of the advantages of mutex locks is that they are supported naturally by the *test-and-set* instruction found on many multiprocessors.

Mutex locks are meant to be used to control access to shared data. The idea is that each piece of shared data has an associated lock, which a process must acquire before it can access the data. We have already seen an example of this; the semaphore `lockSem` in Listing 2.1 is essentially a mutex lock. This idiom can be supported by syntactic sugar; for example, **Modula-3** provides the statement syntax

LOCK *m* **DO** *statements* **END**

which executes by first acquiring the lock *m*, then executing the *statements*, and finally releasing *m*. In **SML**, this idiom might be supported by a higher-order function with the type

```
val withLock : mutex -> ('a -> 'b) -> 'a -> 'b
```

The semantics of the expression

```
withLock mu f x
```

are that first the lock *mu* is acquired, then the function *f* is applied to *x,* and then the function's result is returned after releasing the lock.

Mutex locks are sufficient for insuring mutual exclusion in critical regions, but do not provide an easy way to implement condition synchronization. In our producer/consumer example, if the buffer is empty, then the consumer must wait for the producer to add something to it; likewise, if the buffer is full, the producer must wait for the consumer to remove something. While it is possible to program this using only mutex locks, it is more natural to use *condition variables*. A condition variable is used to delay a process until some condition in a critical region is satisfied (*e.g.*, the buffer is not empty). Just as a mutex lock is specialized to support mutual exclusion synchronization, the condition variable is designed to support condition synchronization.

The basic operations on condition variables are

```
val wait : condition -> unit
```

which causes a process to block on the condition variable, and

```
val signal : condition -> unit
```

which wakes up one waiting process. A condition variable is associated with a specific mutex lock, which must be held when performing a `wait` operation on the variable. The semantics of the `wait` operation are that the mutex lock is released, and then the process is blocked; when the condition is signaled, the next process in the condition's waiting queue is unblocked and it reacquires the mutex lock and proceeds. A `signal` operation on a condition variable that has an empty waiting queue has no effect; in this sense condition variables are *memoryless*.

The implementation of the producer/consumer buffer is much cleaner using mutex locks and condition variables than using semaphores. The code for this is given in Listing 2.3. Here we use the mutex lock `mu` to provide mutual exclusion, and the two condition variables `dataAvail` and `dataEmpty` to block waiting processes. Note that waiting on a condition is implemented as a loop, with the waiting process checking the condition after it wakes up. This is necessary to avoid the potential problem of another

```
datatype 'a buffer = BUF of {
    data      : 'a option ref,
    mu        : mutex,
    dataAvail : condition,
    dataEmpty : condition
  }

fun buffer () = let
      val mu = mutex()
      in
        BUF{
          data      = ref NONE,
          mu        = mu,
          dataAvail = condition mu,
          dataEmpty = condition mu
        }
      end

fun insert (BUF{data, mu, dataAvail, dataEmpty}, v) = let
      fun waitLp NONE = (data := SOME v; signal dataAvail)
        | waitLp (SOME v) = (wait dataEmpty; waitLp(!data))
      in
        withLock mu waitLp (!data)
      end

fun remove (BUF{data, mu, dataAvail, dataEmpty}) = let
      fun waitLp NONE = (wait dataAvail; waitLp(!data))
        | waitLp (SOME v) = (data := NONE; signal dataEmpty; v)
      in
        withLock mu waitLp (!data)
      end
```

Listing 2.3: Producer/consumer buffer implemented with mutex locks

process acquiring the mutex lock and invalidating the condition between the time the waiting process is unblocked and the time it reacquires the lock. This situation is an example of a *race condition*, which is a situation where the relative speed and scheduling of processes can affect the correctness of the program. By rechecking the condition after being signaled, we avoid the possibility of a race. We could use a single condition variable to block waiting processes, but then we would have had to use broadcast to support sharing of the buffer between multiple producers and consumers (as we did in the semaphore implementation).

2.4.3 Monitors

Monitors are a special form of module that can be used to encapsulate shared state. As with a regular module, a monitor provides data abstraction, with access to its state being restricted to a collection of exported procedures. In addition to data abstraction, monitors provide mutual exclusion by only allowing a single process to be executing inside the monitor at a time. In effect, this is equivalent to having a single mutex lock for the whole monitor, and wrapping the body of each exported procedure with a LOCK statement. In addition to the implicit locking provided by the exported procedures, monitors also provide condition variables for condition synchronization. In fact, programming languages with monitors predate the kind of support for mutex locks and condition variables described in the previous section. While monitors provide more linguistic support than mutex locks, it can be argued that providing mutex locks as a separate mechanism is a better approach, since it separates two orthogonal language features (*i.e.*, modules and mutual exclusion).

2.5   Message-passing languages

In the previous section, we used the producer/consumer buffer as an example to illustrate different shared-memory primitives. Message-passing languages support this style of interprocess communication more directly. The basic operations in message-passing languages are "*send a message*" and "*receive a message*." Since a message must be sent before it can be received, message-passing imposes an *causal order* on the actions of the program.

One way to distinguish message-passing languages is by the mechanism used to specify the destination of a send operation and the source of a receive. This pair of names is called a *communication channel*. Different schemes for specifying communication channels support different communication topologies. The most basic way to specify a communication channel is *direct naming*, where the endpoints (*i.e.*, the sending and receiving processes) are named explicitly. In this case, the topology of a channel is a one-to-one connection. A variation on this is to allow receive operations to accept messages from any sending process, which allows many-to-one connections. Direct naming is quite restrictive, so a natural generalization is to allow process names to be stored in variables and sent in messages. In a strongly-typed language direct naming has the additional disadvantage that a process can only receive messages of one type, which means that the programmer must use a union type and case analysis to support multiple types of messages. This problem can be addressed by associating multiple *ports* with each process, where each port can support a different type of message. The send operation then must specify both the destination process and port, while the receive operation specifies an input port. Another common mechanism is to make the communication channels into first-class citizens, and specify them independently of the sender and receiver processes. When communication channels are supported as values, many-to-many connections are possible using a single channel (multiple processes may read and write from the channel). When we discuss message passing in the sequel, we use channels as the naming scheme, and allow multiple processes to read or write on a channel. In addition to point-to-point messages, where each message that is sent is received by only one process, some message-passing schemes support *broadcast* (or *multicast*), where a message can be sent to every process in a group of processes.

Another, more important, way to distinguish between different forms of message passing is the amount of synchronization provided by the message-passing operations. The basic issue is whether an operation is *blocking* or *non-blocking* (the terms *synchronous* and *asynchronous* are sometimes used instead). Since there are two different operations, we can organize the design space into a taxonomy of four choices. In practice, the receive operation is almost always a blocking operation,[2] which leaves us the choice of non-blocking versus blocking send. There is also the question of whether communication is bidirectional (*i.e.*, whether the send operation blocks until a reply is received). In the next three sections, we discuss these choices in more detail.

2.5.1 Asynchronous message passing

An asynchronous message-passing mechanism buffers the communication between the sender and receiver, which allows the sender to continue execution after sending a message. This is analogous to mailing a letter; once the letter is in the postbox, the sender can continue with other tasks. One issue is whether the ordering of messages that the sender sees is also seen by the receiver. Most languages with asynchronous message passing provide FIFO (*First-In, First-Out*) ordering of messages, but FIFO ordering of messages is not guaranteed in distributed systems or in some implementations of asynchronous message passing. Figure 2.2 gives examples of asynchronous message passing. The vertical lines are pictorial representations of the *process histories* (or *time-lines*) for the processes P and Q, with time progressing down the page. Both figures cover a situation in which P sends two messages to Q, and then receives one, and Q receives a message, sends one, and then receives another. The difference is in the ordering of P's messages; in Figure 2.2(a), the messages obey a FIFO ordering, whereas they do not in Figure 2.2(b). An asynchronous channel can be viewed as a semaphore with data. The send operation corresponds to **V**, and the recv operation to **P**. The number of outstanding messages in the buffer represents the value of the semaphore.

Some implementations of asynchronous message passing only provide finite buffering. In this situation, if the producer outpaces the consumer, then the send operation eventually becomes blocking, since the sender must wait for empty space in the buffer. While this violates the spirit of asynchronous message passing, the alternative may be worse.

---

[2]One notable exception is the **SR** language, which allows one to define a receive operation that is asynchronously invoked when a message arrives.

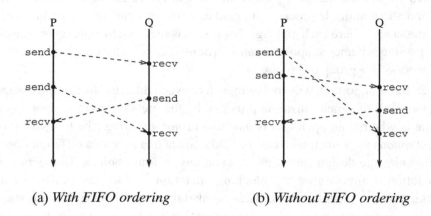

(a) *With FIFO ordering*   (b) *Without FIFO ordering*

Figure 2.2: Asynchronous message passing

If the language implementation allows buffers to grow without bound, then the available memory could be exhausted, causing the system to crash.

The producer/consumer example illustrates this problem well. The producer and consumer processes can be connected directly using an asynchronous communication channel, but if the producer generates new items faster than the consumer uses them, the program will have unbounded space consumption. To avoid this, some form of *flow-control* is required. The finite buffer provides this, since the buffer size limits the distance the producer can get ahead of the consumer. Listing 2.4 gives the code for an implementation of the producer-consumer buffer using asynchronous message passing. This version of the implementation avoids the need for mutual exclusion synchronization, since only one process can access the buffer's state directly. The condition synchronization is provided by the buffer process sending messages on the emptyCh and remCh channels (recall that an asynchronous channel is like a semaphore with data). The producer (or consumer) process must wait for a message to be available, before it can insert (resp. remove) an item. Flow-control is provided by *handshaking* on the remove operation; the buffer process waits for an acknowledgement, before sending the "empty" message. This type of handshaking could also be used for the insert operation, but that would effectively increase the buffer size by the number of producers, since each producer could send a message and then wait for the acknowledgement. Figure 2.3 illustrates the message traffic used in this implementation. It is also interesting to note that the buffer's state is implemented as a pair of mutually recursive functions: empty and full. This is a common idiom when programming message-passing concurrency in **ML**-style languages.

```
datatype 'a buffer = BUF of {
    emptyCh  : unit chan,
    insCh    : 'a chan,
    remCh    : 'a chan,
    remAckCh : unit chan
}

fun buffer () = let
        val emptyCh = channel () and insCh = channel()
        val remCh = channel() and remAckCh = channel()
        fun empty () = (
                send (emptyCh, ());
                full (recv insCh))
        and full x = (
                send (remCh, x);
                empty (recv remAckCh))
    in
        spawn empty;
        BUF{
            emptyCh = emptyCh, insCh   = insCh,
            remCh   = remCh,    remAckCh = remAckCh
        }
    end

fun insert (BUF{insCh, emptyCh, ...}, v) = (
        recv emptyCh; send (insCh, v))

fun remove (BUF{remCh, remAckCh, ...}) =
        (recv remCh) before send(remAckCh, ())
```

Listing 2.4: Producer/consumer buffer implemented with asynchronous message passing

2.5.2 Synchronous message passing

In synchronous message passing, the sender is blocked until its message is received. [3] This is somewhat analogous to making a phone call, where the caller must wait until someone picks up the phone (*i.e.,* accepts the call) before talking. There are two basic scenarios for synchronously sending a message: either the sender waits or the receiver waits. Figure 2.4 shows the process histories for these two scenarios, where the dotted lines correspond to a process being blocked. Because the two processes must wait for each other, synchronous message passing is sometimes called *rendezvous* (or *simple rendezvous*).

Implementing the producer/consumer buffer using synchronous message passing is straightforward; the code is given in Listing 2.5. As with the asynchronous case, a process is used to encapsulate the buffer state, but unlike the asynchronous case, no extra

---

[3]In the case of synchronous message passing, the "recv" operation is sometimes called "accept."

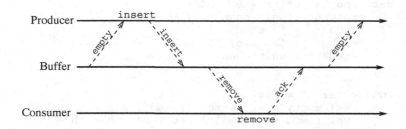

Figure 2.3: Message traffic in asynchronous producer/consumer buffer implementation

communication is required for flow-control. The condition synchronization is implemented by the enabling of communication on the channels. When the buffer is empty, then communication on the channel insCh is enabled, but not on the channel remCh. Conversely, when the buffer is full, the situation is reversed.

While synchronous communication patterns are more common than asynchronous patterns, it is occasionally necessary to communicate asynchronously — for example, when cyclic communication patterns are required that might otherwise result in deadlock. The producer/consumer buffer example illustrates one technique for supporting asynchronous communication in a synchronous language. Another technique is to have the sender dynamically spawn a new process to actually send the message; this way the new process

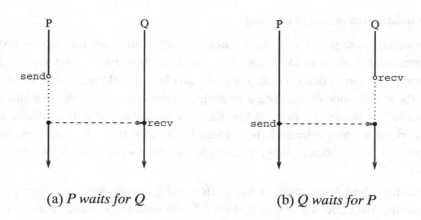

(a) *P waits for Q*   (b) *Q waits for P*

Figure 2.4: Synchronous message passing (simple rendezvous)

```
datatype 'a buffer = BUF of {
    insCh : 'a chan,
    remCh : 'a chan
  }

fun buffer () = let
    val insCh = channel() and remCh = channel()
    fun empty () = full (recv insCh)
    and full x = (send (remCh, x); empty())
    in
      spawn empty;
      BUF{
        insCh = insCh,
        remCh = remCh
      }
    end

fun insert (BUF{insCh, ...}, v) = send (insCh, v)

fun remove (BUF{remCh, ...}) = recv remCh
```

Listing 2.5: Producer/consumer buffer implemented with synchronous message passing

may block, but the sender can continue executing. When process creation is inexpensive, this is a useful technique. Note, however, that unlike using a buffer process, this technique does not guarantee a FIFO ordering of the messages.

2.5.3 Selective communication

In message-passing programs, it is often necessary to manage communication with multiple partners. For example, if we wish to modify the producer/consumer buffer implementation of Listing 2.5 to use a larger buffer, then when the buffer is partially full, the buffer process must be able to handle communications with both the producer and the consumer. There are several ways that this might be accomplished.

It is possible to design a protocol based on the simple operations used in Listing 2.5. The idea is to use a single channel for both `insert` and `remove` requests. The producer (or consumer) first sends a request, and then attempts its operation; when the buffer process receives an insert (or remove) request, it enables communication on the appropriate channel. This becomes quite complicated, however, because the buffer process must also manage outstanding `insert` requests when it is full (and outstanding `remove` requests when it is empty). Another problem is that we have lost the benefits of rendezvous, and have reverted to explicit handshaking. Furthermore, this kind of protocol is not very abstract, and may have to be modified to be used in other contexts (for example, a process that wants to read from two different buffered channels).

To avoid the complexities and inefficiencies of such protocols, most message-passing languages provide a mechanism for selecting from a choice of several blocking communications. One approach is to provide a *polling* operation (or non-blocking `recv` operation) that allows a process to attempt a communication without blocking (if the operation would block, then the attempt fails). Using this, one might implement the buffer by repeatedly polling the `insCh` and `remCh` channels. While this *spinning* provides the desired nondeterministic choice of communications, it is wasteful of computing resources. A better approach is to provide a *selective communication* operation that allows a process to block until one of a choice of operations is possible. Using such a mechanism, the finite producer/consumer buffer process can be implemented quite elegantly as follows (using the previous implementation of `insert` and `remove`):

```
fun loop [] = loop [recv insCh]
  | loop buf = if (length buf > maxLen)
      then (send (remCh, hd buf); loop (tl buf))
      else (select remCh!(hd buf) => loop (tl buf)
               or insCh?x => loop (buf @ [x]))
```

where we are assuming syntactic support for selective communication in the form of the `select` expression, and use a list to represent the buffer. This has two clauses: the first attempts to send the first item in the buffer on the `remCh` channel (the "`!`" operator), and the second attempts to receive a message from the `insCh` channel (the "`?`" operator). The communications in these clauses are called *guards*, because they "guard" the actions following the "`=>`." The `select` operation becomes *enabled*, when one of the guards becomes enabled; if both guards are simultaneously enabled, then one is selected nondeterministically.

There are variations in the design of selective communication mechanisms. Many languages provide *input-only* selective communication, where the guards are restricted to input operations only. For the above example, that would mean that the `remove` operation would have to be implemented using a request from the consumer, so that the buffer process could select on two input operations. When both input and output guards are allowed, the mechanism is called *generalized selective communication*.

2.5.4 Remote procedure call

A common idiom in message-passing programs is the *client-server* structure, where one process, called the *server*, provides some service (usually involving access to shared state) to clients. A typical client-server protocol involves the client sending a request, and then waiting for a reply from the server, where the server is structured as a loop with

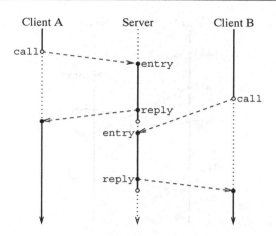

Figure 2.5: Remote procedure call (rendezvous)

each iteration corresponding to the handling of one client request. Because of the importance of this idiom, some languages, such as **Ada**, provide it as the basic communication mechanism. In such a mechanism, the clients use a `call` operation to request a service and wait for the reply, while the server uses the `entry` operation to wait for requests and a `reply` operation to return the result. The server-side entry operations are typically gathered into a selective communication. Figure 2.5 shows a process history for a server responding to requests from two different clients. Languages based on this mechanism typically also supply a selective communication construct to allow the server to offer a choice of different entries.

There are a number of different names for this mechanism. Because it involves blocking both the sender and receiver, it is sometimes called *rendezvous* (or *extended rendezvous*). Others describe the communications as *transactions*. In this book, we use the term *Remote Procedure Call* (RPC), because the request/reply protocol is similar to the procedure call/return linkage. This analogy can be made stronger; the server process is actually playing the rôle of a monitor, with the entries corresponding to the monitor's procedures. The server process provides both data abstraction, by encapsulating its state, and concurrency control, by only accepting one request at a time.

One variant on RPC is the mechanism of *asynchronous RPC*, also called *promises*. The idea is that the client can decouple the sending of a request from the waiting for a reply. When the client sends a request, it gets a promise of a reply; later it can *claim* the promise, which causes the client process to block until the reply is received. Figure 2.6 illustrates this mechanism. This is useful for hiding network and server latency when

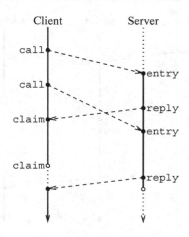

Figure 2.6: Asynchronous RPC

using the client-server paradigm.

2.5.5   Comparison of message-passing mechanisms

Given these various choices of mechanisms, it is worth comparing them (Chapter 6 contains a more technical discussion of some of these issues).

The main argument in favor of asynchronous message passing is performance; both because the implementation overhead of the asynchronous primitives is lower, and because the senders do not have to block. In practice, however, most uses of asynchronous message passing involve synchronization via acknowledgement messages (such as the flow-control in the producer/consumer example). This explicit synchronization loses the advantage of lower overhead; in fact, it is likely to be more expensive than the implicit acknowledgements provided by the synchronous send operation. Using asynchronous messages, one can achieve parallelism by overlapping useful computation with waiting for the acknowledgement. This is not as big of an advantage as it may seem at first for two reasons. Often there is no suitable computation for a thread to do while waiting for the acknowledgement, and when there are multiple threads in a program, parallelism can be gained by running other threads. To use asynchronous message passing correctly without acknowledgements usually requires some a priori knowledge of the system's behavior. The main disadvantages of asynchronous message passing are rooted in the fact that it provides very little synchronization. Thus, the programmer is forced to implement more complicated protocols to achieve the necessary synchronization.

Rendezvous (or blocking send), on the other hand, provides a very strong form of synchronization; namely, the two processes involved in a rendezvous achieve *common knowledge* about the communication. This property makes synchronous message passing easier to reason about, since it avoids a kind of interference where the state of the sender when the message is sent is different than when the message is received. This is also reflected in the typical failure modes of erroneous programs. In asynchronous systems, the typical failure mode is an overflow of the memory used to buffer messages, which is likely to be far removed in time (and possibly place) from the source of the problem. In synchronous systems, the typical failure mode is deadlock, which is immediate and easily detected. Thus, detecting and fixing bugs in a synchronous message-passing program is easier.

Occasionally the buffering provided by asynchronous message passing can be semantically useful, such as in situations where some buffering is required to avoid cyclic dependencies that might cause deadlock. For example, processes can send messages to themselves via a buffered channel, which is not possible over a synchronous channel. In these cases, however, the buffering can be easily provided using an additional process (*à la* the producer/consumer example), or by spawning a new thread to send the message.

The main disadvantage of choosing RPC as the basic communication mechanism is that it is asymmetric. While it makes programming client-server abstractions easier, it does not support other styles, such as producer-consumer networks. For this reason, and because implementing RPC using message passing is more natural than vice versa, message passing is a better choice than RPC for the basic communication primitive of a concurrent language.

A related issue is the choice between generalized selective communication and the input-only form. The advantage of the input-only form is that it is fairly easy to implement efficiently, whereas the generalized form can be quite expensive. On the other hand, the input-only form suffers from the same asymmetry as RPC.

2.6 Parallel programming mechanisms

While the focus of this book is on programming with explicit concurrency, there are some parallel programming mechanisms that are of interest later in the book.

2.6.1 Futures

Various parallel dialects of **Lisp**, such as **Multilisp**, provide a mechanism called *futures* for specifying the parallel evaluation of expressions. Futures combine thread creation, communication, and synchronization into a single mechanism. The **Lisp** expression

```
(let
  ((x (future exp)))
  body)
```

is evaluated by creating a placeholder (sometimes called a *future cell*) binding the variable x to it, and spawning a new process to evaluate *exp*. When the new process has completed the evaluation of *exp*, it fills in the future cell with the result. An attempt to access the value of x in *body* is called *touching* x, and must synchronize on the availability of the value. If the value of x is not available, then the touching process blocks until the evaluation of *exp* is complete and the future cell has been filled.

Futures are not designed to support concurrent programming, rather they are designed to be a parallel programming mechanism. Their main limitation as a concurrent programming notation is that they only provide one chance for communication and synchronization between the parent and child threads. **Multilisp** provides shared memory and low-level locking mechanisms (essentially test-and-set) for supporting other patterns of communication and synchronization. Using other communication and synchronization mechanisms in conjunction with futures can lead to problems, since some implementations consider it optional as to whether a new thread actually gets spawned for each future. For example, if the body of a future has code that synchronizes with its context, this can result in deadlock if the run-time system chooses to use the same process to evaluate both the future's body and its context.

2.6.2 Synchronizing shared-memory

The programming language **ID-90**, and its predecessors, provide *synchronizing shared-memory* for process communication and synchronization. There are two flavors of this: *I-structures* provide write-once semantics, while *M-structures* allow multiple updates.[4] In both cases, the semantics are generalized to various different classes of data structures (*e.g.*, vectors and tuples), but for simplicity, we consider the case of single cells.

An I-structure cell has two states: *empty* and *full*. Unlike variables in **SML** (which are also "single assignment"), an I-structure cell is first allocated and then initialized, which allows one to build up a data structure incrementally. In addition to creation, there are two operations on I-structures: `put`, which puts a value into an empty cell, and `take`, which returns the value of a full cell. Figure 2.7(a) gives the allowed state transitions of an I-structure cell. Applying `put` to a full cell is a dynamic error, while attempting a `take` on an empty cell causes a process to block until the cell is full (*i.e.*, some other process does a `put`). Notice that I-structures capture the basic synchronization mechanism of futures; completing the evaluation of a future causes a `put` of the result, and a touch corresponds to a `get`.

---

[4]The "I" stands for *incremental*, and the "M" for *mutable*.

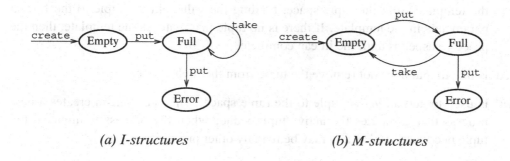

(a) I-structures   *(b) M-structures*

Figure 2.7: Synchronizing-memory state transitions

Like an I-structure, an M-structure cell also has two states (*empty* and *full*). The difference is that a full M-structure becomes empty when a process takes its value (see Figure 2.7(b)). This leads to a protocol for atomic updates: *take-modify-put*. If an M-structure cell is initialized by its creator, and if subsequent to that, every process takes the value, uses it, and then puts a new value back, access to the value will be serialized. This is because taking the value has the effect of locking out other processes until the cell is full again.

A `unit` valued M-structure effectively implements a binary semaphore, with `take` as the **P** operation, and `put` as the **V** operation. Exploiting this fact, we can translate the producer/consumer buffer implementation of Listing 2.2 to one using M-structures, which is given in Listing 2.6. We also make a slight improvement by storing the data value in the `full` M-structure, instead of using a separate reference cell.

2.6.3 Tuple spaces

Tuple spaces are a model of communication for parallel distributed-memory programming. A tuple space is basically an associative memory that is shared by the processes of a system. Unlike hardware memory, the values in a tuple space are tuples of typed fields, which are similar to **SML** tuples. Processes communicate by reading and writing tuple values. Reading a tuple is done by *pattern matching* on a subset of the tuple's fields.

Tuple spaces have been popularized by the **Linda** family of programming languages. The **Linda** languages are traditional sequential languages, such as **C**, extended with a small collection of tuple-space operations. There are four basic operations in the **Linda** model:

out is used to add a tuple to the tuple space.

in takes a tuple *template* (or *pattern*) as an argument, and removes a tuple that matches the template from the tuple space, binding the values in the tuple to the formal parameters in the template. If there is no tuple that matches the template, then the process suspends until the **in** can complete.

rd is like **in**, but does not remove the tuple from the tuple space.

eval is used to add an *active* tuple to the tuple space. This mechanism creates a new process that computes the active tuple value; when the process terminates, the tuple becomes *passive*, and may be read by other processes.

There are also non-blocking variants of **in** and **rd**, called **inp** and **rdp** (the "p" suffix stands for *polling*).

Communication in **Linda** differs from most other distributed-memory communication models, in that the messages (*i.e.*, tuples) are not directed at any particular destination. Instead, once inserted into tuple space, a tuple can be read by any process that executes a matching **rd** operation. This flexibility of communication is further aided by the fact that the templates used in **rd** operations can have undefined fields, called *formals*. A formal matches any field of the right type, no matter what its value. A formal also provides a mechanism to bind the values in the tuple being read to local variables in the process.

As with message passing, tuple spaces can be used directly to provide a connection between a producer and consumer, but, as in the case of asynchronous channels, control-flow must be explicitly programmed. Ensuring FIFO ordering in tuple spaces is also a

```
datatype 'a buffer = BUF of {
    empty : unit m_struct,
    full  : 'a m_struct
}

fun buffer () = let
    val empty = m_struct ()
    in
      put(empty, ());
      BUF{empty = empty, full = m_struct()}
    end

fun insert (BUF{empty, full}, v) = (
    take empty;
    put (full, v))

fun remove (BUF{empty, full}) = (
    (take full) before put(empty, ()))
```

Listing 2.6: Producer/consumer buffer implemented using M-structures

```
fun mkBuffer () = let
        val bufName = a new buffer name
      in
        out ⟨bufName, "empty"⟩;
        bufName
      end

fun insert (bufName, v) = (
      in ⟨bufName, "empty"⟩;
      out ⟨bufName, "full", v⟩)

fun remove bufName = (
      in ⟨bufName, "full", formal v⟩;
      out ⟨bufName, "empty"⟩;
      v)
```

Listing 2.7: Producer/consumer buffer implemented in **Linda**

problem, since reading tuples is nondeterministic. FIFO ordering can be imposed independently of flow-control, by including *sequence numbers* in the tuples, although to support multiple producer or consumer processes requires keeping the sequence counters in tuple space. The implementation of the one-element producer/consumer buffer is given in Listing 2.7 and is quite simple. In this code, v is assumed to be a local variable of the correct type. Unlike in the message-passing case, no extra process is required for the buffer. The tuple ⟨bufName, "empty"⟩ is used to synchronize the producer and consumer; when it is present in the tuple space, the buffer is "empty." The buffer name is a globally unique value used to distinguish one buffer from another. This use of names to tag tuples is very common in **Linda**. It is also one of the weaknesses of **Linda** as a programming notation, since it forces the user to manage the names of the communication channels explicitly. On the other hand, **Linda** does make it easy to support a wide range of different communication patterns, such as multicast and shared work lists.

Notes

There are a number of good surveys of concurrent language design. Bryant and Dennis compare a number of different concurrency mechanisms using two example problems [BD80]. Andrews and Schneider [AS83] survey a broad range of concurrency mechanisms. A more recent survey by Bal, Steiner, and Tanenbaum [BST89] reviews over 90 different concurrent and distributed programming languages, including **CML**'s predecessor **PML** [Rep88]. Wegner and Smolka compare the use of processes and monitors to protect shared state [WS83].

There are also many books on concurrent programming. Andrews [And91] covers concurrent programming using various different languages, as well as covering in detail most of the issues surveyed in this chapter. Birrell gives a tutorial on programming with threads, mutex locks, and condition variables in **Modula-3** [Bir91]. A paper by Hauser et al. describes ten different paradigms of concurrency used in two large interactive applications (one research, one commercial) [HJT+93]. And Gehani and McGettrick [GM88] have collected reprints of significant papers on concurrent languages and programming (including [AS83] and [WS83]).

There are many languages and concurrency libraries based on various shared-memory primitives. Semaphores are often supported by operating systems as a synchronization mechanism (*System V, Release 4* is one example [UNI90]). Monitors were an early attempt to provide more programming language support for shared-memory concurrency [Hoa74]. A number of languages, such as **Concurrent Pascal** [Bri77], **Concurrent Euclid** [Hol83b], and **Mesa** [MMS79, LR80] provide monitors along with condition variables. The experiences with **Mesa** directly influenced the language **Modula-2+** [RLW85] and its successor **Modula-3** [Nel91], which provide independent mutex locks instead of monitors. Following this trend, Cooper and Morrisett, at Carnegie-Mellon University, have developed a concurrency package, called **ML-threads**, which provides threads, mutex locks, and condition variables for **SML** [CM90]. The design of **ML-threads** is owed to the **C-threads** package [CD88], which in turn owes its design to **Modula-2+**. A principal application of the **ML-threads** library is the construction of low-level operating system services, which requires heavy use of shared state [CHL91]. There is also a multiprocessor implementation of a version of **ML-threads** done by Morrisett and Tolmach [MT93]. With the popularity of object-oriented sequential languages, the monitor is making a comeback in the form of synchronizing objects, which provide mutual exclusion in method calls. The most well-known example of this comeback is **Java** [AG98], although **Java** confuses the issue by allowing an object's lock to be used in other ways.

The concept of a set of sequential processes running in parallel and communicating by synchronous message passing was introduced in a seminal paper by Hoare [Hoa78], which described the language **Communicating Sequential Processes (CSP)**. While **CSP** was quite limited as first described (static process creation, direct naming, and input-only guards), it has been the inspiration for many synchronous message-passing languages. The language **occam** [INM84, Bur88] is derived from **CSP**, but includes channels and a limited form of dynamic process creation. The higher-order language **Amber** [Car86] provides generalized selective communication on typed channels, as well as dynamic process and channel creation. Other languages that owe an intellectual debt to **CSP** include **Joyce** [Bri89] and **Pascal-m** [AB86]. A pared down version of **CSP**, called **TCSP**, has been used for theoretical study of concurrent systems [Hoa85].

Actors are a well-known class of concurrent programming languages and systems [Agh86] that are based on asynchronous message passing. The concurrent language **Erlang** is a dynamically typed higher-order language based on asynchronous message passing [AVWW96] and can be viewed as an example of an actor language. It uses dynamic direct naming to specify the destination of messages, and provides an input-only form of selective communication that uses pattern matching to choose between messages in a process's mailbox. **Erlang** was developed at the Ellemtel Computer Science Laboratory for use in programming telephony software. The distributed programming language **SR** provides both shared-memory primitives for local concurrency, and an orthogonal collection of message-passing operations for distributed communication (including an interrupt-driven asynchronous receive mechanism) [AO93].

The choice between asynchronous versus synchronous message passing, and between input-only and generalized selective communication, comes down to two issues: performance and expressiveness. Panangaden and the author have examined the relative expressiveness of different rendezvous primitives [PR97]. These issues are discussed further in Chapter 6.

In the author's personal experience, synchronous message passing is an easier framework for debugging concurrent programs. An early version of the **Pegasus** system [RG86] used asynchronous message passing, but we had great difficulty in debugging our programs. Our experience with implementing **eXene** in **CML** [GR91], on the other hand, demonstrates that large synchronous message-passing programs can be debugged fairly easily, even without debugging tools.

The term "synchronous languages" is used to describe a family of languages that are globally synchronous. The semantics of these languages restrict the history of a system to a totally ordered sequence of *instances* at which events occur. Because of the total ordering of events, these languages are deterministic. Applications of synchronous languages include specifying hardware systems and programming reactive systems. A description of four different synchronous languages and their use in programming reactive systems is given by Halbwachs [Hal93]. Recently, Pucella has been exploring the support of synchronous programming in the context of **SML** (and **CML**) [Puc98].

Futures were originally developed by Halstead in **Multilisp** [Hal85]; they also appear in other parallel **Lisp**s, such as **Mul-T** [KH88]. I-structures and M-structures are from the language **ID** [Nik91]. Arvind, Nikhil, and Pingali discuss the use of I-structures in parallel programs with some small example programs [ANP89]. Barth, Nikhil, and Arvind give some examples of the use of M-structures in **ID** [BNA91]. Milewski proposed a mechanism similar to M-structures for use as an update-in-place data structure in implementations of functional programming languages [Mil90].

The tuple spaces supported by the **Linda** family of languages were first described by Gelernter and Bernstein [GB82, Gel85]. Tuple spaces have been shown to be a portable model of parallel computation, with implementations on machines ranging from shared-memory multiprocessors to distributed-memory multiprocessors to networks of workstations [BCGL87]. A book by Carriero and Gelernter uses **C-Linda** to illustrate parallel programming techniques [CG90]. In Chapter 9, we present a distributed implementation of tuple spaces in the **CML** framework.

While most concurrent languages consist of a sequential sub-language (often a language in its own right) extended with concurrency mechanisms, there are a few languages that have concurrency built in from the ground up. For example, in the language **occam** there are only a few sequential mechanisms, such as iteration [INM84, Bur88]. Another example is the parallel language **ID**, where computation is implicitly parallel, unless explicitly sequenced [Nik91]. An even more extreme case is the recent experimental language **Pict**, in which every construct, including both control and data structures, is expressed in terms of processes and communication [PT97].

There are a number of different approaches to reasoning about concurrent systems. Andrews uses *axiomatic* reasoning based on first-order logic of programs [And91]. While this approach is sufficient to prove safety properties, a richer logic is required to prove liveness properties. Such a logic is called a *temporal logic* and includes *modal operators* for expressing such concepts as *"always"* and *"eventually."* Manna and Pnueli describe the use of temporal logic for specifying reactive and concurrent systems [MP92]. Other approaches to the study of concurrency are the various *process calculi* [Mil89, MPW89a, MPW89b] and *process algebras* [Hen88] that have been developed. These attempt to capture the essence of concurrent computation, much the same way that the λ-calculus captures the essence of sequential computation. While this work is theoretically oriented, it may have an affect on the design of future concurrent languages; for example, the experimental language **Pict** [PT97] is derived from Milner's π-calculus [MPW89a, MPW89b].

Most books on concurrent programming discuss fairness, albeit in an informal way. Kwiatkowska gives a more rigorous treatment in her survey [Kwi89], which is the source of the taxonomy presented in Section 2.3. A wide ranging study of fairness issues can be found in a book by Francez [Fra86]. The fairness requirements on **CML** implementations are discussed in Appendix B.

3

An Introduction to Concurrent ML

This chapter is the first of three tutorial chapters on the basic features and programming techniques of **CML**. This chapter focuses on the features that make up **CML**'s semantic core. The next chapter continues with a discussion of the two most important styles of **CML** programming: *process networks* and *client-server protocols*. Chapter 5 completes the tutorial with further discussion of **CML**'s synchronization and communication mechanisms.

3.1 Sequential programming

As is the case with most concurrent languages, **CML** consists of a sequential core language — Standard ML — extended with concurrency primitives. The individual processes in a **CML** program are programmed using the features of **SML**.[1] While we conceptually view **CML** as a programming language, it is actually implemented as a collection of modules on top of **SML/NJ**. The aspects of **CML** described in this chapter all belong to the core structure of this library, which is named CML. To reduce notational clutter, most of the examples in this chapter are assumed to be given in an environment where the CML structure has been pre-opened (*i.e.*, all of its bindings are at top-level). The CML structure's interface is described in Appendix A, which contains an abridged version of the *CML Reference Manual*.

    CML is a message-passing language, which means that processes are viewed as executing in independent address spaces with their only communication being via messages. But, since **SML** provides updatable references, this is a fiction that must be maintained by programming style and convention. It is good practice to avoid situations where two or more threads share access to a reference or array. Usually, this is not a significant restriction. Shared-state is most likely to be an issue when incorporating existing sequential

---

[1]The term "*communicating sequential processes*" is often used to describe this style of programming.

code into a **CML** application, but even this situation is usually not a problem, since the preferred **ML** programming style is mostly functional. Another potential source of interference is input/output (I/O) using **ML**'s buffered I/O streams. To avoid this problem, **CML** provides its own implementation of the **SML** I/O modules. Discussion of I/O is left to Chapter 5 and the *CML Reference Manual* in Appendix A.

3.2   Basic concurrency primitives

We start with a discussion of the basic concurrency primitives provided by **CML**, which includes process creation and simple message passing via typed channels. In keeping with the flavor of **SML**, both processes and channels are created dynamically.

3.2.1   Threads

Processes in **CML** are called *threads*; this choice of terminology is both to emphasize that they are lightweight, and to distinguish between them and the host operating system's notion of processes. When a **CML** program starts executing, it consists of a single thread of control. This initial thread may create additional threads using the spawn primitive, which has the type

```
val spawn : (unit -> unit) -> thread_id
```

The spawn function takes a function as an argument and creates a new thread of control to evaluate the function applied to the unit value. This use of a function as an argument is a standard technique to delay a computation in a call-by-value language. The newly created thread is called the *child*, and its creator is the *parent*. The return value of spawn is a *thread ID* that uniquely identifies the child thread.[2] The child thread will run until the evaluation of the function application is complete, at which time it terminates. **CML** does not attach any semantics to the parent-child relationship. For example, the termination of the parent thread does not affect the child — once created, the child thread is an independent agent. In particular, this means that the initial thread may terminate without the whole program terminating.

In addition to completing execution of its body, there are two other ways that a thread may terminate. First, it may explicitly terminate itself by calling the exit function, which has the type

```
val exit : unit -> 'a
```

---

[2]See Appendix A for information on the operations on thread IDs.

Like a **raise** expression, the result type of exit is ' a, since it never returns. The other way a thread may terminate is if its execution causes an exception to be raised that is not caught by any handler. Note that such an exception is local to the thread in which it is raised; it does not propagate to its parent.[3]

Since the number of threads in a **CML** program is unbounded and the number of processors on the system is limited, the processors are multiplexed among the threads. This is handled automatically by the **CML** run-time system, which uses periodic timer interrupts to provide preemptive scheduling. This is in contrast with so-called coroutine implementations of concurrency, which require the application programmer to ensure that each thread yields the processor at regular intervals. Preemptive scheduling is important for program modularity, since it allows "off-the-shelf" sequential code, such as libraries, to be used in concurrent programs, without having to add explicit scheduling code. As discussed above, incorporating sequential code into a concurrent program still requires some care, since the code may not be reentrant (*e.g.*, it may use globally allocated mutable data structures).

One important property of threads in **CML** is that they are represented by **SML** values (see Chapter 10). This has two significant consequences: first, they are extremely cheap to create and impose very little space overhead; and second, the storage used to represent a thread is reclaimed by the garbage collector. As we show throughout this book, these properties allow a programming style that uses threads very liberally.

3.2.2 Channels

For multiple threads to be useful, they must have some mechanism for communication and synchronization. **CML** provides a collection of such mechanisms, both as primitives and as libraries. For now, we focus on the most important of these, which is synchronous message passing on typed channels. The type constructor

```
type 'a chan
```

is used to generate the types of channels. A channel for communicating values of type τ has the type τ chan. Two operations are provided for channel communication:[4]

```
val recv : 'a chan -> 'a
val send : ('a chan * 'a) -> unit
```

Message passing is synchronous, which means that both the sender and receiver must be ready to communicate before either can proceed (see Section 2.5.2). When a thread

---

[3]The **CML** run-time system provides a mechanism for reporting the termination of threads as a result of uncaught exceptions. This mechanism is described in the release notes included in the distribution.

[4]Earlier versions of **CML** used the name accept for the recv operation.

executes a `send` or `recv` on a channel, we say that it is *offering* communication. The thread will block until some other thread offers a *matching* communication, that is, the complementary operation on the same channel. When two threads offer matching communications, the message is passed from the sender to the receiver and both threads continue execution. Thus, message passing involves both communication of data and synchronization.

Channels can be viewed as labels for *rendezvous* points — they do not name the sender or receiver, and they do not specify a direction of communication. More than one thread may attempt to `send` or `recv` a message on the same channel. Channels are created dynamically by the function:

```
val channel : unit -> 'a chan
```

3.2.3   Example — Updatable storage cells

A natural first example is the implementation of updatable storage cells on top of threads and channels. We define the following abstract interface to storage cells:

```
signature CELL =
  sig
     type 'a cell

     val cell : 'a -> 'a cell
     val get  : 'a cell -> 'a
     val put  : ('a cell * 'a) -> unit

  end
```

The operation `cell` creates a new cell initialized to the given value; and the operations `get` and `put` are used to read and update a cell's value. Our approach is to represent the state of a cell by a thread, which we call the *server*, and represent the `cell` type as a pair of channels for communicating with the server. The request messages and `cell` type are defined as follows:

```
datatype 'a request = GET | PUT of 'a

datatype 'a cell = CELL of {
     reqCh : 'a request chan,
     replyCh : 'a chan
}
```

The channel `reqCh` carries both `PUT` and `GET` client requests, and the channel `replyCh` carries replies to `GET` requests. The client-side implementation of the `get` and `put` operations is straightforward. Each operation requires sending the appropriate request message, and in the case of `get`, accepting a reply:

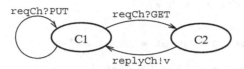

Figure 3.1: The state diagram for the cell server thread

```
fun get (CELL{reqCh, replyCh}) = (
        send (reqCh, GET);
        recv replyCh)

fun put (CELL{reqCh, ...}, x) = send(reqCh, PUT x)
```

Note that this protocol requires that the server send a reply to any GET request it receives. The cell function creates a new cell, which involves allocating the two channels and spawning a new server thread, with the initial value as its state:

```
fun cell x = let
        val reqCh = channel()
        val replyCh = channel()
        fun loop x = (case (recv reqCh)
                of GET => (send (replyCh, x); loop x)
                 | (PUT x') => loop x'
               (* end case *))
        in
          spawn (fn () => loop x);
          CELL{reqCh = reqCh, replyCh = replyCh}
        end
```

Servers are typically implemented as infinite loops, with each iteration corresponding to a single client request (or *transaction*). Since we are programming in **ML**, we use tail recursion to code the loop (*i.e.*, the loop function). These definitions are collected together in the Cell structure, which is shown in Listing 3.1.

While this example is trivial, it illustrates a number of important points. This implementation is a prototypical example of the *client-server* style of concurrent programming (see Section 2.5.4). It is often useful to view a server as a *state machine*; for example, Figure 3.1 gives the state transition diagram for the cell server thread. We use the notation *channel?value* for input transitions and *channel!value* for output transitions (*e.g.*, reqCh?GET means read a GET request from the reqCh channel). In this diagram, State C1 represents the situation where the server is waiting for a message on the reqCh channel, and State C2 represents the situation where a GET request has been received, and the server is attempting to send the reply.

```
structure Cell : CELL =
  struct

    datatype 'a request = GET | PUT of 'a

    datatype 'a cell = CELL of {
        reqCh : 'a request chan,
        replyCh : 'a chan
      }
    fun get (CELL{reqCh, replyCh}) = (
          send (reqCh, GET);
          recv replyCh)

    fun put (CELL{reqCh, ...}, x) = send(reqCh, PUT x)

    fun cell x = let
          val reqCh = channel()
          val replyCh = channel()
          fun loop x = (case (recv reqCh)
                 of GET => (send (replyCh, x); loop x)
                  | (PUT x') => loop x'
                (* end case *))
          in
            spawn (fn () => loop x);
            CELL{reqCh = reqCh, replyCh = replyCh}
          end

  end (* Cell *)
```

Listing 3.1: The complete implementation of updatable cells

These kinds of state diagrams are quite useful for informal reasoning about the behavior of a protocol. For example, the correctness of this implementation relies on the fact that each client's GET request is answered by a server reply, and that each client-server transaction is atomic. The latter fact is a direct result of using synchronous message passing; once the server receives a GET request, it will not accept another request until its reply has been received by the client. This is illustrated in Figure 3.1 by the fact that a GET message causes a transition to State C2, and the only way back to State C1 is by sending the reply message. This guarantees that the transactions are *serialized*, and thus that multiple clients cannot interfere, even though they share the same request and reply channels. If send was not a blocking operation, then we would have to add additional synchronization to guarantee that the reply to a GET request reaches the right client.

This implementation could still be broken by a client violating the protocol (*e.g.*, trying to read a reply without sending a GET request). This problem is avoided by making the cell type abstract, and restricting the user to the get and put operations, which are guaranteed to be well-behaved. For example, the client state transitions associated with the `get` operation are

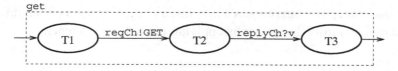

Matching the transitions in this state diagram with those in Figure 3.1 shows that the `get` operation can only proceed when the server is in State C1, and that it completes with the server back in State C1. Looking at the system as a whole, the transitions are

$$(C1, T1) \rightarrow (C2, T2) \rightarrow (C1, T3)$$

Thus, we see that by protecting the implementation inside an abstraction, we can guarantee that clients use it correctly. The use of data and procedural abstraction is an important technique in writing correct concurrent programs (or sequential ones for that matter!).

The above example also illustrates the use of **SML**'s scoping and abstraction mechanisms to implement the hiding of channels. The `cell` function allocates two channels and uses lexical scoping to pass them to the server thread that it spawns (*i.e.*, the channels are in the server's closure). The channels used to communicate with the server are hidden from the client's direct access by the use of an **SML** datatype to hold them, coupled with the `CELL` signature, which does not expose the datatype's representation.

Another important paradigm in message-passing programs is the structuring of computations as networks of processes. These are sometimes called *dataflow networks*, since the data flows from one process to another. The simplest example of this is a *pipeline*, where a group of processes are arranged in series (much like a factory assembly line). Process networks can be viewed as graphs, where the processes are the nodes, and the channels are the edges.

A classic application of dataflow networks is for *stream processing*. A stream can be viewed as a possibly infinite sequence of values. For example, the recurrence

$$nat_0 = 0$$
$$nat_{i+1} = nat_i + 1$$

defines the infinite sequence of natural numbers. This definition can be implemented in **CML** as follows:

```
fun makeNatStream () = let
      val ch = channel()
      fun count i = (send(ch, i); count(i+1))
      in
        spawn (fn () => count 0);
        ch
      end
```

which has the type

$$\textbf{val } \texttt{makeNatStream : unit -> int chan}$$

Each call to `makeNatStream` creates a new instance of the stream of natural numbers. Values are consumed from the stream by applying `recv` to the channel.

3.2.4   Example — Sieve of Eratosthenes

A traditional example of stream programming is computing prime numbers using the *Sieve of Eratosthenes*. We start with the stream of integers beginning with 2 (the first prime). To compute the primes, we filter out multiples of 2, which gives a stream with 3 (the second prime) as its head. We then filter out multiples of 3, giving a stream with 5 (the third prime) as its head. At each step, we take the head of the stream (which is the next prime), and construct a new stream by filtering out multiples of the prime.

The implementation of this sifting process starts with a generalization of the natural number stream that allows us to specify the first number in the sequence. This more general function has the type

$$\textbf{val } \texttt{counter : int -> int chan}$$

The filtering of a stream is provided by the following function, which takes a prime number p and an input stream as arguments, and returns an new stream with multiples of p removed:

```
fun filter (p, inCh) = let
      val outCh = channel()
      fun loop () = let val i = recv inCh
            in
                if ((i mod p) <> 0) then send (outCh, i) else ();
                loop ()
            end
      in
        spawn loop;
        outCh
      end
```

Using the `filter` and `counter` functions, we can define the sieve, which creates a stream of primes:

```
fun sieve () = let
      val primes = channel ()
      fun head ch = let val p = recv ch
            in
                send (primes, p);
                head (filter (p, ch))
            end
      in
        spawn (fn () => head (counter 2));
        primes
      end
```

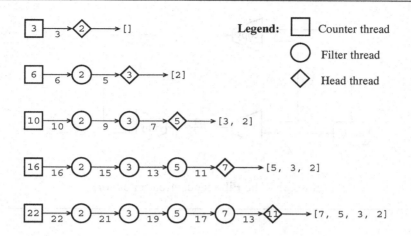

Figure 3.2: Evaluating primes(4)

The sieve function creates a network of threads consisting of a counter thread, which produces the stream of integers, and a chain of filter threads, which end in a head thread. The sieve function returns the channel primes, on which the head thread sends the stream of primes. There is one filter thread in the chain for each prime number sent by the head thread. After the head thread sends a prime p on the primes channel, it spawns a new filter thread to remove multiples of p from the stream, and then reads the next prime from the channel provided by the new filter thread.

The function primes uses the sieve function to compute a list of the first n prime numbers:

```
fun primes n = let
      val ch = sieve ()
      fun loop (0, l) = rev l
        | loop (i, l) = loop (i-1, (recv ch)::l)
      in
        loop (n, [])
      end
```

Figure 3.2 shows the state of the sieve at each iteration of evaluating primes(4). The counter thread is represented as a square labeled by the current counter value. The filters are circles labeled by their prime number, and the head is represented by a diamond labeled with the next prime. The number labeling an arrow between two threads is the value that the thread on the left is offering the thread on the right.

This style of stream processing is similar to the notion of *lazy streams* found in functional languages. The main difference is that there is no mechanism for capturing an

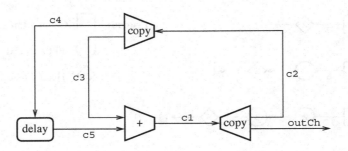

Figure 3.3: The Fibonacci stream network

intermediate value and using it multiple times (the way one can do with a lazy stream).
The streams here are stateful, once a value is read from a stream it cannot be read again.
As we will see in the next example, we can introduce copy nodes when we need to use a
stream in multiple places.

3.2.5   Example — Fibonacci series

Another classic example of dataflow programming is the *Fibonacci series*, which is defined by the recurrence

$$fib_1 = 1$$
$$fib_2 = 1$$
$$fib_{i+2} = fib_i + fib_{i+1}$$

Before implementing a **CML** program that generates this series, let us examine the process network. Each new element in the series is computed from the two previous elements. This means that when the value fib_i is computed, it needs to be fed back into
the network for the computation of fib_{i+1} and fib_{i+2}. This will require nodes that copy
their input to two output channels, and a node that provides a one-element delay. Figure 3.3 gives a picture of this network (the labels on the arcs correspond to the names of
the channels used in the implementation below). When the addition node (labeled by a
"+") produces a result, it is fed back into the computation of the next two elements in the
series.

As shown in Figure 3.3, we can implement the Fibonacci stream using three general
purpose dataflow combinators: *add*, which adds the values from two streams; *delay*,
which provides a one-element delay; and *copy*, which copies its input to two output

```
fun add (inCh1, inCh2, outCh) =
    forever () (fn () =>
      send (outCh, (recv inCh1) + (recv inCh2)))

fun delay init (inCh, outCh) =
    forever init (
      fn NONE => SOME(recv inCh)
       | (SOME x) => (send(outCh, x); NONE)
      (* end fn *))

fun copy (inCh, outCh1, outCh2) =
    forever () (fn () => let
      val x = recv inCh
    in
        send(outCh1, x); send(outCh2, x)
    end)
```

Listing 3.2: Some general dataflow combinators

streams. Each of these combinators is implemented as an infinitely looping thread; the following function is useful in constructing such threads:

```
val forever : 'a -> ('a -> 'a) -> unit
```

The `forever` function takes two arguments: an initial state, and a function from states to states (`forever` is polymorphic in the type of states), and it spawns a thread that repeatedly iterates the function. The implementation is

```
fun forever init f = let
    fun loop s = loop (f s)
  in
      ignore (spawn (fn () => loop init))
  end
```

It is expected that the iterated function does some form of blocking communication. Note that we choose to ignore the thread ID of the spawned thread, which gives `forever` a result type of `unit`.

The implementation of the combinators is given in Listing 3.2. Unlike in the Sieve of Eratosthenes example, the node creation functions do not create their own channels. This is because we need to construct a cyclic process network, which would require a fix-point operator on channel bindings. Instead, we pre-allocate the channels and pass them in as arguments to the node creation functions. The `delay` combinator is essentially the one-element producer/consumer buffer discussed in Chapter 2. Note that the initial state of the buffer is specified as an argument.

The implementation of the network is essentially a direct construction of the picture

```
fun mkFibNetwork () = let
      val outCh = channel()
      val c1 = channel() and c2 = channel() and c3 = channel()
      val c4 = channel() and c5 = channel()
    in
      delay (SOME 0) (c4, c5);
      copy (c2, c3, c4);
      add (c3, c5, c1);
      copy (c1, c2, outCh);
      send (c1, 1);
      outCh
    end
```

Listing 3.3: Implementing the Fibonacci network

in Figure 3.3. As mentioned above, we start by allocating the channels that connect the nodes in the network, and then we create the nodes. Listing 3.3 gives the code for this implementation; note that we use the channel names from the figure in the code. The tricky part in this code is initializing the network. We do this by initializing the delay node to 0 (one may think of this as fib_0), and by sending the value 1 (fib_1) on channel c1. This value then feeds back (via c2 and c3) to be added to 0 to produce the value 1 (fib_2).

There is a subtlety to the implementation of the Fibonacci network that is worth examining. The correctness of this implementation depends on the order in which the copy combinator sends messages on its two output channels, and on the order that the add combinator receives messages on its input channels. If one were to reverse the order of the sends on c3 and c4, the network would deadlock. The problem is that the add node would be attempting to read a value from c3, while the copy node would be attempting to send a value on channel c4, and the delay node would be attempting to send a value to the add node on c5. Although careful coding can avoid this problem in this case, a more robust solution is to make the order of the blocking communication operations nondeterministic. This nondeterminism can be introduced using the mechanism of *selective communication* (see Section 2.5.3).

3.2.6 Selective communication

Selective communication is a key programming mechanism in message-passing concurrent languages. The basic idea is to allow a thread to block on a nondeterministic choice of several blocking communications — the first communication that becomes *enabled* is chosen. If two or more communications are simultaneously enabled, then one is chosen nondeterministically. **CML** provides the select operator for this purpose. This operator takes a list of communications as its argument, and blocks the calling thread until one of the operations is enabled. For example, the add combinator from Listing 3.2 could be recoded to use select to block on reading a value from either inCh1 or inCh2. If it gets a value from inCh1 first, then it must wait to read a value from inCh2 (and vice versa). In **CML**, this is written as:

```
fun add (inCh1, inCh2, outCh) =
      forever () (fn () => let
        val (a, b) = select [
              wrap (recvEvt inCh1, fn a => (a, recv inCh2)),
              wrap (recvEvt inCh2, fn b => (recv inCh1, b))
            ]
      in
         send (outCh, a + b)
      end)
```

This code introduces three new **CML** features: the select operation selects from a choice of communications, the recvEvt function specifies a recv operation inside a select,[5] and the wrap function associates an action with a communication operation. In this example, we are choosing between the operation of receiving a message on inCh1 and the operation of receiving a message on inCh2. In each case, we use wrap to associate the action of waiting for a message on the other channel. The result of this is a pair of values, one from each input channel, that gets summed and sent out on outCh. The body of the add thread executes by blocking until another thread offers a matching send operation on either inCh1 or inCh2, at which point both threads perform the communication. For example, assume that the add thread is blocked on the select operation, and that a thread P executes the following operation:

```
send (inCh1, 17)
```

where inCh1 is bound to the same channel in both threads. Then the add thread receives the value 17 on inCh1, and applies the associated action function to it; in effect, it evaluates the expression

```
(fn a => (a, recv inCh2)) 17
```

which blocks the thread until a value is available from inCh2.

We can also select among output operations, as is illustrated by this recoding of the copy combinator:

---

[5] Earlier versions of **CML** used the name receive instead of recvEvt for this function.

```
fun copy (inCh, outCh1, outCh2) =
    forever () (fn () => let
      val x = recv inCh
    in
      select [
        wrap (sendEvt (outCh1, x),
            fn () => send (outCh2, x)),
        wrap (sendEvt (outCh2, x),
            fn () => send (outCh1, x))
      ]
    end)
```

Similar to `recvEvt`, the `sendEvt` function specifies a `send` operation inside a `select`.[6] A `select` may include both input and output operations. In fact, a thread may even offer to both send and receive a message on the same channel in the same `select`, although this does not allow a thread to communicate with itself, since `select` can only choose one communication.

3.2.7   Example — Updatable cells revisited

An alternative implementation of updatable cells provides a good example of selective communication. Instead of using two different kinds of request messages (GET and PUT), we can use two different channels: one to get the current value from the server, and one to send a new value to the server. Listing 3.4 gives the code for this implementation (the interface is as before). Again the server consists of a tail-recursive loop, with the cell's state as an argument to the function and with each iteration corresponding to one client request. In this implementation, however, the body of the loop consists of a `select` operation. The server offers to either send the current value on the `getCh` channel or receive a new value on the `putCh` channel. The `get` and `put` operations are simply implemented as the complementary message-passing operations on the appropriate channel.

3.3   First-class synchronous operations

We have seen `wrap`, `sendEvt`, and `recvEvt` used to form the clauses of selective communications, but they have another important rôle as part of the general mechanism of *first-class synchronous operations*. The basic idea is to decouple the description of a synchronous operation (*e.g.*, "send the message m on channel c") from the actual act of synchronizing on the operation. We introduce a new kind of abstract value, called an *event*, for representing synchronous operations. **CML** defines the type constructor

```
type 'a event
```

---

[6]Earlier versions of **CML** used the name `transmit` instead of `sendEvt` for this function.

```
datatype 'a cell = CELL of {
    getCh : 'a chan,
    putCh : 'a chan
}

fun get (CELL{getCh, ...}) = recv getCh

fun put (CELL{putCh, ...}, x) = send(putCh, x)

fun cell x = let
    val getCh = channel()
    val putCh = channel()
    fun loop x = select [
            wrap (sendEvt(getCh, x), fn () => loop x),
            wrap (recvEvt putCh, loop)
        ]
    in
        spawn (fn () => loop x);
        CELL{getCh = getCh, putCh = putCh}
    end
```

Listing 3.4: Updatable cells implemented with `select`

which is used to generate the types of abstract synchronous operations. The type τ `event` is the type of a synchronous operation that returns a value of type τ when it is synchronized upon. The aforementioned selective communication operators all produce event values. For example, sending a message returns the type `unit`, so the `sendEvt` operator has the type

```
val sendEvt : ('a chan * 'a) -> unit event
```

The argument to the `chan` type constructor specifies the type of the messages carried by the channel, so the `recvEvt` operation has the type

```
val recvEvt : 'a chan -> 'a event
```

The functions `sendEvt` and `recvEvt` are called *base-event constructors*, because they create event values that describe a single primitive synchronous operation. **CML** follows the convention of appending the "`Evt`" suffix to base-event constructor names.

The power of first-class synchronous operators comes from *event combinators*, which can be used to build more complicated events from the base event values. We have already seen the `wrap` combinator, which has the type

```
val wrap : ('a event * ('a -> 'b)) -> 'b event
```

The `wrap` combinator associates a post-synchronization action, which is called the *wrapper function*, with an event value. For example, synchronizing on

```
wrap (recvEvt ch, fn x => x+1)
```

causes the thread to block until a matching communication is available on `ch`, at which point it completes the communication and applies the wrapper function to the received value (*i.e.*, it adds `1` to it).

This raises the question of how do threads synchronize on events? We have already seen examples of the `select` operator, which has the type:

```
val select : 'a event list -> 'a
```

This takes a list of events and blocks the calling thread until one of the events is enabled, at which point the thread synchronizes on the enabled event. If two or more events in the list are enabled simultaneously, then one is chosen nondeterministically. The `select` operator is actually syntactic sugar for the composition of the `sync` operator and the `choose` event combinator[7]

```
val select = sync o choose
```

The `sync` operator is the basic mechanism for synchronization in **CML**. It takes an event value and synchronizes on it, returning the result. As might be expected, `sync` has the type

```
val sync : 'a event -> 'a
```

The `choose` combinator is used to express nondeterministic choice in an event value, and has the type

```
val choose : 'a event list -> 'a event
```

This combinator takes a list of events and returns an event that represents the nondeterministic choice of the events. When `choose` is applied to the empty list, it returns an event that can never be synchronized on; if a thread attempts to do so, it blocks forever (likewise, executing "`select []`" blocks the thread forever).

As with the `select` operator, we can also view the message-passing operations `recv` and `send` as the composition of `sync` and the corresponding event-valued function

```
val recv = sync o recvEvt
val send = sync o sendEvt
```

---

[7]For performance reasons, `select` is actually implemented as a separate primitive.

This illustrates the decoupling of the description of the operation (*i.e.*, the values created by recvEvt and sendEvt) from the act of synchronization. A good analogy is the use of procedural abstraction, which decouples the description of a computation (the body of the procedure) from the act of computing (the application of the procedure).

The purpose of this separation is to permit user-defined communication and synchronization abstractions that are "first-class citizens." Specifically, these new abstractions can be used in the context of selective communication. We have seen examples of using procedural abstraction to protect the integrity of protocols (the implementation of the Cell structure in Listing 3.1, for example). The limitation of this approach to abstraction is that the operations (*e.g.*, get and put) are functions, which cannot be used as clauses of a selective communication. Procedural abstraction hides too much, because it hides the *synchronous* nature of the operations. While this is not important in the case of updatable cells, there are many examples where this limitation would be a problem. Fortunately, by using **CML**'s first-class synchronous operations, we can have our abstractions and use them too!

It is worth noting that the fact that choose and select take lists of events as arguments makes it easy to support dynamically changing communication structures (an example of this can be found in Chapter 5). This is in contrast with most other message-passing languages, which support selective communication with a select statement. Since any instance of a select statement has a fixed number of clauses, supporting selection from a dynamic number of communications is not possible.

Before looking at examples of using the event constructors and combinators to construct new synchronous abstractions, an informal discussion of their semantics is in order. An event value can be viewed as a tree, where the leaves are the base events (*e.g.*, recvEvt and sendEvt events), and the internal nodes correspond to applications of wrap and choose. For example, consider the event value constructed by

```
val ev = choose [
         wrap (bev₁, w₁),
         wrap (choose [
               wrap (bev₂, w₂),
               wrap (bev₃, w₃),
             ], w₄)
       ]
```

where the bev_i are base events, and the w_i are wrapper functions. This value can be viewed as the tree in Figure 3.4. In this picture, the choose nodes are labeled with $\oplus$, and the wrap nodes are labeled with the wrapper functions. We can understand the semantics of applying sync to the event value *ev* in terms of this picture. The thread blocks until one of the bev_i is enabled by some other thread offering a matching communication. At that point, the communication can proceed, producing result () for the sender, and the sent message for the receiver. The wrapper functions on the path from the selected

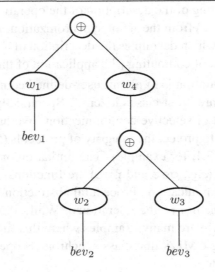

Figure 3.4: An event value tree representation

bev_i to the root are then applied to the result, producing the result of the synchronization. For example, if bev_2 is selected, with result v, then the result of the sync is $w_4(w_2(v))$.

3.3.1   Example — Directional channels

Channels in **CML** are bidirectional; a thread that has access to a channel can both send and receive messages on it. A safer discipline would be to distinguish between input and output accesses to a channel, so that threads could be restricted to only send or receive on a channel. Another way to think of a channel is as a directional pipe, with each end represented by a value of a different type. While such a view of channels could be built into the language, in **CML** we can use events to provide this different style of channels as a *first-class* abstraction. The interface signature for directional channels is given in Listing 3.5. Values of the in_chan type can only be used to read messages, and those of the out_ch type can only be used to send messages. Both procedural and event-valued versions of the channel operations are provided. The implementation is very simple, and can be found in Listing 3.6; note that we use qualified names for the operations from the CML structure, since we use the same names for the directional operations. A directional channel is represented by two values, which share the same underlying bidirectional channel. The communication operations are implemented directly using

```
signature DIR_CHAN =
  sig
    type 'a in_chan and 'a out_chan

    val channel : unit -> ('a in_chan * 'a out_chan)

    val recv    : 'a in_chan -> 'a
    val send    : ('a out_chan * 'a) -> unit

    val recvEvt : 'a in_chan -> 'a event
    val sendEvt : ('a out_chan * 'a) -> unit event

  end; (* DIR_CHAN *)
```

Listing 3.5: Directional channels signature

their bidirectional counterparts. We use **SML** signature matching to control access to the underlying channel.

The importance of this example is that the event-valued operations allow directional channels to be used in selective communications. If we were only interested in providing the procedural operations send and recv, then we could have implemented this abstraction without events. The problem is that send and recv are synchronous operations, and we would like to use them in selective communications, but the procedural

```
structure DirChan : DIR_CHAN =
  struct

    datatype 'a in_chan = IN of 'a CML.chan
    and 'a out_chan = OUT of 'a CML.chan

    fun channel () = let val ch = CML.channel()
        in
          (IN ch, OUT ch)
        end

    fun recv (IN ch) = CML.recv ch
    fun send (OUT ch, x) = CML.send(ch, x)

    fun recvEvt (IN ch) = CML.recvEvt ch
    fun sendEvt (OUT ch, x) = CML.sendEvt(ch, x)

  end;
```

Listing 3.6: The implementation of directional channels

```
fun cell x = let
      val (getInCh, getOutCh) = DirChan.channel()
      val (putInCh, putOutCh) = DirChan.channel()
      fun loop x = select [
              wrap (DirChan.sendEvt(getOutCh, x),
                fn () => loop x),
              wrap (DirChan.recvEvt putInCh, loop)
          ]
      in
        spawn (fn () => loop x);
        (getInCh, putOutCh)
      end
```

Listing 3.7: Updatable cells implemented with directional channels

abstraction used to implement them hides too much. The abstraction provided by events, however, allows access to the channel to be controlled, while not disguising the fact that `recvEvt` and `sendEvt` are synchronous operations. In this sense, the directional channel abstraction is first-class, since its operations can be used in any context that the built in channel operations can be used in. For example, we can implement the updatable cells, using a pair of directional channels to represent each cell. This version does not require `get` or `put` operations; instead, we use directional nature of the channels in the return type of `cell`:

```
val cell : 'a -> ('a DirChan.in_chan * 'a DirChan.out_chan)
```

The cell server must be able to handle either `get` or `put` operations at any time, which means that selective communication is required. But since the directional channel abstraction provides event-valued operations, there is no problem with combining them with selective communication. Listing 3.7 gives this implementation of the `cell` function. We use these directional channels again in the next chapter.

We have seen the `wrap` combinator, which allows a *post*-synchronization action to be associated with an event; **CML** also provides the `guard` combinator, which allows a *pre*-synchronization action to be associated with an event. This is useful to allocate resources, such as reply channels, and to initiate communication with a server. This combinator has the type

```
val guard : (unit -> 'a event) -> 'a event
```

It takes an event-valued function, called a *guard function*, and makes it into an event value; when `sync` is applied to a guard event, the function is first evaluated and then `sync` is applied to its result. Each time a thread synchronizes on the event, the guard function is invoked.

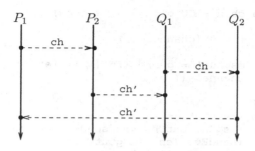

Figure 3.5: A swap mismatch

3.3.2 Example — Swap channels

A simple example of a communication abstraction that uses guards in its implementation is the *swap channel*. This is a new type of channel that allows two processes to swap values when they rendezvous (one might call this *symmetric rendezvous*, since there is no sender/receiver distinction). The interface consists of an abstract type:

```
type 'a swap_chan
```

and functions for creating channels and "*swap*" events:

```
val swapChannel : unit -> 'a swap_chan
val swap        : ('a swap_chan * 'a) -> 'a event
```

When two processes communicate on a swap channel, each sends a value and each receives a value. Implementing this correctly requires some care.

Our implementation is based on the asymmetric message passing operations, so to ensure the symmetry of the operation, each thread in a swap must both offer to send a message and to receive a message on the same channel. We can use the `choose` combinator for this purpose. Once one thread completes a `send` (which means that the other has completed an `recv`), we need to complete the swap, which means sending a value in the other direction. A first solution might be to use another channel for completing the swap, but this results in a race condition when two separate pairs of threads attempt swap operations on the same swap channel at the same time. For example, Figure 3.5 shows what might happen if threads P_1, P_2, Q_1, and Q_2 all attempt a swap operation on the same swap channel at roughly the same time (where the swap channel is represented by the channels ch and ch'). In this scenario, P_1 and P_2 are initially paired, as are Q_1 and Q_2. But there is a race in the second phase of the swaps, and P_1 ends up being paired with Q_2, and P_2 ends up with Q_1 (because Q_1 beats P_1 to reading a value from ch', and P_2 beats Q_2 to sending a value on ch').

```
datatype 'a swap_chan = SC of ('a * 'a chan) chan

fun swapChannel () = SC(channel ())

fun swap (SC ch, msgOut) = guard (fn () => let
      val inCh = channel ()
      in
        choose [
            wrap (recvEvt ch,
              fn (msgIn, outCh) => (send(outCh, msgOut); msgIn)),
            wrap (sendEvt (ch, (msgOut, inCh)),
              fn () => recv inCh)
          ]
      end)
```

Listing 3.8: The swap channel implementation

To avoid this problem, we need to allocate a fresh channel for completing the second phase of the swap operation each time the swap operation is executed. Listing 3.8 shows how the implementation of the swap channel abstraction can allocate a fresh channel for each swap operation. The representation of a swap channel is a single channel that carries both the value communicated in the first phase, and a channel for communicating the other value in the second phase. The channel for the second phase must be allocated before the synchronization on the first message, which is the kind of situation for which guard was designed. The guard function first allocates the channel for the second phase, and then constructs the swap event using the choose combinator. Because of the symmetry of the operation, each side of the swap must allocate a channel, even though only one of them will be used. Fortunately, allocating a channel is very cheap, and the garbage collector takes care of reclaiming it after we are done.

The swap channel example illustrates several important **CML** programming techniques. The use of dynamically allocating a new channel to serve as the unique identifier of a transaction comes up quite often in client-server protocols. It is also an example where the nondeterministic choice is used inside an abstraction, which is why we have both choose and sync, instead of just the select operator. And, lastly, this example illustrates the use of the guard combinator.

3.4 Summary

This chapter has focused on a small core set of **CML** features: thread creation, channel operations, and first-class synchronous operations. The next chapter continues this tutorial with a discussion of more advanced programming techniques. **CML** extends this set of primitives with additional combinators, base-event constructors, and various miscellaneous operations. These are described in Chapter 5 and in Appendix A.

Notes

The use of threads and channels to implement mutable storage cells is one of a number of examples of encoding sequential language features using concurrency. Berry, Milner, and Turner have shown that this encoding is faithful to the sequential semantics of references [BMT92]. Other examples include the **Y** combinator [GMP89, Rep92] and various data structures [PT97]. The **Y** combinator encoding leads to an implementation of reference cells without explicit recursion [Rep92].

4

CML Programming Techniques

This chapter continues the tutorial introduction to **CML** by examining a number of important **CML** programming techniques, as well as introducing some additional **CML** features. The discussion is focused around two important styles of concurrent programming: process networks and client-server programming. We have already seen examples of these styles, but we look at them in much greater depth here.

4.1 Process networks

Process networks are an important tool for structuring concurrent computations. In the previous chapter, we saw two examples of process networks: computing primes using the Sieve of Eratosthenes and generating the Fibonacci series. In this section, we look at two more examples of programming in this style: merge sort, and computing the product of two power series. Both examples illustrate the use of recursively expanding networks, as well as further illustrating the **CML** features that we have seen so far.

4.1.1 Example — Merge sort

Our first example is concerned with sorting a finite sequence of integers using *merge sort*. Merge sort is a divide and conquer algorithm that proceeds by dividing its input into two equal sized sequences, recursively sorting them, and then merging the resulting sorted sequences into a single sorted sequence. The high-level code is

```
fun mergeSort seq = if (length seq = 1)
      then seq
      else let val (s1, s2) = split seq
         in
           merge (mergeSort s1, mergeSort s2)
         end
```

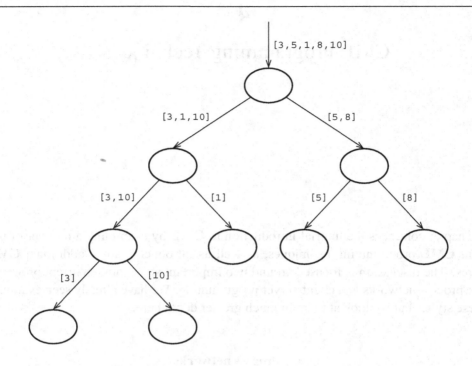

Figure 4.1: Splitting the sequence [3,5,1,8,10]

where the split operation divides the input sequence into two subsequences, which are recursively sorted, and the merge operation merges the two sorted subsequences.

In our **CML** implementation of merge sort, each recursive invocation corresponds to a separate thread, and the sequences are represented by sequences of values sent on a channel. Figure 4.1 shows the downward flow of data in the process network when sorting the sequence [3,5,1,8,10]. Each node represents a thread, and the edges represent the connecting channels. The edges are labeled with the sequence that is passed from the parent to the child.

There are a couple of design details to address. The sequences are finite, so we need a way to mark the end of a sequence. We do this by making the channels carry int option values, and use NONE to represent the end of the sequence. The other issue we need to address is the interface between a merge-sort thread and its two children. We could use two channels for each child thread: one to pass the subsequences from the parent down to the child, and another to pass the sorted subsequences back up. But we can get away with just one channel for each child by exploiting a property of the algorithm. A merge-sort thread will not start reading the sorted subsequences until after

```
fun mergeSort () = let
    val ch = channel()
    fun sort () = (
        case (recv ch)
          of NONE => ()
           | v1 => (case (recv ch)
                of NONE => send(ch, v1)
                 | v2 => let
                     val ch1 = mergeSort ()
                     val ch2 = mergeSort ()
                     in
                        send (ch1, v1); send (ch2, v2);
                        split (ch, ch1, ch2);
                        merge (ch1, ch2, ch)
                     end
                (* end case *))
          (* end case *);
          send (ch, NONE))
    in
      spawn sort;
      ch
    end
```

Listing 4.1: The implementation of a merge-sort thread

it has completely passed both of the unsorted subsequences to its children, and its children must see the entire subsequence before they can pass back the sorted subsequence. Thus, there is no danger of both the child and parent trying to send at the same time.

With these design points decided, we can now look at the implementation. Listing 4.1 gives the code for the body of a merge-sort thread. The mergeSort function creates a new sorting thread and returns the channel for communicating with the thread. It has the type

```
val mergeSort : unit -> int option chan
```

The actual work is done in the sort function, which first attempts to read the first two values in the sequence. If there are fewer than two values, no sorting is required, and it just sends the sequence back. If the sequence has two or more values in it, it recursively creates two sorting threads, with channels ch1 and ch2 as their interfaces. It sends the first two values to its children, and then calls the function split to distribute the rest of the incoming sequence to its children. The implementation of split is given in Listing 4.2. This function is a good example of using the order of arguments to encode state; it alternates between sending a value on ch1 and ch2. The first argument is the incoming value, the second argument is the channel to send the value out on, and the third argument is the other channel. On each iteration, split swaps the second and

```
fun split (inCh, outCh1, outCh2) = let
      fun loop (NONE, _, _) = (
            send (outCh1, NONE); send (outCh2, NONE))
        | loop (x, out1, out2) = (
            send (out1, x);
            loop (recv inCh, out2, out1))
      in
        loop (recv inCh, outCh1, outCh2)
      end

fun merge (inCh1, inCh2, outCh : int option chan) = let
      fun copy (fromCh, toCh) = let
            fun loop v = (
                  send (toCh, v);
                  if (isSome v) then loop(recv fromCh) else ())
            in
              loop (recv fromCh)
            end
      fun merge' (from1, from2) = (
            case (from1, from2)
             of (NONE, NONE) => send (outCh, NONE)
              | (_, NONE) => (
                  send (outCh, from1); copy (inCh1, outCh))
              | (NONE, _) => (
                  send (outCh, from2); copy (inCh2, outCh))
              | (SOME a, SOME b) =>
                  if (a < b)
                    then (
                      send (outCh, from1);
                      merge' (recv inCh1, from2))
                    else (
                      send (outCh, from2);
                      merge' (from1, recv inCh2))
            (* end case *))
      in
        merge' (recv inCh1, recv inCh2)
      end
```

Listing 4.2: The implementation of the `split` and `merge` operations

third arguments. When `split` receives the terminating NONE, it sends NONE to both children.

Once `sort` has received and split its entire input, it then calls the function `merge` to merge the sorted subsequences. The code for this function is also given in Listing 4.2. The `merge` function takes the two input channels to merge and the output channel for the merged sequences as arguments. Its body consists of a loop (the `merge'` function), which repeatedly compares the heads of the two subsequences, sending the smaller value on the output channel. When one of the subsequences is exhausted, the loop continues to copy the other. When both are exhausted, a NONE is sent on the output channel to mark the end of the merge. Note that the merge function does not require selective communication, because we know a priori that there will be values on both input channels until a NONE is encountered.

4.1.2 Example — Power series multiplication

Our second example concerns computations on power series, which are a natural application of stream programming. A power series

$$F(x) = \sum_{i=0}^{\infty} F_i x^i = F_0 + F_1 x + F_2 x^2 + \cdots$$

can be represented as the infinite stream of its coefficients, with the exponents implicit in the position. For notational convenience, we drop the argument x, and write F to denote the power series $F(x)$. In this example, we consider power series with rational coefficients, and assume the existence of a structure named RatNum that implements a rational numbers package. While RatNum presumably provides a full range of operations on rationals, for our example we need only the following limited interface:

```
type rational

val zero : rational

val add : (rational * rational) -> rational
val mul : (rational * rational) -> rational
```

The type rational is the representation of a rational number; the value zero is the representation of 0 as a rational, and the functions add and mul provide rational addition and multiplication, respectively. With this type, a power series can be represented as a channel carrying a sequence of rational coefficients. Since there is a direction to these channels, we use the directional channel abstraction from Listing 3.5. To make the example code more concise, we make the following local structure bindings:[1]

```
structure R = RatNum
structure DC = DirChan
```

With these bindings, the type of a power series stream is

```
type ps_stream = R.rational DC.in_chan
```

The basic structure of a power-series operation is to allocate a channel for the result, spawn a thread to consume the inputs and calculate the result series, and return the input end of the result channel.

---

[1]This kind of local renaming of structures is a much better way to reduce typing than the wanton use of open.

The first power series operation that we consider is the addition of two power series, which is achieved by pointwise addition of coefficients:

$$F + G = \sum_{i=0}^{\infty} (F_i + G_i) x^i$$

This operation is implemented as a `ps_stream` using a thread that repeatedly reads a value from each of two input streams and sends their sum on its output stream. As we saw in the Fibonacci example, we do not want to constrain the order that the inputs are read. It is useful to define a general-purpose function for combining the values from a pair of events that are synchronized in arbitrary order:

```
fun combine f (ev1, ev2) = select [
        wrap (ev1, fn a => f (a, sync ev2)),
        wrap (ev2, fn b => f (sync ev1, b))
      ]
```

This function takes a combining function `f`, and two events as arguments, and synchronizes on the choice of the two events. When one, or the other, event is chosen, `combine` synchronizes on the other, and then returns the result of applying `f` to the pair of synchronization results. It has the type

```
val combine : (('a * 'b) -> 'c) -> ('a event * 'b event) -> 'c
```

In addition, we use the `forever` function defined above (page 49). The implementation of power series addition is similar to the revised version of the `add` function from the Fibonacci example

```
fun psAdd (psF, psG) = let
        val (inCh, outCh) = DC.channel()
        fun add (f, g) = DC.send (outCh, R.add(f, g))
      in
        forever () (fn () =>
          combine add (DC.recvEvt psF, DC.recvEvt psG));
        inCh
      end
```

The main difference is that the `psAdd` function takes its input channels as arguments, but allocates its output channel, which it returns as its result. We structure it this way to exploit the directional nature of the channels.

Multiplying a power series by a constant is defined as multiplying the coefficients by the constant

$$cF = \sum_{i=0}^{\infty} (cF_i) x^i$$

Implementing this as a `ps_stream` is straightforward:

```
fun psMulByConst (c, psF) = let
        val (inCh, outCh) = DC.channel()
    in
        forever () (fn () =>
          DC.send (outCh, R.mul(c, DC.recv psF)));
        inCh
    end
```

Multiplying a power series by a term is slightly more complicated. We have the definition

$$xF = \sum_{i=0}^{\infty} F_i x^{i+1}$$

which can be viewed as the series

$$0 + F_0 x + F_1 x^2 + F_2 x^3 + \cdots$$

In terms of the stream implementation, this is implemented by adding a leading 0 coefficient, and then copying the rest of the stream

```
fun psMulByTerm psF = let
        val (inCh, outCh) = DC.channel()
        fun loop () = (DC.send (outCh, DC.recv psF); loop())
    in
        spawn (fn () => (
          DC.send (outCh, R.zero);
          loop()));
        inCh
    end
```

We now have the building blocks we need for the main part of our example — computing the product of two power series. This is a significantly more complicated problem. The product is defined as

$$P = F \times G$$

Expanding the definitions gives

$$\sum_{i=0}^{\infty} P_i x^i = \left(\sum_{j=0}^{\infty} F_j x^j \right) \times \left(\sum_{k=0}^{\infty} G_k x^k \right)$$

From this we get the definition of the kth coefficient of P:

$$P_k = \sum_{i=0}^{k} (F_i \times G_{k-i})$$

This does not map well onto our streams model, since it requires all of the previous inputs to compute the next output. A better approach is to treat the computation recursively. We

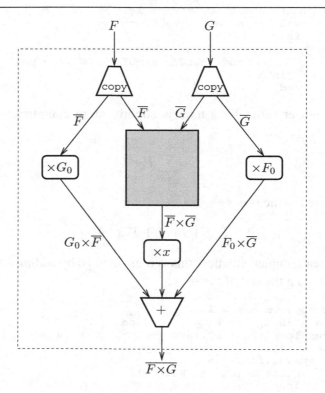

Figure 4.2: The process network for power-series multiplication

use the notation $\overline{F}$ for the power series that forms the *tail* of F; *i.e.*, $F = F_0 + x\overline{F}$. We can then write the product of F and G as

$$P = P_0 + x\overline{P} = F_0 G_0 + x(G_0\overline{F} + F_0\overline{G}) + x^2(\overline{F} \times \overline{G})$$

which gives

$$\begin{aligned} P_0 &= F_0 G_0 \\ \overline{P} &= G_0\overline{F} + F_0\overline{G} + x(\overline{F} \times \overline{G}) \end{aligned}$$

This is much more attractive. The tail of P is the sum of a constant G_0 times the series $\overline{F}$, a constant F_0 times the series $\overline{G}$, and a term times the series formed by multiplying $\overline{F}$ and $\overline{G}$, which we know how to compute by recursion. Figure 4.2 gives the process network for this computation; the shaded box represents the recursive invocation of the network to compute $\overline{F} \times \overline{G}$. Not shown in this picture is the reading of F_0 and G_0 from the input streams, and the output of $F_0 G_0$ as the first coefficient in $F \times G$.

```
fun psCopy psF = let
      val (in1, out1) = DC.channel()
      val (in2, out2) = DC.channel()
      in
        forever () (fn () => let
          val f = DC.recv psF
          in
            combine (fn _ => ())
              (DC.sendEvt(out1, f), DC.sendEvt(out2, f))
          end);
        (in1, in2)
      end
```

Listing 4.3: Copying a power series stream

In addition to multiplication by a constant, and multiplication by a term, this computation also needs to *copy* a stream into two copies. This is done by the function psCopy, which has the type

```
val psCopy : ps_stream -> (ps_stream * ps_stream)
```

The implementation of this function is given in Listing 4.3. Note that we again use combine to synchronize on a pair of events in arbitrary order, although this time the operations are outputs and the resulting unit values are discarded.

Listing 4.4 gives the code for the function psMul, which implements power series multiplication. This function allocates its result channel, and then spawns a thread (the function mul) to implement the network of Figure 4.2. The function mul first reads the heads of the two input streams (f0 and g0). The product of these two values is the first element of the result stream. The remainder of the result stream is copied from the stream psFG, which represents the computation

$$\overline{P} = G_0\overline{F} + F_0\overline{G} + x(\overline{F} \times \overline{G})$$

Note that the streams representing $\overline{F}$ and $\overline{G}$ must be copied.

An important correctness issue with recursive functions is termination. In this case, the corresponding question is can the recursive invocation of the multiplication network get unfolded infinitely deep? We are saved from this problem by the fact that the mul function first reads f0 and g0 before recursively invoking psMul. Since communication is synchronous, the number of recursive invocations is proportional to the number of terms of the result that are demanded (n values require $n + 6$ nested invocations of the network).

Although these two examples of process networks are somewhat contrived, they serve to illustrate many of the techniques used in constructing process networks in **CML**.

```
fun psMul (psF, psG) = let
    val (inCh, outCh) = DC.channel()
    fun mul () = let
        val f0 = DC.recv psF
        val g0 = DC.recv psG
        val (psF', psF'') = psCopy psF
        val (psG', psG'') = psCopy psG
        val psFG = psAdd (
            psMulByTerm (psMul(psF', psG')),
            psAdd (
                psMulByConst (f0, psG''),
                psMulByConst (g0, psF'')))
        fun loop () = (DC.send (outCh, DC.recv psFG); loop())
        in
            DC.send (outCh, R.mul(f0, g0));
            loop ()
        end
    in
        spawn mul; inCh
    end
```

Listing 4.4: Implementing power series multiplication

Chapters 7 and 8 describe more realistic applications that are structured around process networks.

4.2   Client-server programming

The client-server paradigm is a very important model for structuring **CML** programs. Many applications need some notion of shared state; in a message-passing framework, server threads provide a mechanism for mediating access to such shared state. We have already seen simple examples of client-server abstraction in the various versions of updatable cells. In this section, we examine a number of additional examples of client-server protocols.

A typical client-server protocol involves a request message sent by the client to the server, followed by a reply sent by the server to the client. In the simplest case, the request or reply may be implicit in the synchronization. For example, the put operation of the updatable cell example did not involve an explicit reply from the server. The fact that the client's send operation blocks until the server accepts it means that the send serves as its own acknowledgement.

4.2.1 Example — A unique ID service

An example where the request is implicit is a *unique ID server* that provides globally unique IDs (represented by integers) to clients. This service has the following simple interface:

```
val mkUIdSrc : unit -> unit -> int
```

This function creates a fresh source of IDs, which is represented as a function. In a sequential implementation, this would be implemented using an integer counter stored in a reference cell

```
fun mkUIdSrc () = let
        val cnt = ref 0
        fun next () = let val n = !cnt
            in
                cnt := n+1; n
            end
    in
        next
    end
```

This implementation is not safe for **CML**, since accesses to the counter cnt are a potential source of interference. For example, if two threads attempt to get unique IDs from the same source at the same time, they might get the same IDs, which violates the global uniqueness property that we are trying to implement. To provide this service in **CML**, we need to encapsulate the state in a server thread and use a channel to get the IDs. The function mkUIdSrc allocates a new channel, spawns a new server, and returns a function that reads values from the channel:

```
fun mkUIdSrc () = let
        val ch = channel()
        fun loop i = (send(ch, i); loop(i+1))
    in
        spawn (fn () => loop 0);
        fn () => recv ch
    end
```

Instead of using a reference cell as a counter, we keep track of the next ID as the argument to loop. Because communication on the channel is synchronous, we do not need any kind of request or acknowledgement message.

Notice that the mkUIdSrc function is similar to some of the functions we used to generate streams. Sometimes the distinction between stream-style and client-server style programming is fuzzy.

4.2.2 Commit points

While one-way communication is useful in client-server implementations, a more typical interaction involves communication in both directions (*e.g.*, the storage cell in Section 3.2.3). When presenting such a protocol as an abstract synchronous operation, there is a question about when the client should synchronize on the event. For example, consider the following client-side implementation of a simple request-reply protocol:

```
fun rpc req = wrap (
        sendEvt (reqCh, req),
        fn () => recv replyCh)
```

If this is used inside a `select`, the decision to choose this event over another is going to be based on whether the `sendEvt` event is enabled (*i.e.*, whether the server is offering to accept a request). We call the `sendEvt` base event the *commit point* (or *synchronization point*) of the protocol, because of its rôle in a selective communication. Once a thread has synchronized on the commit point of a protocol, it is committed to the choice of that particular protocol.

For client-server protocols that use two-way communication, there are two possible choices for the commit point: either the request message communication or the reply message communication. Which is better depends on the server's semantics and protocol. The simplest choice is to make the request be the commit point, since this has both the client and server agreeing to the transaction up front. We have already seen the `wrap` combinator used to implement this style of protocol; in the remainder of this chapter, we look at the issues related to making the reply be the commit point.

4.2.3 Guards in RPC

The `guard` combinator introduced in the previous chapter is an important mechanism in the implementation of RPC-style protocols; namely, it allows a client to send a request, and then use the acceptance of the server's reply as the commit point. For example, the client-server protocol from above can be recast as follows:

```
fun rpc req = guard (fn () => (
        send(reqCh, req);
        recvEvt replyCh))
```

where the guard function first sends the request, and then returns the event value for accepting the server's reply. In practice, however, there are a number of subtleties to this kind of protocol.

When using `guard` to construct an event value, one must be careful to make sure that the guard function is a "good citizen." It should be written so as to execute in a bounded and reasonably short amount of time, and should not raise exceptions. The most common problem is when a guard involves communication, such as in the example above. Unless one has a priori knowledge that sending the request to the server will not block for an unbounded amount of time, such as in the case when the server is always available, one should use asynchronous communication.

4.2.4 Example — A clock server

A simple example of the use of guards in a client-server protocol, where the client synchronizes on the reply, is the implementation of a *timeout* mechanism using a clock server. We want to define a module, called `ClockServer`, that provides an event constructor `atTimeEvt`, which returns an event for synchronizing on a specified time. This constructor has the signature

```
val atTimeEvt : Time.time -> unit event
```

The basic client-server protocol is for the client to send a request to the clock server, which includes the wake-up time and a fresh reply channel; when the wake-up time arrives, the server sends a message on the reply channel. The reply channel serves as a unique identifier for the client's request. We use a top-level channel for requests:

```
val timerReqCh : (time * unit chan) chan
```

This channel is global in the sense that it is shared by all clients of the server; of course, it is hidden inside the `ClockServer` structure, and clients only access it via the `atTimeEvt` function.[2] The implementation of `atTimeEvt` uses a guard function to allocate the reply channel, and send the request, returning an event that synchronizes on the reply:

```
fun atTimeEvt t = guard (fn () => let
    val replyCh = channel()
    in
        spawn (fn () => send (timerReqCh, (t, replyCh)));
        recvEvt replyCh
    end)
```

Note that the request is sent asynchronously (by spawning a new thread to send it).

The implementation of the clock server is given in Listing 4.5. In this figure, we assume that there is a `unit` event called `tick`, which produces a synchronization event at regular intervals (this can be viewed as a read-only channel that provides a unit message every tick of the clock).[3]

As usual, the clock server is written as a tail-recursive loop; its state is the set of waiting threads, which is represented as a sorted list. Each element contains the time to wake the thread, and the channel on which to send the wake-up message. The function `insert` is used to insert an element into the sorted list. The server waits on the choice of two events: either receiving a client's request or a clock tick. When a client request

---

[2]The initialization and management of global channels and servers requires some special hooks. The *CML Reference Manual* that comes with the **CML** distribution describes these in detail.

[3]Such a channel does *not* exist in **CML**, but **CML** does directly support the timeout mechanism described in this example (see Section 5.2.2).

```
fun server waitingList = let
    fun insert (req as (t, _), []) = [req]
      | insert (req as (t, _), (elem as (t', _))::r) =
        if Time.< (t, t')
          then req::elem::r
          else elem::(insert(req, r))
    fun wakeup () = let
        val now = Time.now()
        fun wake [] = []
          | wake (waiting as ((t, replyCh)::r)) =
            if Time.< (now, t)
              then waiting
              else (
                spawn (fn () => send (replyCh, ()));
                wake r)
        in
          wake waitingList
        end
    in
      select [
          wrap (recvEvt timerReqCh,
              fn req => server (insert (req, waitingList))),
          wrap (tick,
              fn () => server (wakeup ()))
      ]
    end
```

Listing 4.5: The clock server implementation

is received, it is inserted into the waiting list. When a clock tick occurs, the server calls
the wakeup function, which gets the current time and sends wake-up messages to those
clients whose time has come.

The sending of the wake-up messages must be done asynchronously, because the client
may have been synchronizing on the choice of an atTimeEvt event and some other
synchronous operation. If the other operation is chosen before the specified time, then
the client will never accept the wake-up message, and the thread that sends the wake-up
message will deadlock. Therefore, the wakeup function spawns a new thread to send the
wake-up message. Figure 4.3 shows the two possible histories for an interaction between
a client and the clock-server. We assume that the client has executed the expression

```
select [ev, atTimeEvt t]
```

where *ev* is some other synchronous event. In these pictures, the jagged arrows represent
spawning a thread, the open square is the beginning of a thread's execution, and the
filled square represents a thread's termination. In Figure 4.3(a), the waiting time occurs
before the event *ev* was enabled, and the client receives the wake-up message. On the

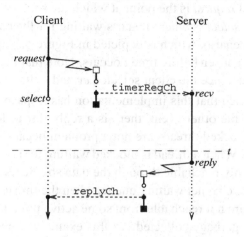

(a) *The client times out*

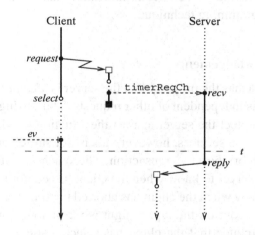

(b) *The client selects some other event ev*

Figure 4.3: Clock-server histories

client's history, the label *request* is the point at which the `atTimeEvt` guard function is evaluated, and the label *select* is where it starts waiting for the base events that make up the choice. The other scenario, which is depicted in Figure 4.3(b), is where the event *ev* becomes enabled and is chosen before time *t* occurs. Note that the thread spawned by the server is blocked forever, since the client selected *ev* and will not accept the reply.

One might be concerned that this implementation has a space leak, since each time a client thread chooses some other event, there is a reply thread left blocked forever. In **CML**, however, these blocked threads are not a problem because they will be automatically *garbage collected*. When a thread is blocked waiting for a synchronous operation to be enabled, its state is only reachable through the data structures associated with the operation (*e.g.*, through the channel waiting queue, when the thread is sending a message). If those data structures are not reachable from some active thread, then both they, and the blocked thread, will be garbage collected. In this example, since neither the client nor the server has a reference to the channel that was allocated for the reply, both it and the thread spawned by the server to send the reply will be garbage collected. This style of speculatively spawning threads to send communication that might never be accepted is an important **CML** programming technique.

4.2.5   Negative acknowledgements

The clock server example has the property that the server is *idempotent*; *i.e.*, that the handling of a given request is independent of other requests. Thus, using a new thread to send a reply is sufficient to protect the server against the situation in which the client selects some other event. For some services, however, this is not sufficient; the server needs to know whether to *commit* or *abort* the transaction. The synchronization involved in sending the reply allows the server to know when the client has committed to the transaction, but there is no way to know when the client has aborted the transaction by selecting some other event. While a timeout on the reply might work in some situations, the absence of a reply does not guarantee that the client has selected some other event; the client might just be slow. To ensure the correct semantics, we need a mechanism for *negative acknowledgements*. The following event combinator provides such a mechanism:

```
val withNack : (unit event -> 'a event) -> 'a event
```

This combinator behaves like `guard`, in that it takes a function whose evaluation is delayed until synchronization time, and returns it as an event value. The main difference is that at synchronization time, the guard function is applied to an *abort event*, which is enabled only if some other event is selected in the synchronization.

To make the workings of negative acknowledgements more concrete, consider the following simple use of `withNack`:

```
fun mkEvent (ev, ackMsg, nackMsg) = withNack (fn nack => (
        spawn (fn () => (sync nack; TextIO.print nackMsg));
        wrap(ev, fn _ => TextIO.print ackMsg))
```

This function takes an event, and returns one that will print the message `ackMsg`, if it is chosen, and the message `nackMsg` if another event is chosen. Printing the acknowledgement is easy — `mkEvent` wraps the event with a wrapper function that prints `ackMsg`. To print the negative acknowledgement message, `mkEvent` spawns a thread that waits for the negative acknowledgement event `nack` and then prints `nackMsg`. If the event is chosen, then the `nack` event will never be enabled, and thus the `nackMsg` will not be printed (instead, the thread will be garbage collected). For example, consider what happens if `ch2` is chosen when executing the following synchronization:

```
select [
    mkEvent (recvEvt ch1, "ch1\n", "not ch1\n"),
    mkEvent (recvEvt ch2, "ch2\n", "not ch2\n")
    ]
```

This will cause the messages "`ch2`" and "`not ch1`" to be printed (the actual order of the messages is nondeterministic).

There are a couple of points about `withNack` that are worth clarification. Let *ev* be an event value constructed by applying `withNack` to a guard function *g*. Then, each time *ev* is involved in a synchronization, *g* will be applied to a fresh abort event. This property holds even in situations such as

$$select \ [ev, \ ev]$$

where there are multiple instances of *ev* in a single synchronization. In this case, each instance of *ev* has its own abort event. If the event value returned by `withNack` is composed of the choice of several base events, then the abort event is only enabled if *none* of the base events is chosen.

4.2.6 Example — Lock server

To illustrate the use of `withNack`, we present the implementation of a *lock server*. This service provides a collection of locks that can be acquired or released (much like mutex locks). The interface is

```
type lock

val acquireLockEvt : lock -> unit event
val releaseLock    : lock -> unit
```

where the abstract type `lock` represents a lock identifier. For purposes of this example, we ignore the question of how lock names are created.

If a client attempts to acquire a lock that is held, then it must wait until the holder of the lock releases it. Since a client may not want to wait indefinitely, the acquireLockEvt function is event-valued so that it can be used in selective communication (with a timeout, for example). This is clearly a case where we want to synchronize on the acquiring of the lock, rather than on the sending of the request. Thus, we need to use a guard function to send the request, and return an event that represents the acquisition of the lock.

The server maintains a set of locks that are currently held; for each lock in the set, it keeps a queue of pending requests for the lock. When a lock is released, the next requesting thread on the queue gets the lock. There is a subtlety to the servicing of pending requests. Consider the case where a client A requests a lock l that is held by some other thread B. By the time B releases l, A may no longer be interested in it (*e.g.*, its attempt to synchronize on acquiring the lock may have timed out). In this case, if the server still thinks that A wants the lock l, it will assign l to A, resulting in starvation for any future attempt to acquire the lock. Clearly, this situation is a problem — we need to structure the protocol so that the server gets the *negative* information that the requesting client is no longer interested in the lock. This problem is what withNack is designed to solve.

The lock type is represented by integer lock IDs wrapped by a datatype constructor:

datatype lock = LOCK **of** int

We assume that there is some mechanism for generating the lock IDs, such as an instance of the unique ID server from above. As with the clock server, we use a top-level channel, called reqCh, for sending requests to the lock server. There are two kinds of request messages, corresponding to the two operations:

```
datatype req_msg
   = ACQ of {
         lock    : int,
         replyCh : unit chan,
         abortEvt : unit event
      }
   | REL of int
```

In these messages, we strip off the LOCK constructor and just send the integer ID of the lock.

The client-side implementation of the acquireLockEvt operation is implemented using withNack applied to a guard function:

```
fun acquireLockEvt (LOCK id) = withNack (fn nack => let
      val replyCh = channel()
   in
      spawn (fn () => send (reqCh, ACQ{
         lock= id, replyCh= replyCh, abortEvt= nack
      }));
      recvEvt replyCh
   end)
```

```
structure M = IntBinaryMap

fun mkLockServer () = let
    fun replyToAcquire (replyCh, abortEvt) = select [
            wrap (sendEvt(replyCh, ()), fn () => true),
            wrap (abortEvt, fn () => false)
        ]
    fun server locks = (case (recv reqCh)
        of (ACQ{lock, replyCh, abortEvt}) => (
            case M.find(locks, lock)
            of NONE =>
                if (replyToAcquire (replyCh, abortEvt))
                then server (M.insert(locks, lock, ref[]))
                else server locks
            | (SOME pending) => (
                pending := !pending @ [(replyCh, abortEvt)];
                server locks)
            (* end case *))
        | (REL lock) => let
            val (locks', pending) = M.remove(locks, lock)
            fun assign [] = locks'
              | assign (req::r) = if (replyToAcquire req)
                then (pending := r; locks)
                else assign r
            in
                server (assign (!pending))
            end
        (* end case *))
    in
        spawn (fn () => server(M.empty)); ()
    end
```

Listing 4.6: The lock server implementation

The guard function allocates a channel for the server's reply, and sends an ACQ request message, containing the lock's ID, the reply channel, and the abort event, to the server. The guard function returns the reply event. The client-side implementation of the releaseLock operation is trivial:

```
fun releaseLock (LOCK id) = send (reqCh, REL id)
```

The implementation of the lock server is given in Listing 4.6. The server's state is represented by finite map from lock IDs to queues of pending acquire requests. We use the **SML/NJ** Library's IntBinaryMap structure to implement the finite map.[4] The ID map has the type

---

[4]The IntBinaryMap structure provides a functional implementation of finite maps with integer keys.

```
(unit chan * unit event) list ref IntBinaryMap.map
```

where each pending acquire request is represented by the pair of the reply channel and abort event. We use a reference to a list to represent the pending request queue, because it simplifies the code for inserting and removing requests for held locks.

When an ACQ request comes in, the server checks to see if the lock is held (*i.e.*, if it is in the domain of `locks`). If so, the request is added to the end of the pending request queue for the lock; otherwise, the server attempts to assign the lock to the requesting client by calling `replyToAcquire`. This function synchronizes on the choice of the client accepting the reply and the transaction's abort event. We are guaranteed that exactly one of these events will be enabled.[5] The function `replyToAcquire` returns `true` if the transaction commits, and `false` if it aborts.

When a REL request comes in, the server checks to see if there are any pending acquire requests for the lock. If there are no pending requests, then the lock is released by removing it from `locks`. In the case that there are pending acquire requests, the server attempts to assign the lock to the next pending request in the queue. The recursive function `assign` repeatedly attempts this until either a client commits to acquiring the lock or the queue is exhausted. In the latter case, the lock is released.

Figure 4.4 shows process histories for the two scenarios that an interaction between a client and the lock server might follow. We assume that the client has executed the expression

```
select [ev, acquireLockEvt l]
```

where *ev* is some other synchronous event, such as a timeout. The picture in Figure 4.4(a) shows the history when the client successfully acquires the lock. The history when the client selects some other event and the transaction is aborted is shown in Figure 4.4(b). The diagonal dashed arrow represents the enabling of the abort event.

Notes

The structuring of programs using *streams* dates back to Landin [Lan65]. Abelson and Sussman discuss the use of streams for programming a number of problems [ASS85]. The realization of streams programs as process networks can be traced to a seminal paper by Kahn and MacQueen [KM77]; for this reason, these are often called *Kahn-MacQueen networks*. The use of process networks to implement power series computations was suggested by Kahn and MacQueen, but not described in any detail. The presentation here is owed to McIlroy, who described implementations of power series multiplication

---

[5]This guarantee assumes well-behaved guards in the client's synchronization expression.

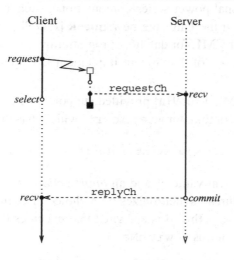

(a) *The client commits*

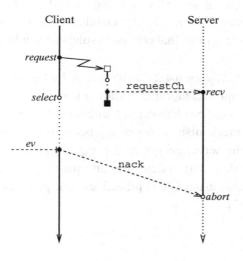

(b) *The client aborts*

Figure 4.4: The commit/abort lock server histories

and a number of additional power series computations, such as composition and exponentiation [McI90], using the language **newsqueak** [Pik89b]. Čubrić has developed a library package on top of **CML** for dataflow programming [Čub94b, Čub94a]. The main focus of her work is the use of dataflow to implement DSP (Digital Signal Processing) applications.

Earlier versions of **CML** [Rep91a] provided support for negative acknowledgements in the form of the event combinator wrapAbort, which has the type

```
val wrapAbort : ('a event * (unit -> unit)) -> 'a event
```

This function takes an event value *ev* and an *abort action* as arguments, and returns an event *ev'*. Whenever a thread synchronizes on a choice of events that includes *ev'*, and chooses some other event, a thread is spawned that executes the abort action. We can define this combinator in terms of withNack

```
fun wrapAbort (ev, abortFn) = withNack (fn nack => (
        spawn (fn () => (sync nack; abortFn()));
        ev))
```

It is also possible to implement withNack using wrapAbort. The main reason for favoring withNack is that it more closely matches common usage. Most uses of wrapAbort involved abort actions that consisted solely of sending a negative acknowledgement message.

The lock server example in Section 4.2 was motivated by Gehani and Roome's description of a **Concurrent C** implementation of a similar server [GR86]. Their implementation uses the *conditional accept* mechanism of **Concurrent C** to accept only requests for locks that are free. This mechanism is necessary because in **Concurrent C** the client can synchronize only on the server accepting the request, and not on the server's reply. Chapter 5 of the author's dissertation describes an implementation of **Concurrent C**'s conditional entry mechanism using **CML** primitives, and presents a version of the lock server built using it [Rep92].

5

Synchronization and Communication Mechanisms

In the previous two chapters, we have studied **CML** as a *message-passing* language. While this is the most natural model of **CML** programming, we can also view it as a language for programming synchronization. **CML**'s event values provide a uniform framework for incorporating a range of synchronous operations. Some are implemented as primitives in the **CML**, while others are provided by libraries, and still others are defined by the application programmer. Independent of their implementation, however, these operations all fit into the same uniform framework of event values. In this chapter, we examine a variety of synchronization mechanisms in the context of **CML**.

5.1   Other base-event constructors

So far, we have seen event constructors for synchronous message passing, but there are a number of other constructors. The simplest of these is the event-valued constant `never`, which has the type

```
val never : 'a event
```

This value will never be enabled for synchronization (it is equivalent to the expression "`choose []`"), and is the identity for the `choose` combinator.

The `alwaysEvt` constructor is used to build an event-value that is always available for synchronization. It has the type

```
val alwaysEvt : 'a -> 'a event
```

When applied to a value *v*, it returns an event value that is always enabled for synchronization with the result *v*. For example, an infinite stream of `1`s can be implemented as

```
val ones = always 1
```

Note that using `alwaysEvt` in a choice does *not* provide a reliable polling mechanism. For example, the following function does not poll a channel for input accurately:

```
fun pollCh ch = select [
        alwaysEvt NONE,
        wrap (recvEvt ch, SOME)
    ]
```

Although it will never block, it may return `NONE` even when there is a matching communication available on `ch`. This result is because there is no priority ordering of base events and the `alwaysEvt` might be chosen over the `recvEvt`.

In general, polling is the wrong technique to use in **CML**. It is much simpler, and more efficient, to use selective communication and additional threads of control. There are some protocols, however, where polling for the availability of a communication may improve efficiency. One example is the implementation of asynchronous RPC (or *promises*) in a distributed setting (see Section 2.5.4). This mechanism might have the interface

```
val promiseEvt : t -> s event
```

where "`t`" is the argument type and "`s`" is the result type of the RPC. The result of calling `promiseEvt` is an event value that represents the promise of a reply from the server.[1] The basic implementation of this might consist of a client-side buffer thread that collects requests and occasionally forwards them to the remote server. The reason that we do not transmit each request directly to the remote server is that by batching the messages, we can reduce system call overhead and make better use of network bandwidth. The buffer thread is also responsible for forwarding the server's replies to the clients. A possible communication pattern for this implementation is given in Figure 5.1. Notice that if the client thread synchronizes on the promise before the buffer thread has forwarded the requests, it will have to wait longer than necessary. We can avoid this inefficiency by polling for the reply in the event value that represents the promise. The following is a sketch of how this might be implemented:

```
fun promiseEvt x = let
        val replyCh = channel ()
        in
          request (x, replyCh);
          guard (fn () => (case (recvPoll replyCh)
            of NONE => (flush(); recvEvt replyCh)
             | (SOME y) => alwaysEvt y
            (* end case *)))
        end
```

In this example, the `request` function is used to initiate the RPC by sending the argument to the buffer thread, and the `flush` function is used to tell the buffer thread to flush

---

[1] Note that unlike some of the other client-server examples we have seen, each synchronization on the promise event does not result in another request.

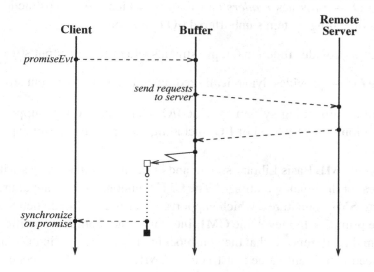

Figure 5.1: Asynchronous remote procedure call

messages to the server. The `recvPoll` function is provided by **CML**, and has the type

```
val recvPoll : 'a chan -> 'a option
```

Notice that in the case where the reply is available already, we use `alwaysEvt` to turn the reply into an event value.[2]

5.2 External synchronous events

In Chapter 1, we argued that concurrency was necessary to handle external synchronous events, but, so far, we have not seen how these external events manifest themselves in **CML** programs. In this section, we describe the **CML** interface to various kinds of external synchronous events. Again, we exploit first-class synchronous operations to treat these in the same framework as internal synchronization.

5.2.1 Input/output

An important form of external event is the availability of user input. The **SML** Basis Library organizes the portable I/O interface into three levels:

---

[2]Note that many of the communication mechanisms provide a primitive polling operation; see Appendix A for details.

1. *Primitive I/O* — provides *readers* and *writers*, which are an abstraction of the underlying operating system's unbuffered I/O operations.

2. *Stream I/O* — provides functional input streams and buffered output streams.

3. *Imperative I/O* — provides dynamically redirectable input and output streams.

In addition, there are operating system specific I/O operations. **CML** supports event-based input operations at every level of I/O, including the operating system specific operations.

CML extends the **SML** Basis Library stream and imperative I/O interfaces with event-value constructors for the input operations.[3] The **CML** versions of these signatures match the corresponding **SML** signatures, which supports easier reuse of code between **CML** and **SML**. At the primitive I/O level, the **CML** interface is not compatible with the **SML** interface — the main difference is that the non-blocking I/O operations in the readers and writers are replaced with event-value constructors. **CML** also provides a mechanism for making a text input or output stream from a string-valued channel.

The availability of event constructors for input operations allows threads to combine them with other synchronous operations. For example, one could read a user-supplied input, such as a password, with a time limit using the following function:

```
fun inputOrTimeOut timeLimit = select [
        wrap (timeOutEvt timeLimit, fn () => NONE),
        wrap (TextIO.inputLineEvt TextIO.stdIn, SOME)
    ]
```

The `timeOutEvt` constructor is described in the next section.

CML does not provide event-value constructors for imperative and stream-level output operations, since output streams are buffered. At the primitive I/O level, however, there are event-value constructors for output operations, but synchronization on output is only useful for devices with flow-control.

5.2.2 Timeouts

Timeouts are another important example of external synchronous events. Most concurrent languages provide special mechanisms for "timing out" on a blocking operation; in **CML** this notion fits naturally into the framework of events. **CML** provides two event constructors for synchronizing on time events:[4]

```
val timeOutEvt : Time.time -> unit event
val atTimeEvt : Time.time -> unit event
```

---

[3]The text versions of these extensions are described in Appendix A.
[4]In earlier versions, these were called `timeout` and `waitUntil`.

The `timeOutEvt` constructor returns an event for synchronizing on a time that is *relative* to time at which synchronization is performed. For example, the following code delays the calling thread for one second:

```
sync (timeOutEvt (Time.fromSeconds 1))
```

The `atTimeEvt` constructor is used to synchronize on an absolute time.

Synchronization on time values is, by necessity, approximate. The granularity of the underlying system's clock, scheduling delays in the underlying operating system, and delays in the **CML** scheduler tend to delay synchronization on a time value slightly. For example, consider the following code for advancing the display of a clock face:

```
fun loop () = (
      sync (timeOutEvt (Time.fromSeconds 60));
      advanceClock();
      loop())
```

Because of the possible delays in resuming the thread, the clock face would slowly lose time. To avoid this kind of problem, one should use `atTimeEvt` when the application is sensitive to clock drift.

When using a timeout in conjunction with other synchronizations, some thought should be given to the desired semantics. For example, consider the buffer thread in the implementation of promises given in Section 5.1. We might program the main loop of this thread as follows:

```
fun loop msgs = select [
      wrap (timeOutEvt tq,
        fn () => (flushMsgs msgs; loop [])),
      wrap (recvEvt reqCh,
        fn (MSG m) => loop (m :: msgs)
         | FLUSH => (flushMsgs msgs; loop []))
      ]
```

where the value `tq` is the amount of time to wait before sending data over the network, the function `flushMsgs` sends the messages over the network, and `reqCh` is the channel on which new messages (`MSG`) and flush requests (`FLUSH`) arrive. The problem with this implementation is that the timeout gets reset each time a new message comes in, which will delay the sending of messages over the network. In fact, if new messages arrive at a rate that is greater than $\frac{1}{tq}$, then the messages will never be sent (unless a `FLUSH` request comes in). To avoid this problem, we could use the `atTimeEvt` constructor, or we could use a separate timer thread. We chose the latter in the following code:

```
fun loop () = let
    fun timerThread () = (sync(timeOutEvt tq); send(reqCh, FLUSH))
    fun empty () = (case (recv reqCh)
            of (MSG m) => (spawn timerThread; nonempty [m])
             | FLUSH => msgs)
            (* end case *))
    and nonempty msgs = (case (recv reqCh)
            of (MSG m) => nonempty (m :: msgs)
             | FLUSH => (flushMsgs msgs; empty())
            (* end case *))
    in
       empty ()
    end
```

In this code, whenever a message is received when the buffer is empty, a new timer thread is spawned. This ensures that a message will have to wait no longer than the time specified by `tq` before being sent over the network.

5.2.3 Signals

Signals are a mechanism for presenting external events to a UNIX process. While they are OS-specific, a small subset of them have equivalents on almost every modern operating system. These include alarms, keyboard interrupts, program termination, and a signal from the run-time system notifying the application that a garbage collection has occurred. Since **CML** already provides a timeout mechanism, it only provides interrupt (`sigINT`), termination (`sigTERM`), and garbage collection (`sigGC`) signals.[5] Signals are delivered to the **CML** application as a buffered stream of messages. Whether a signal is actually delivered to an application depends on the signal's *state*, which can be *handled*, *ignored*, or *default*. In the handled case, when a signal occurs, it is sent on the appropriate signal stream. If a signal is being ignored, then no action is taken when it occurs. The default action depends on the operating system and the signal, but it will either be to ignore the signal or to terminate the program.

For example, an application may wish to print a message and terminate upon receiving a `sigINT` signal. The following initialization code enables this behavior:

```
let fun handler () = let
        val strm = Signals.signalStream()
        in
           Signals.setHandler (Signals.sigINT, Signals.HANDLE strm);
           Signals.recvSig strm;
           TextIO.print "[Interrupt]\n";
           OS.Process.exit OS.Process.failure
        end
    in
       spawn handler
    end
```

---

[5]On some operating systems, such as UNIX, a larger collection of signals is supported. The details are in the documentation distributed with the **CML** software.

The handler thread works by creating a new signal stream and installing it as the stream for sigINT. It then waits for a signal on the stream, and then terminates the program with a failure status code. For further information about **CML**'s signal mechanism, see the documentation distributed with the **CML** software.

5.3 Synchronizing shared-memory

Synchronizing shared-memory provides an attractive alternative to traditional shared-memory mechanisms, since it couples synchronization with memory access. Because of the synchronous aspect of memory accesses, synchronizing shared-memory fits into the **CML** framework in a natural way. In this section, we first show how M-structure cells, which we call *M-variables*, can be implemented as an abstraction. **CML** provides both M-variables and I-variables, and we describe uses of these in Section 5.3.2.

5.3.1 Implementing M-variables

We have seen threads used to hold the state of an updatable cell. This technique can also be used to implement synchronizing memory, such as an M-structure cell. Recall from Section 2.6.2 that M-structure cells are either empty or full, and that the *take* operation blocks until the cell is full, and that attempting to *put* a value into a full cell is an error. The interface is as follows:

```
type 'a mvar

val mVar : unit -> 'a mvar

exception Put

val mTakeEvt : 'a mvar -> 'a event
val mPut      : ('a mvar * 'a) -> unit
```

M-variable cells are created in an empty state. The take operation is supported by the event-value constructor mTakeEvt, since it may block, and the mPut operation raises the Put exception when the cell is already full.

The implementation of this abstraction is given in Listing 5.1. The mvar type is an abstraction of a set of channels for communicating with the server. The getCh channel is used to take values from the server, and the putCh and ackCh channels are used to implement that mPut operation. The mvar function creates the M-variable server and allocates the channels for communicating with clients. The server implementation follows the state machine described in Figure 2.7(b) (page 33), with the exception that there is no error state. The mutually recursive functions empty and full represent the two states of the M-variable. In the empty state, the server will only accept a mPut operation; when it does so, it sends a true acknowledgement and becomes full. In

```
datatype 'a mvar = MV of {
    takeCh : 'a chan,
    putCh : 'a chan,
    ackCh : bool chan
  }

fun mVar () = let
    val takeCh = channel()
    val putCh = channel()
    val ackCh = channel()
    fun empty () = let val x = recv putCh
        in
            send (ackCh, true);
            full x
        end
    and full x = select [
            wrap (sendEvt(takeCh, x), empty),
            wrap (recvEvt putCh,
                fn _ => (send(ackCh, false); full x))
        ]
    in
      spawn empty;
      MV{ takeCh = takeCh, putCh = putCh, ackCh = ackCh }
    end

fun mTakeEvt (MV{takeCh, ...}) = recvEvt takeCh

exception Put

fun mPut (MV{putCh, ackCh, ...}, x) = (
    send (putCh, x);
    if (recv ackCh) then () else raise Put)
```

Listing 5.1: The M-variable implementation

the full state, the server offers its contents on the getCh; when this is taken, the server becomes empty again. The server will also accept a put request when full, but in this case it sends a false acknowledgement and does not change its state.

The mTake operation is very simple: it just attempts to read a value from the getCh channel. Effectively, this implementation uses the channel's waiting queue to manage waiting threads. The mPut operation involves communication in both directions: the client first sends a put request, and then accepts an acknowledgement. If the acknowledgement is true, the cell was empty and the mPut operation succeeded, but if the acknowledgement is false, then the cell was full and the Put exception is raised.

```
exception Put

type 'a ivar

val iVar     : unit -> 'a ivar
val iPut     : ('a ivar * 'a) -> unit
val iGet     : 'a ivar -> 'a
val iGetEvt  : 'a ivar -> 'a CML.event
val iGetPoll : 'a ivar -> 'a option
val sameIVar : ('a ivar * 'a ivar) -> bool
```

Listing 5.2: I-variable operations

5.3.2 Synchronous variables in CML

CML provides "variables" with I-structure and M-structure semantics; these can be found in the `SyncVar` structure (see Appendix A for the full interface). While we have seen how these objects can be implemented in terms of threads and message passing, the actual **CML** implementation is more direct and efficient. Because of this, I-variables and M-variables can often be used to improve performance in situations where the full generality of message passing is overkill. M-variables are used typically to hold some rarely changing shared state (essentially a safe replacement for reference cells). In the remainder of this section, we examine situations where I-variables can be useful. The **CML** interface to the principal I-variable operations is given in Listing 5.2; a complete list can be found in Appendix A (as well as a description of the M-variable operations).

Futures

Futures are a mechanism for specifying parallel computation found in many parallel dialects of **Lisp** (see Section 2.6.1). The future construct wraps up a computation as a logically separate thread, and returns a placeholder, called a *future cell* for the computation's result. The act of attempting to read a value from a future cell is called *touching*. If a thread attempts to touch a future, before the computation of its value is completed, then the touching thread blocks.

Implementing a simple version of futures in **CML** is quite easy. Since touching a future cell is a synchronous operation, we represent the future cells directly as event values (instead of introducing new type), and we use `sync` to touch a value. The future operation has the type:

```
val future : ('a -> 'b) -> 'a -> 'b event
```

We use an I-variable to represent a future cell, since it directly supports the right synchronization semantics. Because the evaluation of a future might result in a raised exception, the I-variable must be able to hold either the result or an exception. The following datatype is used to represent the contents of a future cell:

```
datatype 'a result = RESULT of 'a | EXN of exn
```

The implementation of `future` is straightforward:

```
fun future f x = let
      val futureCell = SyncVar.iVar()
      fun f' () = (RESULT(f x) handle ex => EXN ex)
      in
        spawn (fn () => SyncVar.iPut (futureCell, f'()));
        wrap (
          SyncVar.iGetEvt futureCell,
          fn (RESULT x) => x | (EXN ex) => raise ex)
      end
```

This function spawns a new thread to evaluate its first argument applied to its second, and creates an I-variable for reporting the result. The application of f to x is wrapped up in f'; notice that if the application raises an exception, then it is caught and returned as the result. The result of `future` is an event value that synchronizes on the result of the application being written into `futureCell`. This event is wrapped with a function that strips off the `RESULT` constructor in the normal case, and raises the exception otherwise. Note that the exception is raised in the touching thread's exception context.

RPC protocols

An important use of I-variables is for the efficient implementation of "one-shot" communications. For example, the communication from the timer thread to the buffer thread in Section 5.2.2 is done only once, and could be implemented using an I-variable. A prime example of one-shot communications are the reply communications found in many RPC-style protocols. For example, the clock server of Section 4.2.3 allocated a new reply channel for each request, which was used to send only one reply (the wake-up message). We can reimplement this server using an I-variable to replace the reply channel. The changes are quite simple. We replace the reply channel with an I-variable, and the channel operations with the corresponding I-variable operations, and change the request channel's type to

```
val timerReqCh : (time * unit SyncVar.ivar) chan
```

The advantage of this implementation is that sending a message on a channel is significantly more expensive than writing to an I-variable. An additional benefit is gained by the fact that `writeVar` is a non-blocking operation, which means that the server does not have to spawn a thread to send the wake-up message. Listing 5.3 shows the new implementation of the clock server from Section 4.2.3 (modifications are underlined). The

```
fun atTimeEvt t = guard (fn () => let
    val replyV = SyncVar.iVar()
    in
      spawn (fn () => send (timerReqCh, (t, replyV)));
      SyncVar.iGetEvt replyV
    end)

fun server waitingList = let
    fun insert ...
    fun wakeup () = let
        val now = Time.now()
        fun wake [] = []
          | wake (waiting as ((t, replyV)::r)) =
            if Time.< (now, t)
              then waiting
              else (
              SyncVar.iPut (replyV, ());
              wake r)
        in
          wake waitingList
        end
    in
      ...
    end
```

Listing 5.3: The clock server using I-variables

changes affect only the `atTimeEvt` function and the `wakeup` function in the server.

Measurements suggest that using an I-variable for the reply in an RPC protocol can save around 35% of the synchronization and communication costs. In this example, the savings are even greater, since we avoid spawning a thread for the reply. Of course, we can only use an I-variable when the protocol does not depend on the server synchronizing on its reply being accepted. Protocols that involve negative acknowledgements, such as the lock-server protocol in Section 4.2.5, cannot be implemented using I-variables.

Stream programming

In Chapter 3, we saw several examples of stream-style programming, where streams were represented as channels. The drawback to this representation is that the streams are stateful, once a value is read, it cannot be read again. I-variables can be used to implement "true" streams; *i.e.*, stream values that can be used multiple times without copying.[6] The type of streams as seen by a consumer is

---

[6]This observation should come as no surprise, since I-variables were designed for implementing incremental data structures, such as streams.

```
datatype 'a stream = NIL | HD of ('a * 'a stream event)
```

where NIL represents the termination of a finite stream, and HD represents the head element plus an event for getting the stream's tail. In practice, it is useful to view a stream as represented by a stream event. Using this representation, the following function constructs a list of the first n elements of a stream:

```
fun takeN (s, n) = let
      fun f (0, _, l) = rev l
        | f (_, NIL, l) = rev l
        | f (i, HD(x, s), l) = f (i-1, sync s, x::l)
      in
        f (n, sync s, [])
      end
```

The recursion here is quite similar to the recursion used to iterate on lists; the only difference is that we synchronize to get the next element of the stream. The difference between this view of streams, and that of Chapter 3 is that a stream value is "functional." Reading from it multiple times will always produce the same answer.

We could implement this representation using threads and channels. It requires creating a new thread and channel for each element in the stream, where the thread repeatedly offers to send the element's value on the channel. A more direct approach is to implement these streams using I-variables. For the producer of a stream, each element of a stream is represented as an I-variable:

```
type 'a stream_elem = 'a stream SyncVar.ivar
```

The following function creates a new stream and returns the pair of the producer's view and the consumer's view:

```
fun stream () = let
      val iv = SyncVar.iVar ()
      in
        (iv, SyncVar.iGetEvt iv)
      end
```

A producer can extend or terminate a stream using the following two functions:

```
fun extendStream (iv, v) = let
      val iv' = SyncVar.iVar ()
      in
        SyncVar.iPut (iv, HD(v, SyncVar.iGetEvt iv'));
        iv'
      end

fun terminateStream iv = SyncVar.iPut (iv, NIL)
```

A simple example of a producer is a thread that generates a finite stream of integers from i to j:

```
fun fromTo (i, j) = let
      val (iv, strm) = stream()
      fun iter (iv, i) = if (i < j)
            then iter (extendStream (iv, i), i+1)
            else terminateStream iv
    in
      spawn (fn () => iter (iv, i));
      strm
    end
```

Careful examination of this program reveals a fatal flaw in this representation of streams — these streams are being evaluated *eagerly* instead of *lazily*. For example, calling the function `fromTo` will immediately result in the entire stream being computed. The problem is that writing to an I-variable is an asynchronous operation, so there is no flow-control to inhibit evaluation (see Section 2.5.1). As is shown in Section 5.5, there are situations where the eager version of streams is useful, but for the stream algorithms given in Chapter 3 we need lazy evaluation.

To force lazy evaluation, we need to introduce synchronization to inhibit the producer from racing ahead of the consumer. This synchronization can be achieved either by having the consumer *demand* the next value or by having the consumer *acknowledge* the consumption of a value. A potential problem with these schemes is that multiple consumers may demand (or acknowledge) the same value, but only the first of these communications matters. One solution is to use a datatype to represent the forward link, with constructors for evaluated and unevaluated links, and an M-variable to hold the link. To get the next element, one can take the value from the variable, and if it is evaluated follow it (after putting it back), and if it is unevaluated demand the value. **CML** uses a mechanism similar to this one to implement the functional input streams described in Section 5.2.1.

5.4 Buffered channels

Buffered channels provide a mechanism for asynchronous communication between threads. Buffering of communication is useful in a number of situations. One important example is when a cyclic communication pattern is required, which would result in deadlock if programmed using synchronous communication. Sometimes this buffering can be provided by having additional threads on the communication path (the copy nodes played this rôle in the Fibonacci example in Section 3.2), but in other cases it is necessary to introduce unbounded buffering.

A buffered channel consists of a queue of messages; when a thread sends a message on a buffered channel, it is added to the queue without blocking the sender. If a thread attempts to read a message from an empty buffered channel, then it blocks until some other thread sends a message. This design is a generalization of the one-element producer/consumer buffer that was used as a running example in Chapter 2. The signature

```
signature BUFFER_CHAN =
sig
  type 'a buffer_chan

  val bufferChannel : unit -> 'a buffer_chan

  val send    : ('a buffer_chan * 'a) -> unit
  val recvEvt : 'a buffer_chan -> 'a event

end; (* BUFFER_CHAN *)
```

Listing 5.4: The buffered channels interface

of this abstraction is given in Listing 5.4. Sending a message is non-blocking, so the send operation is provided as a unit-valued function (`send`), while a thread attempting to receive a message may block, so the receive operation is provided as an event constructor (`recvEvt`).

The queue of messages is maintained by a *buffer thread*. Communication to the buffer thread is via a pair of channels, one for `send` operations, and one for `recvEvt` operations. The implementation is given in Listing 5.5. The function `bufferChannel` creates the channels that represent the buffer channel, and spawns the buffer thread. The channel `inCh` is used to send messages to the buffer thread, while the channel `outCh` is used to receive messages from the buffer. As usual, the buffer thread is a tail-recursive function, with its state maintained in its arguments. The state is the message queue, which is represented using the functional queues provided by the `Fifo` structure from the **SML/NJ** Library. When the queue is empty, the buffer thread can only offer to accept messages from `inCh`, which means that any attempt to read a message from the buffer will block. When there is at least one message in the queue, the buffer thread offers to both accept an additional message, which gets added to the rear of the queue, and to send the queue's first message on the `outCh`. The operations `send` and `recvEvt` perform the corresponding **CML** operation on the appropriate channel in the buffer channel's representation. Note that although `send` is implemented using the blocking `send` operation, it cannot be delayed indefinitely, since the buffer thread is always willing to accept a communication on the `inCh`. Sometimes it is useful to apply a filter or translation to the messages in the buffer, in which case the implementation described here can be easily modified. **CML** supports buffered asynchronous communication via the `mailbox` abstract type, which is described in the reference manual (see Appendix A).

```
structure BufferChan : BUFFER_CHAN =
  struct

    datatype 'a buffer_chan = BC of {
        inCh : 'a chan,
        outCh : 'a chan
      }

    structure Q = Fifo

    fun bufferChannel () = let
        val inCh = channel() and outCh = channel()
        fun loop q = if (Q.isEmpty q)
            then loop(Q.enqueue(q, recv inCh))
            else select [
              wrap (recvEvt inCh,
                fn y => loop(Q.enqueue(q, y))),
              wrap (sendEvt(outCh, Q.head q),
                fn () => loop(#1(Q.dequeue q)))
              ]
      in
        spawn (fn () => loop(Q.empty));
        BC{inCh=inCh, outCh=outCh}
      end

    fun send (BC{inCh, ...}, x) = CML.send (inCh, x)

    fun recvEvt (BC{outCh, ...}) = CML.recvEvt outCh

  end; (* BufferChan *)
```

Listing 5.5: The implementation of buffered channels

5.5 Multicast channels

Another useful abstraction is a *buffered multicast channel*, which builds on the buffered channel abstraction by providing *fan-out* to multiple readers. A multicast channel has a single input port and number of output ports. When a thread sends a message on a multicast channel, it is delivered once to each output port. The interface to the multicast channel abstraction is given in Listing 5.6. The type constructor mchan generates the types of multicast channels, and port is the corresponding type of output ports. The interface includes operations for creating a new channel (mChannel), asynchronously sending a message to the ports of a channel (multicast), creating a new output port (port), and constructing an event for receiving a message from a port (recvEvt).

A multicast channel is implemented as a process network, consisting of a server thread that supports the multicast and port operations, and a chain of ports ending in a sink. Figure 5.2 gives a pictorial view of this process network. Each port consists of a pair

```
signature MULTICAST =
  sig

    type 'a mchan
    type 'a port

    val mChannel  : unit -> 'a mchan
    val port      : 'a mchan -> 'a port
    val multicast : ('a mchan * 'a) -> unit
    val recvEvt   : 'a port -> 'a event

  end (* MULTICAST *)
```

Listing 5.6: The multicast channel interface

of threads: a *tee* thread that provides the linkage between the ports, and a buffer thread that provides the output buffering for the port. For the buffer, we use **CML** *mailboxes*, which are similar to the buffered channels described in the previous section. When a message is multicast, the server sends it to the first thread in the chain. When a tee thread gets a message, it sends the message to the corresponding mailbox and to the next tee thread in the chain (or to the sink). New ports are added to the front of the chain by the server.

The implementation of the multicast abstraction is given in Listing 5.7. A multicast channel value is represented by a request/reply channel pair that provides an interface

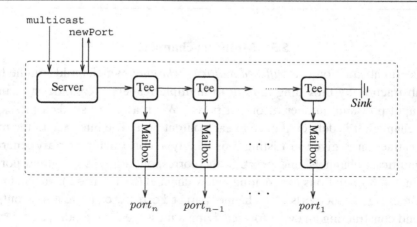

Figure 5.2: Multicast channel process network

```
structure Multicast : MULTICAST =
  struct

    structure MB = Mailbox

    datatype 'a port = Port of 'a MB.mbox

    datatype 'a mchan = MChan of ('a request chan * 'a port chan)
    and 'a request
      = Message of 'a
      | NewPort

    fun mChannel () = let
        val reqCh = channel() and replyCh = channel()
        fun mkPort outFn = let
            val mbox = MB.mailbox()
            val inCh = channel()
            fun tee () = let val m = recv inCh
                in
                    MB.send(mbox, m);
                    outFn m;
                    tee()
                end
            in
              spawn tee;
              (fn msg => send(inCh, msg), Port mbox)
            end
        fun server outFn = (case (recv reqCh)
            of NewPort => let val (outFn', port) = mkPort outFn
                in
                    send (replyCh, port);
                    server outFn'
                end
             | (Message m) => (outFn m; server outFn)
            (* end case *))
        in
          spawn (fn () => server (fn _ => ()));
          MChan(reqCh, replyCh)
        end

    fun multicast (MChan(ch, _), m) = send (ch, Message m)

    fun port (MChan(reqCh, replyCh)) = (
        send (reqCh, NewPort);
        recv replyCh)

    fun recvEvt (Port mbox) = MB.recvEvt mbox

  end (* Multicast *)
```

Listing 5.7: The implementation of multicast channels

to the server thread. A request is either a message to be broadcast or a request for a new port. The `multicast` and `port` functions are trivial; the interesting function is `mChannel`, which implements the process network in Figure 5.2.

The `mChannel` function creates the request and reply channels, and spawns the server thread. In its initial state, any messages that are sent on the channel will just be dumped in the sink. Instead of directly representing the links in the chain of ports as channels, which would require making the sink a thread, we use an abstract output function (`outFn`) to implement the links (*i.e.*, the right-pointing arrows in Figure 5.2). For the sink, this output function is a no-op, and for the other links, it is implemented using `send`. The server thread's state consists of the output function for the current head of the chain. As usual, each iteration of the server handles a client request. When the server gets a `Message` request, it simply passes the message on to the head of the chain. When it gets a `NewPort` request, it calls the `mkPort` function with the current output function as an argument. This returns a new output function for the server and the event value that represents the port, which the server sends back to the requesting client. The `mkPort` function creates the new tee thread and buffer channel, and connects them together.

There are problems with this implementation of the multicast-channel abstraction. Once a thread acquires a port, it must consume all future messages that are sent on the channel. If it stops consuming messages while another process is still producing them, the buffering of these messages in the port becomes a space leak. Of course this problem can occur with the simple buffered channel abstraction of the previous section, but it is a greater restriction in the case of the multicast channel, since often the set of consumers is dynamic. For example, multicast channels can be used in GUIs to support multiple views of a shared object. If the user closes one of the views, then some provision for releasing the corresponding port must be made. There are several possible solutions to this problem:

- A client can attach a "*sink*" thread to the port, which consumes any future messages. This addresses the main source of space leaks, but does not work very well in the situation where clients are repeatedly creating and discarding ports, since the chain of ports continues to grow. It also has the disadvantage of requiring the client to manage the freeing of ports explicitly.

- The abstraction can be extended to include a `delete` operation that removes the port from the multicast network. This approach avoids the problem of the monotonically growing chain of ports, but the implementation is fairly complicated, and it also requires explicit management of ports by the client.

- One might use some form of finalization mechanism (as provided by the **SML/NJ** garbage collector), but this does not address the basic complexity of the deleting ports from the chain.

Another approach, which is much more attractive, uses a completely different implementation of the abstraction. The idea is to generalize the "true" streams implementation described in Section 5.3.2. These streams allow multiple threads to read the same value, which is the essence of multicast. We can view the sequence of values sent on a multicast channel as a stream, and the state of each multicast port as a point in the stream. Reading a value from a port advances that port's view of the stream, but does not affect the other ports. Using a stream obviates the need for providing a port for each buffer, but we still use a tee thread for each port to keep track of the port's state and to map the stream value to a message on a channel.

An element v in the stream of values is represented by the pair (v, iv), where iv is the I-variable that refers to the next stream element. The concrete representation of a stream cell is the recursive datatype

```
datatype 'a mc_state = MCState of ('a * 'a mc_state SyncVar.ivar)
```

The type name includes the word *state*, because the state of a port is one of these values.

The stream-based implementation has the same interface as the previous version (see Listing 5.6), and the representation of multicast channels and the implementation of the `multicast` and `port` operations is almost identical to those given in Listing 5.7. The only difference is that we use a synchronous channel to connect the tee thread with the client of a port — this has the effect of reducing space consumption. Most of the changes are localized to the `mChannel` operation, which is shown in Listing 5.8. The body of the server thread handles `newPort` messages in essentially the same way as before. The main difference in the server thread is that its state is now represented by the I-variable that will hold the next stream value (`iv`). When the server receives a `Message` request, it allocates a new I-variable (`nextIV`) for the next stream element, and writes the pair of the message value and `nextIV` into `iv`; `nextIV` then becomes the server's new state. The main difference in the `mkPort` function is in the `tee` thread, which now consumes the stream of values, sending each one on its output channel.

Figure 5.3 gives a pictorial view of the process network for the stream-based version of Figure 5.2. In this picture, the shaded band represents the stream of values that have been multicast (v_1 through v_5 so far). Each element in the stream is represented as a pair of the value and a reference to the next value in the stream; the symbol Λ is used to represent the empty I-variable. The dotted lines connect the threads (represented as rounded rectangles) with the stream element that they are currently holding. For example, the client of $port_1$ will see v_4 as its next message. The initial I-variable and the first stream cell, which holds v_1, are not referenced by any thread and thus can be reclaimed by the garbage collector.

```
structure Multicast : MULTICAST =
  struct

    datatype 'a port = Port of 'a chan

    datatype 'a mchan = MChan of ('a request chan * 'a port chan)

    and 'a request
      = Message of 'a
      | NewPort

    datatype 'a mc_state = MCState of ('a * 'a mc_state SyncVar.ivar)

    fun mChannel () = let
        val reqCh = channel() and replyCh = channel()
        fun mkPort iv = let
            val outCh = channel()
            fun tee iv = let
                val (MCState(v, nextIV)) = SyncVar.iGet iv
                in
                    send (outCh, v);
                    tee nextIV
                end
            in
              spawn (fn () => tee iv);
              Port outCh
            end
        fun server iv = (case (recv reqCh)
            of NewPort => (
                send (replyCh, mkPort iv);
                server iv)
             | (Message m) => let val nextIV = SyncVar.iVar()
                in
                    SyncVar.iPut (iv, MCState(m, nextIV));
                    server nextIV
                end
            (* end case *))
        in
          spawn (fn () => server (SyncVar.iVar()));
          MChan(reqCh, replyCh)
        end

    ...

  end (* Multicast *)
```

Listing 5.8: Multicast channels using I-variables

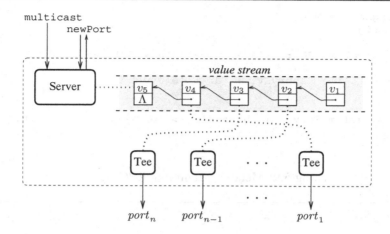

Figure 5.3: Stream-based multicast network

5.6 Meta-programming RPC protocols

As we have seen, client-server (or RPC) communication structures are very important in many concurrent programs. This importance has led the designers of several languages, such as **Ada** and **Concurrent C**, to provide RPC-style communication as the basic communication and synchronization mechanism (see Section 2.5.4). Unfortunately, this approach has the disadvantage of making other communication patterns, such as process networks, more difficult to program. **CML** takes the alternative approach of providing one-way communication as its primitive, and providing an abstraction mechanism for building more complicated protocols such as RPC. Of course, the **CML** approach has the disadvantage of requiring more programming when using RPC-style protocols. In this section, we show how a combination of higher-order functions and event values can be used to provide a "*meta-programming*" facility for RPC-style protocols, which eliminates most of the programming overhead.

5.6.1 Simple RPC

The basic idea is to take a definition of a server operation and package up the communication protocol as a pair of operations: one for the server and one for the client. A server operation is an instance of the polymorphic type:

```
('a * 'b) -> ('a * 'c)
```

```
signature MAKE_RPC =
  sig

    val mkRPC : (('a * 'b) -> ('a * 'c)) -> {
           call     : 'b -> 'c,
           entryEvt : 'a -> 'a event
         }

    val mkServer : 'a -> ('a -> 'a event) list -> unit

  end;
```

Listing 5.9: Meta-programming RPC signature

where the type variable ′a is the type of the server's state, the variable ′b is the type of the operation's argument, and the variable ′c is the type of the operation's result. Thus, a server operation takes a state and an argument and returns a new state and result.

The RPC meta-programming module, called MakeRPC,[7] has two operations: mkRPC, which implements the client and server-side operations for a given server operation, and mkServer, which implements the server from a list of server operations. Listing 5.9 gives the interface of these operations. The mkRPC function takes a server operation, and returns a record consisting of the client-side call, and the server-side entryEvt. The resulting entryEvt function maps the server's state to an event that returns the new state as a synchronization result. The mkServer function takes an initial server state and a list of entries, and spawns a server that handles the entries.

Listing 5.10 gives the implementation of the MakeRPC structure. The mkRPC function implements a vanilla RPC protocol with the client-side call operation represented as a blocking function call. On the client side, the call function allocates an I-variable for the reply, sends the server a request consisting of the call's arguments and the reply variable, and then waits for the reply. The server-side entryEvt function is not much more complicated. It wraps the doCall function around the receiving of a client's request. The doCall wrapper evaluates the operation on the given state and arguments, sends the result back to the client, and returns the new state as the synchronization state. The mkServer function is quite simple. It spawns a thread that repeatedly synchronizes on the choice of the list of entry events. The selection is constructed by applying each entry event function to the current state. The result of the selection is the server's next state.

---

[7]The **CML** Library also provides an RPC meta-programming module called SimpleRPC. See the *CML Reference Manual* in Appendix A for details.

```
structure MakeRPC : MAKE_RPC =
  struct

    fun mkRPC f = let
          val reqCh = channel ()
          fun call arg = let
                val reply = SyncVar.iVar ()
                in
                  send (reqCh, (arg, reply));
                  SyncVar.iGet reply
                end
          fun entryEvt state = let
                fun doCall (arg, replyV) = let
                      val (newState, result) = f (state, arg)
                      in
                        SyncVar.iPut (replyV, result);
                        newState
                      end
                in
                  wrap(recvEvt reqCh, doCall)
                end
          in
            {call=call, entryEvt=entryEvt}
          end

    fun mkServer initState entries = let
          fun selectEntries state =
                select (map (fn f => f state) entries)
          fun loop state = loop (selectEntries state)
          in
            spawn (fn () => loop initState);
            ()
          end

  end;
```

Listing 5.10: The `MakeRPC` structure

We use an I-variable for the reply message in order to improve performance. We could also use asynchronous communication (*e.g.*, a mailbox) to communicate the request to the server. We choose not to do this because the examples in the sequel require the extra synchronization provided by synchronous message passing.

To illustrate the use of the `MakeRPC` module, we revisit the updatable cells example from Chapter 3. Recall that the updatable cell abstraction supports two RPC-style operations: `get`, which gets the cell's current state, and `put`, which updates the cell's state. Listing 5.11 shows how we can use meta-programming to implement this abstraction.

```
fun mkCell initVal = let
      val {call=get, entryEvt=get'} =
            MakeRPC.mkRPC (fn (x, _) => (x, x))
      val {call=put, entryEvt=put'} =
            MakeRPC.mkRPC (fn (_, x) => (x, ()))
      in
        MakeRPC.mkServer initVal [get', put'];
        {get = get, put = put}
      end
```

Listing 5.11: Example of `MakeRPC`: updatable cells

5.6.2　Event-valued RPC

The `MakeRPC` structure provides support for the asymmetric **Ada**-style extended rendezvous, where the client-side operation cannot be used in selective communication. In **CML**, we can extend this package to provide an event-valued interface to the client by adding the following function:

```
val mkRPCEvt : (('a * 'b) -> ('a * 'c)) -> {
      call     : 'b -> 'c event,
      entryEvt : 'a -> 'a event
      }
```

There are two possible implementations of this operation, depending on whether the client's request or the server's reply is the commit event (see Section 4.2.2). For this example, we choose the client's request as the commit event. The `mkRPCEvt` function can then be implemented by a small modification to the `mkRPC` function from Listing 5.10:

```
fun mkRPCEvt f = let
      val reqCh = channel ()
      fun call arg = guard (fn () => let
            val reply = SyncVar.iVar ()
            in
              wrap (
                  sendEvt (reqCh, (arg, reply)),
                  fn () => SyncVar.iGet reply)
            end)
      fun entryEvt state = ...
      in
        {call=call, entryEvt=entryEvt}
      end
```

As before, we underline the changes. The server-side `entryEvt` function is unchanged, but we now implement the `call` function as a guard event. We could also provide functions to create RPC protocols where the server's response is the commit point (with or without negative acknowledgements); how to implement this form is left as an exercise.

5.6.3 Conditional RPC

In systems programming, it is often necessary to deal with the possibility that some expected event might not occur. To this end, **Ada** supports several variations on its basic rendezvous mechanism — namely, a *delay* clause in the server's select statement, a *timed* entry call, and a *conditional* entry call. These operations can be implemented easily in **CML**. The server-side delay clause is implemented using the following function:

```
fun delay (tim, act) state =
    wrap (timeOutEvt tim, fn () => act state)
```

This takes a timeout interval and an associated action, and returns a function that can be used as an argument to `mkServer`. Using event-valued client-side calls, we can implement the timed entry call as

```
select [
    wrap (timeOutEvt t, timeout action),
    wrap (call args, call action)
    ]
```

where *t* is the timeout interval and *call* is the RPC event

An implementation of Ada's conditional entry requires modifying the `call` function in `mkRPC` (see Listing 5.10) to *poll* the server to see if it will accept a request:

```
fun condCall arg = let
    val reply = SyncVar.iVar ()
    in
      if sendPoll(reqCh, (arg, reply))
        then SOME(SyncVar.iGet reply)
        else NONE
    end
```

Modifying `mkRPCEvt` to support conditional entry requires a more complicated protocol, since even if the poll of the server succeeds, the client may still choose a different event and the transaction will have to be aborted. Implementing this protocol can be done using negative acknowledgements, and is left as an exercise.

Some languages, such as **Concurrent C** and **SR**, go further in their support for conditional entry and provide a mechanism for a server to conditionally accept a request based on a boolean predicate. This predicate can depend on both the state of the server, and on the contents of the message. In this section, we look at how we can emulate this mechanism in **CML**.

In the case where this predicate only depends on the server's state, there are a couple of ways to program it in **CML**. For the buffered channel example in Section 5.4, we structured the server to select from different sets of events in different states. The other technique is to use `guard` to test the predicate. For example, the following event constructor takes a predicate on states (`pred`) and a function for making an event from a state (`mkEvt`), and returns a function for conditionally making an event from a state:

```
fun condEvt (pred, mkEvt) state = guard (fn () => (
        if (pred state) then mkEvt state else never))
```

This function returns the event value `never` when the predicate is false, which is the identity for `choose`. It has the type

```
val condEvt : (('a -> bool) * ('a -> 'b event)) -> 'a -> 'b event
```

where "`'a`" is the type of the server's state.

When the predicate depends on the message's contents, the techniques of the previous paragraph do not apply. We have already seen one example where this situation arises. The lock server presented in Section 4.2.5 can only handle a request when the lock specified in the request message is not held. This can be described as a predicate on the server's state and the request message's contents. The approach used in the lock server to handle this case is to tentatively accept any request, but to only commit to accepting a request when the requested lock is actually available. In the remainder of this section, we examine ways to support conditional acceptance of RPCs as an abstraction.

We can extend the RPC meta-programming module to support conditional acceptance of requests. We extend the interface of Listing 5.9 with the following function:

```
val mkCondRPC : (('a -> 'b -> bool) * (('a * 'b) -> ('a * 'c)))
    -> {
          call     : 'b -> 'c,
          entryEvt : 'a -> 'a event
       }
```

This function is like the `makeRPC` function in Section 5.6.1, except that it also takes a predicate function as an argument. The predicate is curried over the state and the call argument. As an illustration of this abstraction, Listing 5.12 gives the implementation of a lock server using the `MakeRPC` structure. Note that this implementation can represent the set of held locks as a set of integers, instead of as a map from integers to outstanding requests (*cf.*, Listing 4.6).

Our implementation of `makeCondRPC` uses a buffer thread between the client and the server. When the client executes a call, it sends a request message to the buffer thread, which tracks the outstanding requests. The buffer thread is also responsible for testing requests against the predicate; when the server offers to accept an entry, it partially evaluates the predicate against its current state, and then sends the partially evaluated predicate to the buffer. When the buffer finds a request that satisfies the predicate, it forwards the call to the server; the server's reply goes directly back to the client. Figure 5.4 illustrates this communication network.

The communication pattern described above is a simplification, however, since it does not address the issue of selective communication in the server (recall that `mkServer` can handle a list of entries). For this we must use negative acknowledgements to inform

```
datatype lock = LOCK of int

fun mkLockServer () = let
      fun isLocked locks (LOCK lock) =
            IntBinarySet.member(locks, lock)
      fun lockFn (locks, LOCK lock) =
            (IntBinarySet.add(locks, lock), ())
      val {call=lock, entryEvt=lockEntryEvt} =
            MakeRPC.mkCondRPC (isLocked, lockFn)
      fun unlockFn (locks, LOCK lock) =
            (IntBinarySet.delete(locks, lock), ())
      val {call=unlock, entryEvt=unlockEntryEvt} =
            MakeRPC.mkRPC unlockFn
      in
        MakeRPC.mkServer IntBinarySet.empty [
            lockEntryEvt,
            unlockEntryEvt
          ];
        {lock=lock, unlock=unlock}
      end
```

Listing 5.12: Lock server implemented using `mkCondRPC`

the buffer thread that the predicate it has is stale. We split `mkCondRPC`'s implementation into the construction of the client and server operations, and the implementation of the buffer. Listing 5.13 gives the code for `makeRPC`. This code is a slight modification of the code in Listing 5.10 and again we underline the changes. In addition to the request channel (`reqCh`), the `mkCondRPC` function also allocates a channel for the server to send the predicate to the buffer (`predCh`), and a channel for the buffer to forward client messages to the server (`forwCh`). The client-side operation (`call`) is identical to the unconditional version, but the server side is more complicated. The `entryEvt` function now constructs an event using the `withNack` combinator. The guard function first sends

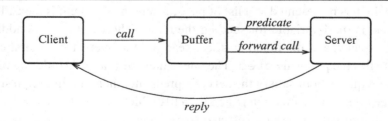

Figure 5.4: The conditional client/server communication network

```
fun mkCondRPC (pred, f) = let
    val reqCh = channel()
    val predCh = channel()
    val forwCh = channel()
(* the client side call *)
    fun call arg = let
        val reply = SyncVar.iVar ()
        in
            send (reqCh, (arg, reply));
            SyncVar.iGet reply
        end
(* the server side entry event *)
    fun entryEvt state = withNack (fn nak => let
        fun doCall (arg, replyV) = let
            val (newState, result) = f (state, arg)
            in
                send (predCh, (pred state, nak));
                SyncVar.iPut (replyV, result);
                newState
            end
        in
            wrap (recvEvt forwCh, doCall)
        end)
    in
        condBuffer (recvEvt predCh, recvEvt reqCh, forwCh);
        {call=call, entryEvt=entryEvt}
    end
```

Listing 5.13: Making a conditional RPC operation

the partially applied predicate and the negative acknowledgement event to the buffer, and then constructs the entry event.

The most complicated part of makeCondRPC is in the implementation of the condition buffer, which is given in Listing 5.14. The buffer maintains a queue of outstanding client calls, which is represented as a list of pairs, where the first item is the call argument and the second is the I-variable for sending the reply. The function ins adds a call to the end of the queue, and the function scan searches the queue for the first call whose argument satisfies the predicate pred. The queue maintains a FIFO ordering of requests, so that if two requests both satisfy the server's predicate, then the first request is chosen by scan. The other utility function is forwCall, which is used to forward a call to the server. Since the server might have selected some other entry, forwCall selects on the choice of the negative acknowledgement (disable) and the server accepting the call; it returns true, if the call is accepted. The buffer can be in one of two states: it is said to be *enabled* if it has a valid predicate from the server; otherwise, it is *disabled*. The

5.6 Meta-programming RPC protocols

fun condBuffer (predEvt, reqEvt, forwCh) = let
    fun forwCall (call, disable) = select [
            wrap (disable, fn _ => false),
            wrap (sendEvt(forwCh, call), fn () => true)
        ]
    fun ins (calls, call) = calls @ [call]
    fun scan (pred, calls) = let
        fun scan' ([], _) = NONE
          | scan' ((call as (req, _))::r, front) =
                if (pred req)
                    then SOME(call, List.revAppend(front, r))
                    else scan'(r, call::front)
        in
            scan' (calls, [])
        end
    fun enabledBuf (calls, pred, disable) = select [
            wrap (disable, fn () => disabledBuf calls),
            wrap (reqEvt, fn (call as (req, _)) => (
              if (pred req)
                  then if (forwCall (call, disable))
                      then disabledBuf calls
                      else disabledBuf (ins(calls, call))
                  else enabledBuf (ins(calls, call), pred, disable)))
        ]
    and disabledBuf calls = select [
            wrap (reqEvt, fn call =>
              disabledBuf (ins(calls, call))),
            wrap (predEvt, fn (pred, disable) => (
              case (scan (pred, calls))
               of NONE => enabledBuf (calls, pred, disable)
                | (SOME(call, calls')) =>
                    if (forwCall (call, disable))
                        then disabledBuf calls'
                        else disabledBuf calls
              (* end case *)))
        ]
    in
      spawn (fn () => disabledBuf []); ()
    end
```

Listing 5.14: The condition buffer
```

mutually recursive functions `enabledBuf` and `disabledBuf` are used to represent these states.

The `enabledBuf` function synchronizes on the choice of two events: either receiving a call request (`reqEvt`) or being informed that the predicate is stale because the server has selected some other entry (`disable`). This function maintains the invariant that no outstanding call satisfies the predicate. When a new call comes in, it checks it against the predicate; if it is not satisfied, then the message is added to the outstanding call queue. If the new call satisfies the predicate, then the call is forwarded to the server. As mentioned above, forwarding a message may fail if the predicate is stale; in this case, the new call is added to the outstanding call queue, but independent of whether the call is forwarded successfully, the buffer becomes disabled.

The `disabledBuf` function also synchronizes on the choice of two events: either receiving a call request (`reqEvt`) or receiving a new predicate from the server (`predEvt`). When a new call request is received, it adds the request to the outstanding call queue. If a new predicate is received, then the outstanding queue must be checked for any calls that match the predicate. If no such calls are found, then the buffer becomes enabled (note that the enabled state invariant is satisfied). Otherwise, the matching call is forwarded to the server.

One might complain that this abstraction does not provide a way for the client to use its side of the protocol in a selective communication. One can imagine combining the `mkRPCEvt` function of Section 5.6.2 with a form of conditional accept mechanism implemented using the condition buffer from above. Unfortunately, this is provably impossible. The problem is that such an implementation would require a *three-way rendezvous* between the client, buffer, and server, and it is not possible to implement a three-way rendezvous in **CML**, since it only provides two-way rendezvous as a primitive.[8] It should be noted, however, that if we move the predicate test into the server thread (reducing the number of threads involved to two), then it would work. But this would lose the modularity of the meta-programming approach.

Notes

While we have now covered most of the features of **CML** in this and the previous two chapters, the reader is referred to the *CML Reference Manual* for a complete description of **CML**. The core parts of the reference manual can be found in Appendix A.

CML's I-variables and M-variables are taken from the parallel language **ID** [ANP89, Nik91]. Earlier versions of **CML** did not provide M-variables, and used the name "*condition variable*" instead of I-variable. An implementation of condition variables using

---

[8]By n-way rendezvous, we mean a synchronous communication involving n processes. Since message passing in **CML** is synchronous, it provides a 2-way rendezvous. This problem is discussed in greater detail in Section 6.4.

channels and threads can be found in the author's dissertation [Rep92]. The language **Concurrent Haskell** [PGF96] also provides M-variables as a primitive; in fact, it is the only synchronization and communication mechanism in the language.

Futures were developed originally by Halstead in the language **Multilisp** [Hal85]; they also appear in other parallel **Lisp**s, such as **Mul-T** [KH88]. Most implementations of futures are designed to support parallel programming, and so must deal with issues such as task granularity and throttling excessive parallelism. One way to do this is for the run-time system to decide dynamically whether to evaluate the body of a future inline, or in parallel. Mohr, Kranz, and Halstead have developed an approach to inlining futures called *lazy task creation*, which has the advantage of being deadlock free [MKH91]. An implementation of futures in **CML** that uses lazy task creation is described in Chapter 12 of the author's dissertation [Rep92].

The buffered channel abstraction in Section 5.4 provides the communication mechanism found in asynchronous message-passing languages, such as **Erlang** [AVWW96] and actor languages [Agh86].

The multicast channels described in Section 5.5 are quite useful for implementing so-called publish and subscribe interactions (also known as the *Observer* design pattern [GHJV95]), which is why they are provided as a module in the **CML** Library. Examples of their use can be found in Chapters 7, 8, and 9.

The RPC, or extended rendezvous, mechanisms of Sections 5.6, 5.6.2, and 5.6.3 are found in a number of languages. **Ada** [DoD83] and **Concurrent C** [GR86] both use extended rendezvous as their basic communication mechanism. **Concurrent C** extends the basic mechanism by allowing the server to accept requests conditionally (as in Section 5.6.3). And the *synchronization expressions* found in **SR** are also a form of conditional accept [AO93].

A different approach to providing extended rendezvous in **CML** is to define an abstract type

```
type ('a, 'b) entry
```

where the first type argument is the entry argument type, and the second is the entry's result type. This abstraction provides a name for an extended rendezvous in the same way that a channel names a simple rendezvous [Rep92].

The problems with supporting three-way rendezvous in **CML** were discussed informally in the author's dissertation [Rep92]. More recently, Panangaden and the author have developed a formal model for reasoning about these questions [PR97]; this topic is discussed in the next chapter. Charlesworth has proposed a generalized *multiway rendezvous* mechanism as an extension for **Ada** [Cha87]. Another proposed mechanism for defining multi-party interactions are *scripts* [FHT86, EFK89]. Multiway rendezvous is an instance of the *committee coordination* problem [CM88].

6

The Rationale for CML

The design of **CML** has been driven by practical experience. In particular, the mechanism of first-class synchronous operations is motivated by the fundamental conflict between selective communication and abstraction. This chapter explains the rationale for the design of **CML**, and especially for first-class synchronous operations. It is aimed at people interested in language design, and is not required to understand the remainder of the book. In this chapter, we focus on *core* **CML** — synchronous message passing plus the event combinators — the other synchronization mechanisms found in **CML**, such as mailboxes, I-variables, and M-variables, can be viewed as derived forms. Some of the discussion here repeats earlier arguments, but is included for coherence.

6.1 Basic design choices

As surveyed in Chapter 2, there are many possible choices for the design of a concurrent language. **CML** chooses message passing over shared memory, synchronous communication over asynchronous, and simple rendezvous over extended rendezvous. This section argues in favor of these choices.

While **SML** is an imperative language, its design greatly encourages a mostly functional style of programming.[1] Mutable values must be declared explicitly as such, and there is syntactic overhead on their use. For these reasons, extending **SML** with shared-memory concurrency primitives is not true to the "spirit" of the language. Message passing, on the other hand, encourages a mostly functional programming style that fits well with **ML**. As we have seen, much of the state in typical **CML** programs is represented as immutable arguments to the tail-recursive functions that implement threads. The actual side-effects are hidden in the context switching and communication operations. Furthermore, combining synchronization and communication into the same mechanism provides

---

[1]One might call this *"value-oriented"* programming.

a more robust programming model than shared-memory with mutex locks and condition variables.

Given the choice of message passing as the basic communication and synchronization mechanism, the next decision is how much synchronization should be provided. There is an obvious trade-off between the efficiency of the communication primitives and the amount of synchronization they provide. Asynchronous message passing can be implemented with very low overhead, but provides no synchronization information to the sender. In synchronous message passing, on the other hand, the sender and receiver attain *common knowledge* of the message transmission, which makes synchronous message passing easier to reason about and to program with. For example, using synchronous message passing, we can use a single pair of channels to implement a client-server protocol (as shown in Section 3.2.3), whereas implementing the same protocol using asynchronous message passing requires dynamic allocation of reply channels. Furthermore, programs based on asynchronous message passing often require sending acknowledgement messages explicitly; once the cost of these extra messages is factored in, the performance advantages of asynchronous message passing may be lost. Synchronous message passing also has the advantage that its failure mode is typically deadlock, whereas asynchronous message passing will often postpone the detection of errors until the channel buffers are exhausted.[2] For these reasons, we rejected asynchronous message passing as the basis of **CML**. Since this design decision was made, we have proven that the synchronous communication provided by **CML** is inherently more powerful than asynchronous communication (see Section 6.4).

Another argument in favor of asynchronous message passing is that it supports the transparent distribution of an application (*e.g.*, a client does not need to know if communication with a server is done locally, or remotely via a proxy). Figure 6.1 illustrates this situation when the client-server protocol is visible to the client. If this protocol is based on synchronous message passing, then the semantics of the local and distributed implementations are different. If the client sends a request in the local case, then it knows that the server has accepted the request, whereas in the distributed case, the proxy has accepted the request, but the server may still refuse it. On the other hand, if the protocol is based on asynchronous message passing, then the client knows nothing about the server's state in either case. Effectively, because asynchronous message passing is a weaker mechanism, it reduces the local case to the distributed case. For some, this is a compelling argument in favor of asynchronous communication. There are two reasons, however, why this argument does not justify the choice of asynchronous message passing over synchronous message passing.

First, there is a real distinction between local and distributed communication. If the

---

[2]If the channel buffers are unbounded, this is when memory is exhausted.

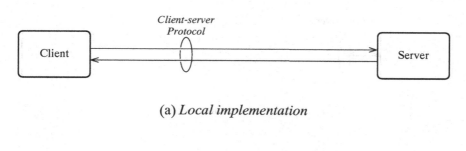

(a) *Local implementation*

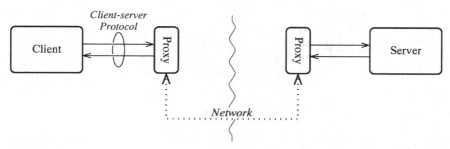

(b) *Distributed implementation*

Figure 6.1: A client-server protocol

client and server are executing on physically different processors, they may suffer independent processor failure, or their communication link may fail. A robust distributed program must be able to handle these situations. Furthermore, distributed communication has higher latency and lower bandwidth than local communication. A program that fails to note these performance differences may be wildly inefficient. For this reason, distributed programming is qualitatively different from concurrent programming, and requires a different programming model.

Second, even if we assume a reliable distributed setting, this argument draws the wrong conclusion from the example. The real problem with the protocol in Figure 6.1 is that the client should not be exposed to the implementation details of the protocol. The protocol should be abstract, so that the client cannot distinguish between local and remote servers. Figure 6.2 illustrates an abstract client-server protocol.

Another possible design choice is the extended rendezvous mechanism, which involves two-way message traffic; languages such as **Ada** and **Concurrent C** are based on such mechanisms. There are two problems with choosing extended rendezvous as the base mechanism: it is not clear which of the many forms of extended rendezvous should be chosen, and extended rendezvous does not support producer-consumer communication

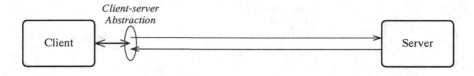

(a) *Local implementation*

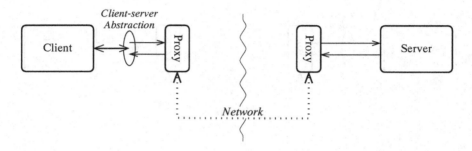

(b) *Distributed implementation*

Figure 6.2: An abstract client-server protocol

very well, where communication is unidirectional. Given the extensibility afforded by **CML**'s events, it is clear that starting with the more primitive simple rendezvous operation is a better choice than building in some complicated extended rendezvous mechanism.

6.2   First-class synchronous operations

The support for first-class synchronous operations is the major distinguishing feature of **CML**. In this section, we describe the motivation for this approach.

6.2.1   The need for selective communication

A language, such as **CML**, with synchronous communication must provide some mechanism for selecting between communication alternatives. For example, Figure 6.3 gives the communication network for a terminal server. The terminal server must be able to accept output from the client (on the `outstream`) and from the keyboard. Since there is no a priori way to know which input is next, the server must be able to accept either.

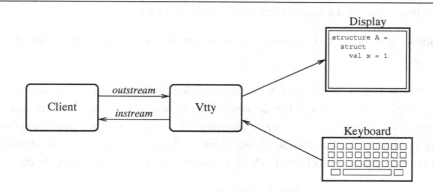

Figure 6.3: A terminal manager network

To address this need, synchronous message-passing languages provide a *selective communication* mechanism. For example, in an **Amber**-style notation, the body of the terminal server might be implemented as

select kbd?key **=>** *code to handle key press messages*
    or outstrm?c **=>** *code to handle client output*

where kbd is the keyboard channel, outstrm is the outstream channel, and "?" is the input operation on channels. The semantics of this operation is to wait until there is input on either kbd or outstrm, bind the input message to the corresponding variable (*i.e.,* key or c), and then take the associated action.

6.2.2 The need for abstraction

Abstraction is the principal mechanism for structuring software. In concurrent programming, we use abstraction to hide the details of process interactions. For example, consider a server thread that provides a service via a *request-reply* (or RPC) protocol. The server side of this protocol is something like

```
fun serverLoop () = if serviceAvailable()
    then let
      val request = recv reqCh
    in
        send (replyCh, doit request);
        serverLoop ()
    end
    else doSomethingElse()
```

where the function doit actually implements the service. Note that the service is not always available. This protocol requires that clients obey the following two rules:

1. A client must send a request before trying to read a reply.

2. Following a request, the client must read exactly one reply before issuing another request.

If all clients obey these rules, then we can guarantee that each request is answered with the correct reply, but if a client breaks one of these rules, then the requests and replies will be out of sync. An obvious way to improve the reliability of programs that use this service is to bundle the client-side protocol into a function that hides the details, thus ensuring that the rules are followed. The following code implements this abstraction:

```
fun clientCall x = (
        send (reqCh, x);
        recv replyCh)
```

By hiding the request and reply channels (*e.g.*, by using the module system), we can guarantee that clients of this implementation interact with the server correctly.

6.2.3 Selective communication vs. abstraction

Unfortunately, there is a conflict between selective communication and using procedural abstraction to implement abstract protocols. For example, while the `clientCall` function given above ensures that the protocol is observed, it hides too much. If a client blocks on a call to `clientCall` (*e.g.*, because the server is not available), then it cannot respond to other communications. Avoiding this situation requires using selective communication, but the client cannot do this because the abstraction hides the synchronous aspect of the protocol. This is the fundamental conflict between selective communication and existing forms of abstraction. If we make the operation abstract, we lose the flexibility of selective communication, but if we expose the protocol to allow selective communication, we lose the safety and ease of maintenance provided by abstraction. Resolving this conflict requires introducing a new abstraction mechanism that preserves the synchronous nature of the abstraction. This is the rôle of first-class synchronous operations.

6.2.4 The facets of selective communication

The motivation for first-class synchronous operations is to provide a way to do selective communication with abstract communication protocols as the choices. For this purpose we introduce a new type of value, called an *event*, that represents an abstract communication protocol. In addition to the new type, we need to define a collection of constructors, combinators, and operators on event values. The design of these is guided by the natural decomposition of the traditional `select` construct.

This decomposition is best explained using an example. Consider the following loop (again using **Amber**-style notation):

```
fun accum sum = (
        select addCh?x => accum(sum+x)
            or subCh?x => accum(sum-x)
            or readCh!sum => accum sum)
```

This code implements the body of an accumulator thread that supports three operations: addition, subtraction, and read the current value. Each of these operations is implemented as a clause in the `select`, consisting of a channel I/O operation and an associated action:

Operation	I/O operation	Action
addition	`addCh?`	`x => accum(sum+x)`
subtraction	`subCh?`	`x => accum(sum-x)`
read current value	`readCh!sum`	`=> accum sum`

These clauses are joined in a nondeterministic choice, which forms the body of the synchronization operation. This example illustrates the four facets of the traditional `select` construct:

1. the communication operations,

2. the actions associated with the communications,

3. the nondeterministic choice of multiple communications, and

4. the synchronization operation.

Our approach is to unbundle these facets and support each one independently. Most important is the separation of the description of the synchronous operations (the first three facets) from the synchronization itself. We introduce the type of *events* to describe synchronous operations, and a collection of constructors, combinators, and operations to support the different facets of selective communication:

1. the base-event constructors (*e.g.*, `recvEvt` and `sendEvt`) are used to create the event values that describe the communication operations,

2. the `wrap` combinator is used to associate an action with a synchronous operation,

3. the `choose` combinator is used to define the nondeterministic choice of a collection of synchronous operations, and

4. the `sync` operator is used to synchronize on a synchronous operation (*i.e.*, event value).

For example, we write the accumulator example in **CML** as follows:

```
fun accum sum = sync (
      choose [
          wrap (recvEvt addCh, fn x => accum(sum+x)),
          wrap (recvEvt subCh, fn x => accum(sum-x)),
          wrap (sendEvt (readCh, sum), fn () => accum sum)
      ])
```

By starting with *base-event* values to represent the communication operations, and providing combinators to associate actions with events and to build nondeterministic choices of events, we provide a flexible mechanism for building new synchronization and communication abstractions.[3] Event values provide a mechanism for building an abstract representation of a protocol without obscuring its synchronous nature. For example, the client-call abstraction from page 122 can be implemented as an event-value constructor:

```
fun clientCallEvt x = wrap (
        sendEvt (reqCh, x),
        fn () => recv replyCh)
```

This abstraction is "first-class" in the sense that it has the same status as the built-in event-value constructors.

This formulation of first-class synchronous operations corresponds to the mechanism first proposed in the **PML** language. **CML** extends this mechanism in a number of significant ways; the next section motivates these extensions.

6.3   Extending PML events

The previous discussion explains the motivation for first-class synchronous operations as found in the language **PML**. There are some limitations with this mechanism, however, which are addressed by the richer set of event combinators provided by **CML**.

6.3.1   The need for guards

Consider a protocol consisting of a sequence of communications: $c_1; c_2; \cdots; c_n$. When this protocol is used in a selective communication, one of the c_i must be designated as the *commit point*; *i.e.*, the communication by which this protocol is chosen instead of the others in the select. For example, in the events constructed by the `clientCallEvt` function above, the `sendEvt` on `reqCh` is the commit point. Using the **PML** set of event combinators, the only possible commit point is c_1. The `wrap` combinator allows one to tack on $c_2; \cdots; c_n$ after c_1 is chosen, but there is no way to make any of the other c_i the commit point.

---

[3] Chapter 5 gives numerous examples.

This asymmetry seriously limits the kinds of protocols that can be implemented as abstractions. A simple example of this is the implementation of a timer service. Suppose that we want to provide the event constructor

```
val atTimeEvt : Time.time -> unit event
```

which constructs an event that is enabled at the specified time. This can be implemented using a request-reply protocol with a clock server. The client's request specifies a wake-up time for the server, and the server's reply is sent to notify the client that the requested time has come. Obviously, the client needs to synchronize on the server's reply, which is not possible using only the **PML** subset of events. To address this limitation, **CML** provides the guard combinator

```
val guard : (unit -> 'a event) -> 'a event
```

This combinator allows computation, including communication, prior to the commit point to be included in the abstract representation of a protocol. Using the guard combinator, we can easily implement the atTimeEvt constructor[4]

```
fun atTimeEvt t = guard (fn () => let
        val replyCh = channel()
        in
          send (reqCh, (t, replyCh));
          recvEvt replyCh
        end)
```

This example also illustrates the use of guard to include other pre-commit computation in a protocol, such as allocating a reply channel.

Returning to the idealized client-server interaction that we have been examining, we see that there are two basic forms for the abstraction. The form where the client's request is the commit point:

```
fun clientCallEvt1 x = wrap (
        sendEvt (reqCh, x),
        fn () => recv replyCh)
```

and the form where the server's reply is the commit point:

```
fun clientCallEvt2 x = guard (fn () => (
        send (reqCh, x);
        recvEvt replyCh))
```

The choice, of course, depends on the semantics of the service.

There are some additional problems caused by our use of synchronous message passing for the request and reply. For example, if the server is not available, the sending of the request in clientCallEvt2 will block the client. This is solved by making the request asynchronous:

---

[4]This is a simplified presentation of the example on page 75 (Section 4.2.4).

```
fun clientCallEvt3 x = guard (fn () => (
        spawn (fn () => send (reqCh, x));
        recvEvt replyCh))
```

There is also the problem that the client might commit to a different communication in a choice involving this protocol; in this case, the server would block forever on trying to send the reply. In the case of idempotent services, such as the clock server, we can again solve this by making the communication asynchronous. There are situations, however, where this is insufficient.

6.3.2 The need for negative acknowledgements

Once we introduce the ability to communicate with a server prior to the commit point, we are faced with the problem of how to inform the server that the client has decided to abort the transaction. As discussed above, this is not necessary for idempotent services, but it is sometimes necessary for the server to know whether to *commit* or *abort* the transaction. The synchronization involved in sending the reply allows the server to know when the client has committed to the transaction, but there is no way to know when the client has aborted the transaction by selecting some other event. While a timeout on the reply might work in some situations, the absence of a reply does not guarantee that the client has selected some other event; the client just might be slow. To address this problem, **CML** extends the traditional synchronous message-passing operations with support for *negative acknowledgements*.

To illustrate, consider the implementation of an input-stream abstraction using a client-server model. Input streams provide several different operations for reading different amounts of data (a single character, a whole line, *etc.*). Furthermore, input streams should be smoothly integrated into the concurrency model, which means that the input operations should be event-valued. For example, the function

$$\textbf{val } \text{input1} : \text{instream} \rightarrow \text{char event}$$

is used to read a single character.[5] Let us assume that the implementation of these operations uses a request-reply protocol; thus, a successful input operation involves the communication sequence

$$\text{send } (ch_{req}, \; request); \quad \text{recv}(ch_{reply})$$

where ch_{req} and ch_{reply} are the request and reply channels. As in the case of atTimeEvt, it is necessary for the client to synchronize on receiving the reply, so the request is sent prior to the commit point. But what if the client does not complete the transaction? If the server were to just send the input character to the client asynchronously, it

---

[5]Note that these operations should not be confused with the actual I/O stream interface provided by **CML**.

would be lost. In order for the server to ensure that each character of input is received by one client exactly once, it needs a confirmation of both the successful completion and abortion of each transaction. The synchronization of sending a reply can provide the confirmation of the completion, but we also need a *negative acknowledgement* mechanism to signal that the transaction should be aborted. Furthermore, this mechanism should be compatible with the abstraction provided by event values.

CML supports negative acknowledgements by providing the event combinator

```
val withNack : (unit event -> 'a event) -> 'a event
```

which is an extension of the guard combinator.[6] As does the guard combinator, withNack takes a function whose evaluation is delayed until synchronization time, and returns an event value. The main difference is that at synchronization time, the guard function is applied to an *abort event*, which is enabled only if some other event is selected in the synchronization (this is more fully described in Section 4.2.5).

Returning to the input stream example, the client-side implementation of the input event becomes something like

```
withNack (fn nack => let
  val replyCh = channel()
  in
    spawn (fn () => send(reqCh, REQ_INPUT(replyCh, nack)));
    recvEvt replyCh
  end)
```

When the server is ready to reply to a request, it synchronizes on the choice of sending the reply, and the negative acknowledgement event

```
sync (choose [
    wrap (sendEvt(replyCh, data), fn () => commit),
    wrap (nack,                   fn () => abort),
  ])
```

6.4 The expressiveness of CML

The orthogonality between the primitive communication operations and the event combinators in **CML** raises an interesting expressiveness question. Given a certain set of primitive event constructors (*e.g.*, sendEvt and recvEvt), what kinds of event values can be implemented? For example, can one implement a three-way rendezvous primitive? Unfortunately, the answer to this question is negative, as stated in the following theorem:

---

[6]Earlier versions of **CML** used a different combinator for supporting abort actions, called wrapAbort. The two combinators have the same expressive power, but the withNack combinator is more natural to use. See the Notes section in Chapter 4 for more discussion.

Theorem 6.1 Given the standard **CML** event combinators and an n-way rendezvous base-event constructor, one *cannot* implement an $(n+1)$-way rendezvous operation abstractly (*i.e.*, as an event value).

For **CML**, which provides two-way rendezvous primitives, this means that it is impossible to construct an event-valued implementation of three-way rendezvous.

While the technical arguments are beyond the scope of this book, the intuition behind them is fairly straightforward. An n-way rendezvous mechanism is a way for n processes to agree simultaneously. For example, in a synchronous message transmission, both the sender and receiver agree to the communication at the same instant. Another way of viewing this is that the processes involved in an n-way rendezvous achieve some form of *common knowledge*. The intuition behind the theorem is that if a language provides a primitive mechanism for n-way agreement, there is no way to ensure that $(n+1)$ processes agree in an abstract fashion; *i.e.*, in a way that is independent of context. The problem is that while one can get n of the processes in agreement, the $(n+1)$th process is not constrained to make the same choice.

One of the immediate conclusions from these results is that there is a real difference in the expressiveness of synchronous and asynchronous message passing (in the presence of general choice). A language based on asynchronous message passing, even if it supports first-class synchronous operations, cannot support abstract implementations of synchronous message passing. For the programmer, this means that situations that require both synchronous message passing and selective communication will have to be programmed on a case-by-case basis. It is interesting to note, however, that in a language with asynchronous communication and input-only choice, it is possible to implement synchronous communication (two-way rendezvous) with input-only choice as an abstraction, using a simple acknowledgement-based protocol. From this, we conclude that generalized selective communication is strictly more expressive than the input-only form found in many languages. Furthermore, given a language with two-way rendezvous and with input-only choice, one cannot implement a communication abstraction that would allow output guards.

These arguments also explain why the two implementations of the client-server protocol in Figure 6.1 are distinct in the synchronous case. For the distributed implementation to mimic the local one would require a four-way rendezvous between the two proxies, client and server processes, which is not possible in the **CML** framework. The reason that we can avoid trouble in the abstract case is that we can allow for the reduced amount of synchronization in the distributed setting without having to modify the client's code. Of course, not all protocols allow such adjustments, but essentially all of the client-server protocols encountered in practice are amenable to distribution.

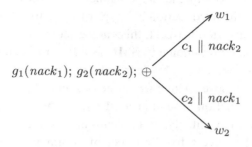

Figure 6.4: The diagram for $(g_1(nack_1); c_1; w_1) \oplus (g_2(nack_1); c_2; w_2)$

6.5 Discussion

CML provides four basic event combinators: `choose`, `wrap`, `guard`, and `withNack`.

The first three combinators have analogs in many concurrent languages, but the `withNack` combinator is unique to **CML**. Adding support for negative acknowledgements was motivated originally by the need to program protocols, such as the input stream example above. But further analysis shows that the concept of negative acknowledgements is a natural part of the design space. To illustrate this, consider the most general form of event value without internal choice, which has the abstract form

$$g(nack); c; w$$

where g is the guard function (parameterized by the negative acknowledgement event $nack$), c is the commit point, and w is the wrapper function. Figure 6.4 gives a diagrammatic view of the possible synchronization on the choice of two such generalized event values. We see from this diagram that the negative acknowledgement event is the complement of the commit event.

The choice of synchronous message passing for **PML** and **CML** was based on experience and intuition, but as we see from the discussion in Section 6.4, there are strong technical arguments for it as well. In practice, however, one needs a richer collection of synchronization primitives. Support for timeouts and operating system events are obvious extensions, but it is also useful to have other flavors of communication primitives, such as asynchronous channels and synchronizing memory. A nice aspect of first-class synchronous operations is that additional synchronous operations can be easily incorporated in the framework as new types and event-value constructors. Furthermore, these additional operators can be implemented either as primitives or on top of the existing primitives without affecting their semantics.

The fact that **CML** is a library on top of **SML/NJ** forces certain design choices, such as the use of functions to create threads and channels dynamically. The most interesting of these forced choices is the introduction of a type of value to represent communications and their associated actions. In retrospect, this choice seems to be a natural consequence of adding message passing with choice to **SML** as a library.[7] This is best explained by an example. Assume that we have a boolean valued channel cb and an integer valued channel ci, and want to choose a value from one of them. To make the types work out, we must use a wrapper function around at least one of the recvEvt operations (*e.g.*, wrapping a function that maps integers to booleans around the recvEvt on ci). Since type constructors in **SML** have a fixed number of arguments, we are forced to represent the result of wrapping a channel I/O operation as an abstract value (the underlying type of the channel cannot be part of the result type), which requires a type constructor for the type of these abstract values.[8] If we are willing to restrict ourselves to *homogeneous* choice, then first-class synchronous operations are not required (for example, see Section 10.4.3).

Notes

The idea of first-class synchronous operations was first incorporated in the design of concurrency mechanisms for **PML** [Rep88], which was in turn influenced by Cardelli's language **Amber** [Car86]. The design of **CML** has also been discussed in [Rep91a], [Rep92], and [PR97]. As mentioned above, adding message passing with selection to an **ML**-like language seems to result in something similar to first-class synchronous operations. Two other examples of this are Holmström's language **PFL**, and Ramsey's concurrency primitives for **SML** [Ram90]. These designs, however, were not motivated by the need to support abstraction.

The expressiveness results presented in Section 6.4 are joint work between the author and Panangaden [PR97]. They are proven using an abstract model of process interaction and knowledge theoretic arguments. The strength of the common knowledge achieved by a rendezvous operation depends on the form of the rendezvous mechanism. For example, a primitive notion of atomic rendezvous achieves common knowledge in the sense of Halpern and Moses [HM90], while a rendezvous protocol achieves the weaker *concurrent common knowledge* [PT92].

---

[7]The original design of events in **PML** was not forced in this way, since communication was built into the language with special syntactic forms.

[8]If the **SML** type system were extended to support existential types, this would no longer be the case.

7

A Software Build System

A natural application of concurrency is the management of multiple independent tasks. For example, building a large **C** program involves a number of individual compilations, each of which is run as a separate UNIX command. Since these compilations are independent, they may be run at the same time (possibly on different machines). In this chapter, we describe the implementation of a "parallel" build system using **CML**.

7.1 The problem

The basic problem is that we are given a set of objects, and a set of dependencies between the objects. Associated with some objects is an *action* that describes how to build the object; other objects (*e.g.*, source files) do not have associated actions. Taken together, they form an acyclic *dependency graph*, whose topological order defines the order in which objects should be built. We use the term *antecedents* to denote the nodes that a node depends on, and *successors* to denote the nodes that depend on it. The nodes of the graph are classified into *internal* nodes (those that have non-zero in-degree), *leaf* nodes (those with no antecedents), and the *root* node (which has no successors). We restrict ourselves to graphs with exactly one root. For the graph to be well formed, any internal node should have an associated action. Leaf nodes may also have actions.

Also associated with each object is a *timestamp* that tells when the object was last built or modified. If a node in the graph has a timestamp that is earlier than the timestamp of one of its antecedents, then we say that the graph is *inconsistent*. The problem of incrementally rebuilding a system is that of making the dependency graph consistent.

In more concrete terms, the objects are files in the system, and the actions are UNIX commands. We specify these dependencies using a UNIX-style makefile, which consists of a sequence of rules, possibly separated by blank lines. Each rule is two lines: the first is the object dependency information, and the second line is the associated action. The action is a command in the underlying system's command shell (*e.g.*, /bin/sh in

```
prog : main.o util.o
   cc -o prog main.o util.o

main.o : main.c util.h
   cc -c main.c

util.o : util.c util.h
   cc -c util.c
```

Listing 7.1: A simple makefile

UNIX systems). The first rule in the makefile defines the root object. More formally, our makefiles have the following simple grammar:

File	$\rightarrow$	*Root Rule**
Root	$\rightarrow$	*Rule*
Rule	$\rightarrow$	*Dependency* EndOfLine Action EndOfLine
Dependency	$\rightarrow$	Object : Object*

Where EndOfLine is the end-of-line marker, Action is an action, and Object is an object name token (in our case, this is a sequence of characters not containing whitespace). Listing 7.1 gives a simple example of a makefile in this syntax. This makefile defines dependencies and actions for the objects prog, main.o, and util.o. The dependency graph for this system is given in Figure 7.1. Looking at this graph, one can see the potential for parallelism: namely, that the objects util.o and main.o can be built independently.

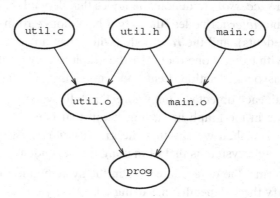

Figure 7.1: The dependency graph for the makefile in Listing 7.1

7.2   The design

Our make system is implemented as a function that takes a filename, and returns a function for rebuilding the system:

```
val make : string -> unit -> bool
```

If the build operation is successful, then `true` is returned; a result of `false` signifies that an error occurred in one of the actions.

The system translates the makefile into a dataflow network that represents the dependency graph, with nodes for the objects, and communication channels for the dependency edges. The messages sent along the dependency edges provide double duty: in addition to notifying an object that its antecedents are available, we also use them to communicate the timestamp of the antecedent object. We use the following datatype to represent these messages:

```
datatype stamp
  = STAMP of Time.time
  | ERROR
```

A stamp is either the timestamp of the antecedent object or `ERROR`. In the latter case, the antecedent is not available.

Each node in the graph is implemented as a separate thread. The outgoing edges of a node (*i.e.*, the edges to its immediate successors) are represented as a multicast channel, provided by the **CML** Library.[1] Using a single multicast channel to represent all outgoing edges from a node has the advantage that it simplifies the construction of the graph, since at the time that the node and its channel are created we do not need to know how many successors it has. Furthermore, it avoids introducing artificial orderings among the successors, which could inhibit parallelism or cause deadlock.

The system also has a controller thread that has a multicast channel to each of the leaf nodes. Figure 7.2 gives the process network for the simple dependency graph of Figure 7.1. In this picture, the ellipses represent the threads for the leaf objects, the rectangles are the internal objects (the controller thread is also a rectangle), and the grey bars represent the multicast channels. The controller thread initiates a build sequence by sending a unit message to the leaves, which in turn send timestamps to their successors. Once an internal node has received timestamps from all of its antecedents, it executes its action to build its object and then multicasts the timestamp of the newly created object. Once the root receives timestamps from all of its antecedents, the build is complete, and it notifies the controller.

We describe the implementation details of this design in the remainder of this chapter. First we describe the construction of the dataflow network from a list of rules, then we

---

[1] Multicast channels were also described in Section 5.5.

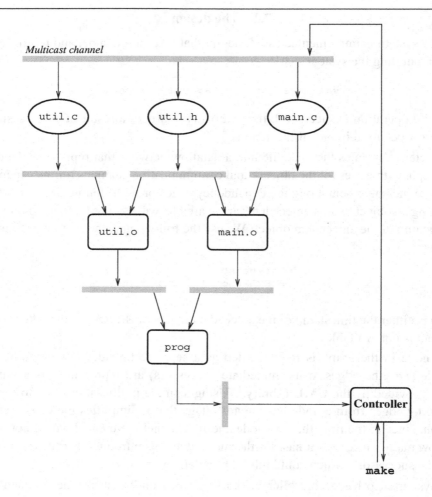

Figure 7.2: The process network for the simple dependency graph

describe the implementation details of the threads at the nodes and leaves. We complete the discussion by describing the makefile parser and the top-level glue that pulls it all together. The Notes section at the end of this chapter offers implementation alternatives and possible extensions.

7.3   Building the dependency graph

The construction of the dependency graph network is done by the `makeGraph` function (see Listing 7.2). The creation of the threads that represent the leaves and internal nodes

```
fun makeGraph (signalCh, {root, rules}) = let
      val makeLeaf = makeLeaf signalCh
      datatype objnd_state
        = DEF of stamp Multicast.mchan
        | MARK
        | UNDEF of {
             target : string,
             antecedents : string list,
             action : string
          }
      val objTbl = ObjTbl.mkTable (2 * length rules, Fail "ObjTbl")
      val insert = ObjTbl.insert objTbl
      val find = ObjTbl.find objTbl
      fun getNd objName = (case (find objName)
            of SOME(DEF nd) => Multicast.port nd
             | _ => raise Fail "missing definition"
            (* end case *))
      fun addNd {target, antecedents=[], action} =
            insert (target, DEF(makeLeaf{
               target=target, action=SOME action
            }))
        | addNd {target, antecedents, action} = (
            insert (target, MARK);
            app insNd antecedents;
            insert (target, DEF(
              makeNode {
                 target = target,
                 antecedents = map getNd antecedents,
                 action = action
              }))))
      and addLeaf target =
            insert (target, DEF(makeLeaf{
               target=target, action=NONE
            }))
      and insNd target = (case (find target)
            of (SOME(DEF nd)) => ()
             | (SOME MARK) => raise Fail "cyclic dependency"
             | (SOME(UNDEF nd)) => addNd nd
             | NONE => addLeaf target
           (* end case *))
    in
      app (fn nd => insert(#target nd, UNDEF nd)) rules;
      app (fn nd => insNd(#target nd)) rules;
      case (find root)
       of (SOME(DEF nd)) => nd
        | _ => raise Fail "impossible: missing root definition"
      (* end case *)
    end
```

Listing 7.2: The implementation of `makeGraph`

are provided, respectively, by the functions `makeLeaf`

```
val makeLeaf : unit Multicast.mchan -> {
        target      : string,
        action      : string option
     } -> stamp Multicast.mchan
```

and `makeNode`

```
val makeNode : {
        target      : string,
        antecedents : stamp Multicast.port list,
        action      : string
     } -> stamp Multicast.mchan
```

These functions are described in Section 7.4.

The input to the `makeGraph` function is the multicast channel for signaling the start of a build cycle, and a record consisting of the name of the root object and the list of rules. Each rule in the list is a record of the target name, list of antecedent names, and the string specifying the action. To translate this list-based representation of the graph into the network, we need a mechanism to map object names to nodes in the network. For this purpose, we define the structure `ObjTbl`:

```
structure ObjTbl = HashTableFn (
   struct
     type hash_key = string
     val hashVal = HashString.hashString
     fun sameKey (s1 : string, s2) = (s1 = s2)
   end)
```

which implements hash tables on object names using the `HashTableFn` functor from the **SML/NJ** Library.

The `makeGraph` function begins by creating a fresh hash table for mapping object names to the state of its network node. These states are represented by the following datatype:

```
datatype objnd_state
  = DEF of stamp Multicast.mchan
  | MARK
  | UNDEF of {
        target : string,
        antecedents : string list,
        action : string
      }
```

Initially, for each rule in the input, `makeGraph` maps the object defined by the rule to the UNDEF state. There are actually four states that a node might be in during construction of the network:

1. *Defined* — when the node and all of its antecedents have been created and linked into the network. This state is represented by mapping the node to DEF (mc),

where *mc* is the multicast channel used by the node to send currency information to its successors.

2. *Marked* — when the antecedents of the node are being constructed, prior to defining the node itself. This state is necessary to detect cycles in the dependency graph, and is represented by mapping the node to MARK.

3. *Undefined internal node* — when the node has not been encountered yet. This state is represented by mapping the node to UNDEF (*info*), where *info* is the initial rule information for the node.

4. *Undefined leaf* — when the leaf node has not been encountered yet. This state is represented by the node not being mapped (recall that a leaf node does not have antecedents and thus may not be the target of any rule in the makefile).

Once the hash table has been initialized, we construct the network by applying the function insNd to the target object of each rule. This function looks the target up in the hash table and processes it according to which of the four possible states it is in. If the target node is defined, then there is no further action required. If the target node is marked, then there is a cycle and the Fail exception is raised (this case occurs on recursive calls to insNd). In the case that the target node is undefined, we call the function addNd, which does a depth-first traversal of the subgraph rooted at the target node. As each internal node is visited in this traversal, it is first marked, and then we apply insNd to its antecedents, and finally we create the network node for the object using makeNode. Lastly, if the target node is an undefined leaf (*i.e.*, not in the table), then we call addLeaf, which adds it to the table as a defined leaf node.

7.4 Creating the graph nodes

The main work of the system is performed by the threads that represent the nodes in the dependency graph. As mentioned above, there are two functions for creating the leaf and internal nodes. The threads spawned by these functions are responsible for running actions and getting currency information from the file system. To help with this, we define a few useful system operations (see Listing 7.3). The function getMTime gets the timestamp of a file (or ERROR if the file does not exist); the function fileStatus checks to see if a file exists, and if so returns SOME of its modification time — otherwise it returns NONE; and the function runProcess runs an action and returns true if the execution was successful.

The function makeNode is used to create a thread for an internal node in the graph. It takes as arguments the name of the object corresponding to the node, a list of antecedent events, and the action that builds the object. It creates the thread for the object,

```
fun getMTime objName =
      STAMP(OS.FileSys.modTime objName)
        handle _ => ERROR

fun fileStatus path = if (OS.FileSys.access (path, []))
        then SOME(OS.FileSys.modTime path)
        else NONE

fun runProcess prog =
      (OS.Process.system prog = OS.Process.success)
        handle _ => false
```

Listing 7.3: Useful system operations

and returns the multicast channel used to communicate with the node's successors. The implementation of makeNode is given in Listing 7.4.

The body of a the thread is a loop (the function objThread) that iterates once for each build cycle. On each iteration it first waits for all of its antecedents to be made current.[2] Once it has received stamps from all of its antecedents, it determines the most recent stamp. If an ERROR stamp was received, the thread immediately propagates the ERROR stamp. Otherwise, it checks the currency of the object by comparing the most recent antecedent stamp with the modification time of the object. In the case that the object does not exist, we use time zero for its timestamp. If the object's timestamp predates the antecedent's, then the object needs to be rebuilt. Finally, the object's timestamp (after rebuilding) is multicast to its successors. If an error occurs while rebuilding the object (signaled by an exception), an error message is printed and the ERROR stamp is sent instead of the timestamp.

The implementation of makeLeaf is somewhat simpler, since there are no antecedents; the implementation is given in Listing 7.5. The makeLeaf function takes as arguments the signal channel that the controller uses to start a build cycle, and the object name and an optional action. The function allocates a new multicast channel for sending the objects currency information to its successors; this channel is returned as the result. This distinction between leaves with actions and those without is encapsulated in the doAction function. Where there is an action, doAction runs it; otherwise, it just returns true (signifying a successful execution).

As with makeNode, the body of a leaf thread is a loop (the function waiting) that iterates once for each build cycle. An iteration is triggered by a signal coming in from the controller via the multicast channel signalCh. Each iteration consists of executing

---

[2]Note that since the multicast channel is asynchronous, we can synchronize on the antecedent events in any order without risking deadlock. If we were using synchronous message passing, then we would have to use selective communication.

```
fun makeNode {target, antecedents, action} = let
    val status = Multicast.mChannel ()
    fun notify msg = Multicast.multicast (status, msg)
    fun objThread () = let
        val stamps = map Multicast.recv antecedents
        fun maxStamp (STAMP t1, STAMP t2) =
                if (Time.< (t1, t2))
                    then STAMP t2 else STAMP t1
          | maxStamp _ = ERROR
        in
            case foldr maxStamp (STAMP Time.zeroTime) stamps
              of ERROR => notify ERROR
               | (STAMP t) => let
                    fun doAction () = if (runProcess action)
                        then notify (getMTime target)
                        else (
                            TextIO.output (TextIO.stdErr, concat [
                                "Error making \"", target, "\"\n"
                                ]);
                            notify ERROR)
                    in
                        case (fileStatus target)
                          of (SOME objTime) =>
                                if (Time.<= (objTime, t))
                                    then doAction ()
                                    else notify (STAMP objTime)
                           | NONE => doAction ()
                        (* endcase *)
                    end
            (* end case *);
            objThread ()
        end
    in
        spawn objThread;
        status
    end
```

Listing 7.4: The implementation of `makeNode`

the action (if any), getting the timestamp of the object, and then sending the stamp out on the multicast channel to the leaf's successors. If executing the action results in an error, then the thread prints an error message and sends the ERROR stamp.

7.5 Parsing makefiles

The other major portion of the system is the parser that translates a makefile to a form suitable for `makeGraph`. We implement a low-tech parser for the grammar given in Section 7.1; a full-featured make system would require a richer grammar and might better

```
fun makeLeaf signalCh {target, action} = let
    val start = Multicast.port signalCh
    val status = Multicast.mChannel ()
    fun notify msg = Multicast.multicast (status, msg)
    val doAction = (case action
            of (SOME act) => (fn () => runProcess act)
             | NONE => (fn () => true)
            (* end case *))
    fun waiting () = (
        Multicast.recv start;
        if (doAction())
          then notify (getMTime target)
          else (
            TextIO.output(TextIO.stdErr, concat [
                "Error making \"", target, "\"\n"
                ]);
            notify ERROR);
        waiting ())
in
  spawn waiting;
  status
end
```

Listing 7.5: The implementation of `makeLeaf`

be handled using an automatic parser-generation tool, such as **ML-Yacc**. The code for the parser is given in Listing 7.6. The parser works by parsing rules until the end-of-file is encountered (signified by the empty string). We use the `Substring` module from the **SML** Basis Library to implement various string manipulations. The function `stripWS` takes a line and strips any leading and trailing whitespace from it; `stripWS` returns a `substring` for further manipulation. The function `getRule` is responsible for parsing the two lines that comprise a rule. It uses `parseRule` to parse the dependency line into the target and antecedents. If the dependency information is not well formed, or if the action is missing, then the `Fail` exception is raised. The action part of the rule is not analyzed beyond stripping any leading or trailing white space from the line (in particular, we do not check for empty actions).

7.6　Putting it all together

The final step is to glue the parser with the graph-builder, and to define the controller thread. These tasks are handled in the body of the `make` function, which is given in Listing 7.7. This function parses the makefile and builds the dependency graph from it. It then creates the controller thread, and returns a request/reply interface to the controller.

The controller thread is a loop consisting of three simple steps. Each iteration begins

```sml
structure SS = Substring

fun parseMakefile strm = let
    fun stripWS l = SS.dropl Char.isSpace
            (SS.dropr Char.isSpace (SS.all l))
    fun getLine () = (case (TextIO.inputLine strm)
            of "" => NONE
             | l => SOME(stripWS l)
            (* end case *))
    fun getNonBlankLine () = (case getLine()
            of NONE => NONE
             | (SOME l) => if (SS.isEmpty l)
                then getNonBlankLine()
                else SOME l
            (* end case *))
    fun parseRule l =
        map (SS.tokens Char.isSpace)
            (SS.fields (Char.contains ":") l)
    fun getRule () = (case (getNonBlankLine ())
            of NONE => NONE
             | (SOME l) => (case (parseRule l)
                of [[dst], srcLst] => (case getLine()
                    of (SOME act) => SOME{
                        target = SS.string dst,
                        antecedents = map SS.string srcLst,
                        action = SS.string act
                        }
                     | NONE => raise Fail "Missing action"
                    (* end case *))
                 | _ => raise Fail "Rule syntax"
                (* end case *))
            (* end case *))
    fun parse rules = (case getRule()
            of (SOME rule) => parse (rule::rules)
             | NONE => rev rules
            (* end case *))
    in
      case parse []
       of [] => raise Fail "Empty makefile"
        | (rules as ({target, ...} :: _)) =>
            {root = target, rules = rules}
      (* end case *)
    end
```

Listing 7.6: The makefile parser

```
fun make file = let
    val reqCh = channel() and replCh = channel()
    val signalCh = Multicast.mChannel()
    val inStrm = TextIO.openIn file
    val rootCh = makeGraph (signalCh, parseMakefile inStrm)
        handle ex => (TextIO.closeIn inStrm; raise ex)
    val root = Multicast.port rootCh
    fun controller () = (
        recv reqCh;
        Multicast.multicast(signalCh, ());
        case (Multicast.recv root)
         of (STAMP _) => send (replCh, true)
          | ERROR => send (replCh, false)
        (* end case *);
        controller ())
    in
      TextIO.closeIn inStrm;
      spawn controller;
      fn () => (send(reqCh, ()); recv replCh)
    end
```

Listing 7.7: The implementation of make

with the controller waiting for a request to initiate a build of the system. When a request is received, the controller sends out a signal to the leaves on the multicast channel `signalCh`. The controller then waits for the currency information from the root object. If it receives a timestamp, then it reports success on the reply channel; otherwise it reports failure. At this point, the system is ready for another iteration.

Notes

This chapter illustrates the use of **CML** as a concurrent *shell* language. Many applications of shell languages provide opportunity for parallelism — either using a uniprocessor's multitasking or by exploiting multiprocessors or local area networks of workstations. In this chapter, we have seen how **CML** can be used to structure parallel execution of system processes. More traditional shells have also been used for this purpose. For example, Fowler describes a version of **sh** that supports execution on remote processors in a local area network [Fow93], and the **Condor** system developed at the University of Wisconsin provides an infrastructure for using a local area network as a parallel processor [BLL92].

The make system described in this chapter is quite restricted in its function. There are a number of obvious extensions that the reader may wish to consider. For example, the system could support multiple root objects and allow the desired target to be defined as an argument to the make function. This would require a very different pattern of communication, since only the antecedents of the target should be built. We might also want to allow any arbitrary node to be the target. Another example is to support tools that produce multiple objects. A common example are parser builders, such as **ML-Yacc**, which produces both an interface and an implementation.

Another issue is the mechanism used to trigger rebuilds. In most make systems, this is under user control, but it might be useful to have a system that automatically rebuilds the system when any leaf object changes. There are many applications of such event-driven systems, and this may be a fruitful area for the use of languages like **CML**. For example, an effort is underway to implement a version of the **Yeast** system in **CML**,[3] which is a general-purpose tool for implementing event-driven applications [KR95].

The UNIX **make** program was invented by Feldman in the late '70s [Fel79], and has been a mainstay of the UNIX development environment ever since. Oram and Talbott discuss the UNIX **make** program in detail [OT91], while Fowler discusses many of the issues related to the design and implementation of **make** and related tools [Fow90].

Another way to organize this type of system is as a *demand-driven* computation. Instead of objects sending their timestamp to their successors, they could demand the timestamps of their antecedents. This kind of communication pattern would be able to support the multiple root objects suggested above.

---

[3] Balachandra Krishnamurthy, personal communication, 1995.

8

A Concurrent Window System

The control structure of an interactive program can be quite complex when implemented in a sequential language. This problem arises because interactive programs must be able to deal with asynchronous external events responsively, while also executing the application code. The usual solution to this problem is to structure the program around a central *event loop*, which dispatches control to parts of the application in reaction to external events. Often, the event-loop is part of a library, and applications are programmed using the so-called *"inverted program structure."* [1] This is not too bad when the application is purely reactive, that is, it only does something as a reaction to user input, but many interactive applications do not fit this model. In such cases, the application must define special call-backs to perform computation when the system is otherwise idle. In order to guarantee responsiveness, these call-backs must execute quickly and then pass control back to the event loop. In effect, the use of an event-loop is a "poor man's concurrency." This structure makes programming computationally significant algorithms difficult, and leads to a bias towards reactive, or input-driven, systems. [2]

A more natural way to program these systems is as a set of communicating processes. Some window systems, such as the X Window System, provide concurrency between applications by using multiple system processes, but the individual applications are sequential and suffer from the problems mentioned above. Using a concurrent language to program all aspects of the window system, from the window manager to application code, leads to a much cleaner structure and exposes more of the system's natural concurrency.

In this chapter, we examine a toy window system implemented in **CML**, along with a simple example application. Compared to the latest graphical web applets and fancy user interface builders, this system is primitive and crude. The reader should understand that

---

[1] Inverted in the sense that the *library* has control and calls application code, instead of the other way around.

[2] The reader may recall that these issues were discussed in somewhat greater detail in Section 1.1.1.

the focus of this chapter is on the use of concurrency to handle user interaction. While the graphics side of the system is primitive, it is sufficient to provide a realistic context.

8.1 Overview

The rôle of a window system is to manage multiple windows on a display, which are being used by independent client applications. The window system provides the client applications with access to their subset of the display, and to the multiplexed keyboard and mouse input devices. To the clients, it is as if they are executing with their own display, keyboard, and mouse. Thus we can view a client as a function that takes a window, keyboard, and mouse as arguments. Pictorially, we can view a client as

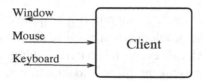

Since the window system itself executes in an environment consisting of a window, keyboard, and mouse, we can view it as a client too.

The function of a window system is typically divided into three logically distinct components: a *display system* that multiplexes the display, mouse, and keyboard among multiple clients, and provides an abstraction layer over the hardware; a *user-interface library* that provides an API for graphics and user input; and a *window manager* that allows the user to manage applications. To simplify the presentation, we assume the existence of the display system and user-interface library, which are described in the next two sections, and focus on the implementation of the window manager and sample clients.

8.2 Geometry

The display has the standard rectilinear geometry, with one unit representing one pixel on the screen. As is conventional, the origin is in the upper-left-hand corner, x coordinates increasing to the right and y coordinates increasing downwards. There are two geometric types used in this chapter: points and rectangles. These types are defined in the structure `Geom`. In addition, the `Geom` structure also provides a small collection of standard operations on points and rectangles. Its signature is given in Listing 8.1. Most of these operations have the obvious semantics, but a few of them may be unfamiliar:

`ptLess` (p_1, p_2) returns `true` if p_1 is above and to the left of p_2.

`rectOrigin` (r) returns the upper left-hand corner of the rectangle.

```
datatype point = PT of {
    x : int, y : int
}

datatype rect = RECT of {
    x : int, y : int,
    wid : int, ht : int
}

val origin : point
val ptAdd : point * point -> point
val ptSub : point * point -> point
val ptLess : point * point -> bool
val ptInRect : point * rect -> bool

val rectOrigin : rect -> point
val rectWid : rect -> int
val rectHt : rect -> int
val rectMove : (rect * point) -> rect
val rectInset : (rect * int) -> rect
val rectAdd : (rect * point) -> rect
val rectSub : (rect * point) -> rect
val rectWithin : (rect * rect) -> rect
```

Listing 8.1: The `Geom` structure's signature

rectMove (r, p) moves the origin of r to p and returns the new rectangle.

rectInset (r, n) returns a rectangle that is inset from r by n pixels in each dimension (*i.e.*, the origin is moved down and to the right by n pixels, and the width and height are decreased by $2 * n$ each). Note that by specifying a negative value for n, we can grow the rectangle.

rectAdd (r, p) adds p to the origin of r and returns the new rectangle.

rectSub (r, p) subtracts p from the origin of r and returns the new rectangle.

rectWithin (r_1, r_2) returns a rectangle with the size of r_2 that is within r_1. It does this by moving r_2 the minimum distance required for it to be contained by r_1. If r_2 is wider (resp. higher) than r_1, then r_2's left side (resp. top) is aligned with r_1's.

8.3   The display system

Our display system provides a simple black and white bitmap-graphics model with a small collection of drawing operations. For input devices, the display system provides a simple keyboard and a single-button mouse. The `DpySystem` structure implements an

```
signature DPY_SYSTEM =
  sig
    ...
    datatype rastor_op = CPY | XOR | OR | AND | CLR | SET

    datatype texture = SOLID | TEXTURE of word list

    val drawLine : bitmap -> rastor_op -> (Geom.point * Geom.point) -> unit
    val drawRect : bitmap -> rastor_op -> Geom.rect -> unit
    val fillRect : bitmap -> (rastor_op * texture) -> Geom.rect -> unit

    val bitblt : {
            dst : bitmap,
            rop : rastor_op,
            pt : Geom.point,
            src : bitmap,
            srcRect : Geom.rect
          } -> unit

    val drawText : bitmap -> rastor_op -> (Geom.point * string) -> unit

    val stringSize : (bitmap * string)
          -> {wid : int, ht : int, ascent : int}
    ...
  end; (* DPY_SYSTEM *)
```

Listing 8.2: Graphical types and operations

interface to the display system; it has the signature DPY_SYSTEM, which is detailed in
the rest of this section.

8.3.1   The graphics model

The display system provides *bitmaps*, which are rectangular collections of one-bit pixels.
A small set of standard graphical operations is provided; Listing 8.2 gives the signature of
these operations. Each operation takes a raster_op as an argument, which determines
the effect of the drawing operation. Each raster operator is a different function of the
source and destination pixels; Table 8.1 gives the semantics of these operators. For the
drawText, drawLine, and drawRect operations, the   source pixel is always black.
For the fillRect operation, the source pixels are specified by the   texture argument,
and for bitblt operation, the source pixels are taken from the source bitmap.

The function drawLine draws a line between the given points, which includes the
end points. Applying drawLine to the argument (p,p) draws a single pixel at the
point p. The function drawRect draws a rectangle, and the function fillRect fills
a rectangle with a given texture.   A texture is a 16×16 array of pixels; it can either

Table 8.1: Rastor operator semantics (○ = white, ● = black)

	(source destination)			
Operator	(○ ○)	(○ ●)	(● ○)	(● ●)
CPY	○	○	●	●
XOR	○	●	●	○
OR	○	●	●	●
AND	○	○	○	●
CLR	○	○	○	○
SET	●	●	●	●

be SOLID (*i.e.*, all 1's) or represented as a list of 16 words, with the high-order bit of the first word being the upper-left-hand corner (*i.e.*, row-major order). A bit value of 0 is drawn as white and a 1 is drawn as black. There is an important difference between the way that drawRect and fillRect interpret their arguments: drawRect draws a rectangle that is wid + 1 pixels wide and ht + 1 pixels high, while fillRect fills a wid × ht block of pixels.

The most complicated operation is bitblt, which copies a rectangle of pixels from one bitmap (src) to another (dst). The srcRect argument specifies the rectangle to copy in the source bitmap, and the pt argument specifies the upper-left-hand corner of the rectangle in the destination.

There are two functions that support the drawing of text: drawText draws the given string starting at the given point, and stringSize returns the size that the rendered image of a string would have. The size of a piece of text is described in terms of the rectangle that it occupies (with height ht and width wid), and the distance from the top of the rectangle to the *baseline* (the ascent). When drawing text, its position is given in terms of the baseline (*i.e.*, the y coordinate of the point given to drawText specifies the position of the text's baseline).

8.3.2 Layers

Most modern window systems support the "*covered window*" paradigm, in which windows are allowed to overlap.[3] When a portion of a window is covered by another window

---

[3]Some early window systems used the "*tiling*" paradigm, in which the total area covered by windows is limited to the size of the display.

```
signature DPY_SYSTEM =
  sig
    ...
    type bitmap

    val mkBitmap : (bitmap * Geom.rect) -> bitmap
    val toFront : bitmap -> unit
    val toBack : bitmap -> unit
    val move : (bitmap * Geom.point) -> unit
    val delete : bitmap -> unit

    val sameBitmap : (bitmap * bitmap) -> bool
    val bitmapRect : bitmap -> Geom.rect
    val bitmapClr  : bitmap -> unit
    ...
  end; (* DPY_SYSTEM *)
```

Listing 8.3: Layer operations

and then becomes uncovered, the newly unobscured area must be displayed on the screen. There are various techniques for supporting covered windows. The Toy Display System uses the "*layers*" approach, which is perhaps the simplest technique from the point of view of the window system. In this model, the display system is responsible for keeping track of the contents of any obscured regions. The refreshing of obscured regions is handled completely by the display system, and does not require window system or client action.

A common alternative to the layers approach is the so-called "*damage control*" model. In this scheme, the display system informs the client when an obscured portion of its window has become exposed. The client is responsible for redisplaying the obscured portion. While this is much simpler for the display system implementation, it adds an implementation burden to the client code, which is why we use the layers model here.

Listing 8.3 gives the signature of the operations provided by the Toy Display System to support overlapping windows. In this scheme, we use the `bitmap` type to represent windows. The function `mkBitmap` creates a new *subwindow* of the given bitmap. The rectangle argument specifies the position and size of the subwindow with respect to its parent's origin. The newly created bitmap will have its own coordinate system with its origin at its upper-left-hand corner, and the contents of the new bitmap will occlude its parent. Using the `mkBitmap` function, one can create a tree-structured hierarchy of windows. At each level of the hierarchy, there is also a front-to-back ordering on the windows. For the children of a single parent, this order is initially determined by the order of creation (windows are created in front), but it can be changed by the `toFront` and `toBack` functions, which move the specified window to the front (resp. back) of all

```
signature DPY_SYSTEM =
  sig
    ...
    datatype mouse_msg = M of {btn : bool, pos : Geom.point}

    val mouseUp    : mouse_msg -> bool
    val mouseDn    : mouse_msg -> bool
    val mousePos   : mouse_msg -> Geom.point
    val mouseTrans : Geom.point -> mouse_msg -> mouse_msg

    datatype key_press = K of char

    val keyDEL : key_press
    val keyBS  : key_press
    val keyRET : key_press
    val keyTAB : key_press
    ...
  end; (* DPY_SYSTEM *)
```

Listing 8.4: Keyboard and mouse messages

of its siblings. If two windows at the same level in the hierarchy have different parents, then their order is defined by the order of their parents. The position of a window with respect to its parent can be changed by the move operation. The move operation also has the effect of moving the window to the front of its siblings. Lastly, the delete operation deletes a window, and all of its subwindows.

Listing 8.3 also includes three other operations on bitmaps. The sameBitmap function returns true when its two arguments are the same bitmap. The bitmapRect function returns the rectangle that a bitmap occupies in its parent's coordinate system. And the bitmapClr function clears all the pixels in the bitmap to white.

8.3.3 Keyboard and mouse input

The keyboard and mouse input devices each generate a stream of *input messages*. [4] Mouse messages carry information about the mouse's button and the current position of the mouse cursor in the display's coordinate system. The representation of mouse messages is given in Listing 8.4. Together, these values constitute the *mouse state*. The DpySystem structure provides a small collection of functions for examining mouse messages and a function (mouseTrans) for translating the mouse position relative to a point. The latter function is used when propagating mouse messages from parents to

---

[4]These are often called *input events*, but we wish to avoid confusion with **CML**'s events.

children. Each time the mouse state changes, the display system sends a new mouse message.

Likewise, whenever the user presses a key on the keyboard, the display system sends a new `key_press` message, which is also defined in Listing 8.4. We assume a simple keyboard with the printable characters, and a few special keys.   Symbolic values are defined for some of the special keys: return (`keyRET`), backspace (`keyBS`), delete (`keyDEL`), and tab (`keyTAB`). As one would expect, the interface to these streams of input messages is event-valued.

8.3.4   Initialization

The last part of the display system interface is the initialization function, which has the following specification:

```
signature DPY_SYSTEM =
  sig
    ...
    val display : string option -> {
           dpy   : bitmap,
           mouse : mouse_msg event,
           kbd   : key_press event
         }
    ...
  end; (* DPY_SYSTEM *)
```

The `display` function initializes the display system and returns the display bitmap and the mouse and keyboard input streams (represented as event values). The display system is shut down when either the **CML** program exits or when the display bitmap is deleted.

8.4   The Toy Window System architecture

The display system described above provides a way to create bitmaps and to draw on them, and it provides a single point of access to the mouse and keyboard input devices. In order to write graphical applications that can run concurrently, we need mechanisms for managing bitmaps and for distributing input. These mechanisms are the job of the window system. The window system defines a *policy* for how windows and their associated threads interact, and provides code that supports the implementation of that policy in graphical components and applications.

In the Toy Window System, a graphical component has a bitmap associated with it that it uses to display information to the user. In many cases, the component may also have sub-components, which, in turn, have their own associated bitmaps. This hierarchy of nested components is supported by the display system's `mkBitmap` function, which takes the parent bitmap as an argument. We also use this hierarchy of nested components to guide the distribution of user input. We use the same interface and interaction protocols for all graphical components in the system, ranging from simple components like push buttons, through applications to even the window manager.

As we noted above, a graphical component or application can be viewed as a function that takes its window, keyboard, and mouse as arguments, but in practice things are a bit more complicated. In addition to the mouse and keyboard, components need to communicate *control information* to their parent and children. Thus, we represent a *window environment* as a record type (`win_env`) consisting of a bitmap, three input channels (mouse, keyboard, and control in), and a mailbox for outbound control messages. We use a mailbox for the command-out communication channel, instead of a channel, as a way to break the cyclic dependency between the parent and child. If not broken, this dependency could result in deadlock (*e.g.*, the child is trying to send a control message to its parent, while the parent is trying to send the child a mouse message).

The `win_env` type is defined in the `WSys` structure, whose signature can be found in Listing 8.5. The `WSys` structure defines a collection of types (including `win_env`) that specifies the interface between components. It also implements a mapping from the display manager's interface to the interface defined by these types. The functions `bmap`, `mouse`, `kbd`, `cmdIn`,   and `cmdOut` may be used to project the components of a window environment. The `rect` function returns the rectangle of the environment's bitmap.

The `sameBitmap` function returns true if the two argument environments contain the same bitmap; it is used to check the identity of environments. Sometimes it is useful to ignore all of the messages on one of an environment's channels; the `sink` function serves this purpose. The `init` function initializes the display system and then wraps up the root bitmap and raw input channels provided as a window environment. Sending a delete command (described below) on the command-out mailbox of this environment causes the display system to shut down. We describe the other operations in the `WSys` structure in the remainder of this section.

8.4.1   The window manager

The window manager is an application that supports creating and destroying applications and their windows. As noted above, the window manager has exactly the same interface to its parent as any other component or application, which means that it is possible to recursively run a copy of the window manager inside an application window.

8.4.2   Input routing policy

A distinguishing feature of a window system is the policy used to decide which client should receive a particular user input event. For our system, which uses a top-down

```
signature WSYS =
  sig

    type bitmap = DpySystem.bitmap

    datatype mouse_msg = datatype DpySystem.mouse_msg
    datatype key_press = datatype DpySystem.key_press
    datatype cntl_msg = CMD of {
        msg  : string,
        rect : Geom.rect option
    }

    datatype win_env = WEnv of {
        win : bitmap,
        m   : mouse_msg chan,
        k   : key_press chan,
        ci  : cntl_msg chan,
        co  : cntl_msg Mailbox.mbox
    }

    val mkEnv : bitmap -> win_env
    val realize : (bitmap * Geom.rect) -> (win_env -> 'a) -> 'a

    val bmap    : win_env -> bitmap
    val mouse   : win_env -> mouse_msg chan
    val kbd     : win_env -> key_press chan
    val cmdIn   : win_env -> cntl_msg chan
    val cmdOut  : win_env -> cntl_msg Mailbox.mbox
    val rect    : win_env -> Geom.rect

    val sameBitmap : (win_env * win_env) -> bool

    val sink : 'a chan -> unit

    val init : string option -> win_env
  end; (* WSYS *)
```

Listing 8.5: The window system interface

distribution of input messages, the choice of policy determines the implementation of routing by the window manager.

Many window managers for the X Window System use the so-called *"focus follows mouse"* policy, in which the current location of the mouse cursor determines which client receives any keyboard or mouse input events. One wrinkle to this policy is the *mouse grab*. Consider an application menu that pops up when the mouse is depressed; we would like the menu to stay active as long as the mouse button is depressed, even if the mouse leaves the area of the application. The window manager's input-event router provides this behavior by declaring that the application has *grabbed* the mouse when the button is depressed (*i.e.*, all mouse messages are routed to the application until the button is released).

The other common policy is to distinguish a particular window, called the *current window*, and to direct all input messages to that window. The user is required to change the current window explicitly by clicking with the mouse (hence the name "*click to type*" for this policy). There are two versions of this policy, which are distinguished by the treatment of mouse messages generated when the mouse is outside the current application window. One approach is to discard any mouse message that is generated outside the current window. In this case, the router must support the mouse-grab mechanism. The other approach is to route all input messages (except the down-click used to select a new current window) to the current window. This approach does not require a special mouse-grab mechanism, since all messages are being routed to the current window.

For the Toy Window System, we choose the last of these policies, as it is the simplest to implement. The others are left as an exercise for the reader. Note that under any of these routing policies, components must be able to handle mouse messages with coordinates outside their window.

8.4.3 Window creation and deletion

In addition to the input routing policy, we need protocols to specify how parent and child windows interact. In a full-fledged system, this interaction would include window movement and resizing, but to keep things simple, we are concerned only with window creation and deletion.

As noted above, the window hierarchy is created top-down. First a parent creates the bitmap and window environment for its child. Then the parent calls the child's *realization function*, passing in the child's window environment. The realization function creates the various threads that implement the child, and any descendants of the child. The `WSys` structure (see Listing 8.5) provides two functions to help with creating the hierarchy: the function `mkEnv` creates a window environment given a bitmap (*i.e.*, it allocates the communication channels); and the function `realize` takes a parent bitmap, a child rectangle and realization function, and realizes the child.

When the window system wants to delete an application window, it sends a `"Delete"` message on the application's `ci` channel. When an application receives a deletion request, it is responsible for suspending any activity, and then sending its parent a `"Delete"` message via its `co` mailbox. When the window system receives a `"Delete"` request, it is free to delete the application's bitmap (which also has the effect of deleting all child bitmaps in the application). The application is also free to initiate its own deletion by sending a request to the window manager (*i.e.*, skipping the first step of the protocol).

```
signature FRAME =
  sig

    type frame

    val frameWid  : int
    val mkFrame   : (WSys.win_env -> 'a)
                    -> WSys.win_env -> (frame * 'a)
    val sameFrame : (frame * frame) -> bool
    val frameEnv  : frame -> WSys.win_env
    val highlight : (frame * bool) -> unit

  end;
```

Listing 8.6: The frame interface

8.4.4   Naming conventions

In the rest of this chapter, we follow the convention of introducing local names for the common modules. The bindings we use are

```
structure G = Geom
structure D = DpySystem
structure W = WSys
```

8.5   Some simple components

Before diving into the full complexity of the window system implementation, let us consider three simple examples of UI components in this framework.

8.5.1   Window frames

It is very common to decorate a window with a border or frame, and often the frame may have both normal and highlighted modes (in fact, we use this in the window manager below). While many window systems build this feature into their windows, it is natural in our approach to implement a frame by embedding the window in a frame window that is a few pixels larger in each dimension.

Since the frame window is the parent of the window being framed, it must be allocated first. The mkFrame function (see Listing 8.6) handles this by taking a *realization* function as an argument, and returning both the frame and the result of realizing the child. The Frame structure provides a few additional operations on frames: the sameFrame function tests for equality, the frameEnv function returns the environment used to communicate with the frame component, and the highlight function

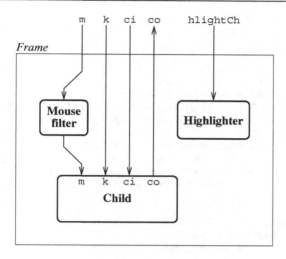

Figure 8.1: The Frame communication network

turns the highlighting of the frame's border on and off. The `Frame` structure also exports the value `frameWid`, which is the width of the frame in pixels, so that clients can compute layouts correctly.

For the most part, the implementation of frames is straightforward. Figure 8.1 shows the communication network that `mkFrame` sets up. Mouse messages must be filtered to get the coordinate system right, but all other messages are passed directly through without intervention. In addition, there is a thread for managing the highlighting state of the frame.

Listing 8.7 gives the code for the frame implementation. Most of the implementation of `mkFrame` is concerned with the geometry computations and highlighting support. First, we compute three rectangles: `frameRect` is the rectangle we draw for the outer frame; `highlightRect` is inset one pixel from `frameRect` and is drawn when the frame is highlighted (giving a two pixel wide frame); lastly, `childRect` is the rectangle that defines the child bitmap extent. Then we allocate the child's environment, which consists of a new sub-bitmap, a new mouse channel, and the other channels from the frame's environment. The `mouseLp` function is the body of the thread that translates mouse messages from the frame's coordinate system to the child's, before passing them onto the child. The `highlightLp` function provides control of the frame's highlighting; it keeps track of the current highlighting state and accepts requests on the `hlightCh` channel. After initializing the frame's graphics and spawning the mouse filter and highlighting

```
datatype frame = F of {
    env : WSys.win_env,
    hlightCh : bool chan
  }

fun mkFrame realize wenv = let
      val frameBM = WSys.bmap wenv
      val (frameRect, highlightRect, childRect) = let
            val G.RECT{wid, ht, ...} = D.bitmapRect frameBM
            in
              ( G.RECT{x=0, y=0, wid=wid-1, ht=ht-1},
                G.RECT{x=1, y=1, wid=wid-3, ht=ht-3},
                G.RECT{x=frameWid, y=frameWid,
                    wid=wid-2*frameWid, ht=ht-2*frameWid
                  }
              )
            end
      val childEnv = WSys.WEnv{
            win = D.mkBitmap (frameBM, childRect),
            m = channel(),
            k = WSys.kbd wenv,
            ci = WSys.cmdIn wenv,
            co = WSys.cmdOut wenv
          }
      val mTrans = D.mouseTrans (G.PT{x=frameWid, y=frameWid})
      fun mouseLp () = (
            send (
              WSys.mouse childEnv,
              mTrans (recv (WSys.mouse wenv)));
            mouseLp ())
      val hlightCh = channel()
      fun drawHL rator = D.drawRect frameBM rator highlightRect
      fun hlightLp isOn = (case (isOn, recv hlightCh)
            of (true, false) => (drawHL D.CLR; hlightLp false)
             | (false, true) => (drawHL D.SET; hlightLp true)
             | _ => hlightLp isOn
            (* end case *))
      in
        D.bitmapClr frameBM;
        D.drawRect frameBM D.SET frameRect;
        ignore (spawn mouseLp);
        ignore (spawn (fn () => hlightLp false));
        (F{env = wenv, hlightCh = hlightCh}, realize childEnv)
      end

fun sameFrame (F{env=e1, ...}, F{env=e2, ...}) =
      D.sameBitmap(WSys.bmap e1, WSys.bmap e2)
fun frameEnv (F{env, ...}) = env
fun highlight (F{hlightCh, ...}, b) = send(hlightCh, b)
```

Listing 8.7: The frame implementation

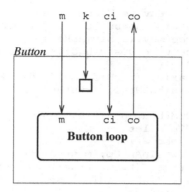

Figure 8.2: The Button communication network

threads, the `mkFrame` function returns the frame and the result of realizing its child. The representation of a frame is a record of its environment and the channel for changing the highlighting; the other frame operations work on this representation in the obvious way.

The observant reader will note that the frame implementation ignores the deletion protocol described above (Section 8.4.3). We can get away with this for two reasons: since the frame component is just a filter on mouse messages (and completely ignores all other messages), it can rely on its child to handle the deletion protocol interaction; and once the child has sent the `"Delete"` message on its command-out mailbox, the parent of the frame will delete the frame's bitmap, which also has the effect of deleting the frame's child's bitmap.

8.5.2 Buttons

Another standard component in user interfaces is the *button*. We implement buttons in the `Button` structure, with the following interface:

```
val mkButton : (string * (unit -> unit))
        -> WSys.win_env -> WSys.win_env
```

The `mkButton` function takes a string, which is the button's label, and an action function, and returns the button's realization function. The communication network for the button component is quite simple: a single thread monitors both the mouse and command-in channels, while the keyboard channel is diverted to a sink. Figure 8.2 shows this network.

The button's implementation is given in Listing 8.8. As with the frame component,

```
fun mkButton (msg, act) (wenv as W.WEnv{win, m, k, ci, co}) = let
      val G.RECT{wid=butWid, ht=butHt, ...} = D.bitmapRect win
      val butRect = G.rectMove(D.bitmapRect win, G.origin)
      val {ht, wid, ascent} = D.stringSize (win, msg)
      val txtOrigin = G.PT{
              x = Int.max(0, (butWid - wid) div 2),
              y = Int.min(butHt-1, ((butHt - ht) div 2) + ascent)
            }
      fun mouseState (D.M{btn, pos}) = (btn, G.ptInRect(pos, butRect))
      fun loop wasInAndUp = let
            fun handleM msg = (
                  case (wasInAndUp, mouseState msg)
                   of (true, (true, true)) => (act(); loop false)
                    | (_, (isDn, isIn)) => loop(not isDn andalso isIn)
                  (* end case *))
            fun handleC (m as W.CMD{msg="Delete", ...}) =
                  Mailbox.send (co, m)
              | handleC _ = loop wasInAndUp
            in
              select [
                  wrap (recvEvt m, handleM),
                  wrap (recvEvt ci, handleC)
                ]
            end
      in
        D.drawRect win D.SET
          (G.RECT{x=0, y=0, wid=butWid-1, ht=butHt-1});
        D.drawText win D.CPY (txtOrigin, msg);
        W.sink k;
        ignore (spawn(fn () => loop false));
        wenv
      end
```

Listing 8.8: The button implementation

much of the button component's implementation is concerned with geometry and graphics, but there is a non-trivial control part as well, which is contained in the `loop` function. In order to detect the difference between the mouse moving into the button's window while the mouse button is depressed and a genuine mouse-click in the button, the `loop` function keeps track of the previous mouse state. The variable `wasInAndUp` is true if the previous mouse message was in the window with the button not depressed. If `wasInAndUp` is true and the new state is also in the window with the mouse button depressed, then a mouse-click has occurred and the button's action is executed.[5] The control loop also monitors the command-in channel for `"Delete"` commands. If it

---

[5]Given the routing policy described above, one might wonder how the button can see the mouse outside its window. This happens because of the *mouse grab* policy; if the mouse button is depressed in the window and then moved out, the button continues to see mouse messages.

sees such a message, it echoes it back on the command-out channel and terminates. This fulfills the requirements of the deletion protocol.

8.5.3 Popup menus

Our last example component is a *popup* menu. Unlike the previous two examples, this is a *transient* component, and as such, does not follow the standard creation and deletion protocols. Instead, when it is determined that a mouse message has triggered the menu, we pass control of the mouse channel to the menu function, which has the following specification:

```
val menu : (WSys.win_env * Geom.point * 'a item list) -> 'a option
```

The arguments to the menu function are: the caller's window environment, the position at which to place the upper-left-hand corner of the menu, and the list of menu items. A menu item is a pair of the menu label and some associated information, and has the following type:

```
type 'a item = (string * 'a)
```

The menu function creates a new bitmap for the menu at the requested position, and monitors the caller's mouse channel until the mouse button is released. If the mouse is inside the menu when it is released, then the selected item is returned; otherwise NONE is returned.

Popup menus are implemented by the Menu structure. There are two steps to executing the menu function: first, we compute the layout of the menu items and the total size of the menu, and then we draw it and track the mouse until its button is released. The first step is handled by the layout function, which is given in Listing 8.9. This function first computes the total height of the items (including inter-item padding) and the maximum item width. It then uses the rectWithin function from the Geom structure to ensure that the menu fits into its parent's window. Finally, it computes and returns the menu's rectangle and a list of layout information for each menu item.

Once the menu layout has been computed, we need to display it and then track the mouse. This is handled by the body of the menu function, which can be found in Listing 8.10. Given the layout, we first allocate the menu bitmap and set up the drawing functions, which are used to draw the menu items (drawText) and highlight the items (fillRect). The menu function uses a simple helper function to map mouse coordinates to menu items:

```
fun whichItem (items : 'a item_info list) pt =
    List.find (fn item => G.ptInRect(pt, #rect item)) items
```

```
type 'a item_info = {
    lab : string,
    value : 'a,
    pt : G.point,
    rect : G.rect
  }

val itemSep = 2

fun layout (w, G.PT{x, y}, items) = let
    fun f ((s, _), (maxWid, totHt, posns)) = let
            val {wid, ht, ascent} = D.stringSize(w, s)
            val y = totHt + itemSep
            val ys = (y, y + ascent, ht)
            in
                (Int.max(maxWid, wid), y+ht, ys::posns)
            end
        val (wid, ht, posns) = List.foldl f (0, 0, []) items
        val menuRect = G.rectWithin (
                D.bitmapRect w,
                G.RECT{
                    x = x, y = y,
                    wid = wid+2*itemSep, ht = ht+itemSep
                })
        fun mkItemInfo ((s, v), (y, base, ht)) = {
                lab = s, value = v,
                pt = G.PT{x=itemSep, y=base},
                rect = G.RECT{x=itemSep, y=y, ht=ht, wid=wid}
            }
    in
        (menuRect, ListPair.map mkItemInfo (items, rev posns))
    end
```

Listing 8.9: Computing menu layout information

We use this function to determine which menu item is under the initial mouse position (this may not be the first item, since the `layout` function may move the position of the menu). Since the `layout` function has already determined the locations of the text for the items, drawing the menu is quite simple. We then highlight the initial item and invoke the mouse tracking loop with it. This loop consumes mouse messages and provides feedback by highlighting the current item until the mouse button is released. When this happens, the tracking loop terminates and returns the current item to the `menu` function, which deletes the menu window before passing the selected item to the caller.

```
fun menu (W.WEnv{win, m, ...}, pt, items) = let
    val (menuRect, items) = layout (win, pt, items)
    val menuWin = D.mkBitmap (win, menuRect)
    val drawText = D.drawText menuWin D.SET
    val fillRect = D.fillRect menuWin (D.XOR, D.SOLID)
    val whichItem = whichItem items
    fun highlight (item : 'a item_info) = fillRect (#rect item)
    fun loop curItem = (
        case (D.mouseTrans (G.rectOrigin menuRect) (recv m))
        of (W.M{btn=true, pos}) => let
            val newCur = whichItem pos
            in
                case (curItem, newCur)
                of (NONE, SOME item) => highlight item
                 | (SOME item, NONE) => highlight item
                 | (SOME item, SOME item') =>
                    if (#pt item <> #pt item')
                    then (highlight item; highlight item')
                    else ()
                 | (NONE, NONE) => ()
                (* end case *);
                loop newCur
            end
         | (W.M{pos, ...}) => Option.map #value (whichItem pos)
        (* end case *))
    val initialItem = whichItem pt
    in
        List.app (fn item => drawText (#pt item, #lab item)) items;
        ignore(Option.map highlight initialItem);
        loop initialItem before D.delete menuWin
    end
```

Listing 8.10: The menu function

8.6   The implementation of a window manager

We are now ready to examine the implementation of a window manager for the Toy
Window System. As we described above, a window manager is responsible for managing a dynamic collection of application windows. This includes supporting creation of
new application windows, routing of input to the appropriate application, and deletion of
applications. It is implemented in the WinMngr structure, and has a simple interface:

```
signature WIN_MNGR =
  sig

    type client = {
        name : string,
        size : Geom.rect,
        realize : WSys.win_env -> unit
    }

    val winManager : (WSys.win_env * client list) -> unit

  end;
```

We create a window manager by calling the `winManager` function with the manager's
environment and a list of client applications. For each client, we specify its name, size
(as a zero-based rectangle), and realization function. The window manager uses this list
to create a popup menu that can be used to start new applications. In the remainder of
this section, we describe the implementation of the window manager.

8.6.1   The window map

A key ingredient of the window system is the *window map*, which is a data structure used
to map messages to the correct sub-window. It keeps track of the existing windows, their
corresponding environments, and their relative stacking order. Since the window map is
useful outside the window manager, it is implemented as a separate module (structure
`WinMap`), which has the signature given in Listing 8.11. A window map also allows
additional information to be associated with each window; the type of the information
is given as the argument to the `win_map` type constructor. A window map is created
by calling the `mkWinMap` function with the environment for the parent window and
its associated information. The functions `insert` and `delete` are used to add and
remove child windows   from the map, and the `listAll` function returns a list of
all of the children. The `delete` function also takes care of deleting the child bitmap.
The window map is also used to change the stacking order of the windows (since it must
keep track of this information anyway).   The functions `toFront`, `toBack`, and `move`
have the same effect as their counterparts in the `DpySystem` structure. The `mapMouse`
function maps a mouse message to the foremost child window that includes the mouse
location (or to the parent, if no child covers that point). It also translates the mouse
position to the coordinate system of the window that includes it. Note that the window
map is only responsible for mapping a point to a window environment; it does not handle
the actual routing of messages. There are also two functions for looking up information
in the map; `findByPt` returns the foremost window containing the given point, while
`findByEnv` returns the information associated with the given window environment.
The `findByPt` returns the parent window and its information when the given point is
not contained in any child window.

```
signature WINMAP =
  sig

    type 'a win_map

    val mkWinMap : (WSys.win_env * 'a) -> 'a win_map

    val parent  : 'a win_map -> (WSys.win_env * 'a)
    val insert  : ('a win_map * WSys.win_env * 'a) -> unit
    val delete  : ('a win_map * WSys.win_env) -> unit
    val listAll : 'a win_map -> (WSys.win_env * 'a) list

    val toFront : ('a win_map * WSys.win_env) -> unit
    val toBack  : ('a win_map * WSys.win_env) -> unit
    val move    : ('a win_map * WSys.win_env * Geom.point) -> unit

    val mapMouse  : ('a win_map * WSys.mouse_msg)
                      -> (WSys.mouse_msg * WSys.win_env * 'a)
    val findByPt  : ('a win_map * Geom.point) -> (WSys.win_env * 'a)
    val findByEnv : ('a win_map * WSys.win_env) -> 'a

  end;
```

Listing 8.11: The window map interface

The implementation of the window map is straightforward, so we just sketch it without presenting the code. The window map maintains the list of window environments and their associated information as its state. The list is ordered from front to back (note that for non-overlapping windows, the order does not matter). Inserting and removing windows from the managed list is straightforward. The window map implements the toFront and toBack functions by reordering its list of windows, and having the display system reorder the windows on the screen. A point in the parent window coordinate system is mapped to a specific subwindow by searching the window list. Because the list is ordered front to back, if the point occurs in a region where two windows overlap, the front window will be chosen.

8.6.2 The window mananger

The window manager is created by the winManager function, whose implementation is partially given in Listing 8.12. The window manager consists of three threads: the *controller*, the *keyboard router*, and the *command-in router*. These threads share a global M-variable (curFrame), which is used to keep track of the current application window (more precisely, it holds the frame of the current application, or NONE if there is no current application). There is also a global I-variable (quitFlg), which is used by the

```
structure MB = Mailbox
structure F = Frame

fun highlight (SOME f, onOrOff) = F.highlight (f, onOrOff)
  | highlight _ = ()

fun sameFrame (SOME f1, SOME f2) = F.sameFrame(f1, f2)
  | sameFrame _ = false

fun winManager (rootEnv as W.WEnv{m, k, ci, co, ...}, clients) = let
      val quitFlg = SyncVar.iVar()
      val curFrame = SyncVar.mVarInit NONE
      fun controller () = let
            val wMap =
                WinMap.mkWinMap (rootEnv, {name="", frame=NONE})
            fun trackMouse () = let
                fun cmdWrap (wenv, {name, frame}) =
                    wrap (MB.recvEvt(W.cmdOut wenv),
                        fn msg => (msg, wenv, valOf frame))
                val childCmdEvt =
                    choose (map cmdWrap (WinMap.listAll wMap))
                in
                  mouseRouter (false, childCmdEvt)
                end
            and mouseRouter (wasDn, childCmdEvt) = ...
            and doMenu pos = ...
            in
              trackMouse ()
            end
      fun kbdRouter () = let
            val msg = recv k
            val current = SyncVar.mTake curFrame
            in
              case current
                of NONE => ()
                 | (SOME f) => send(W.kbd(F.frameEnv f), msg)
                (* end case *);
                SyncVar.mPut(curFrame, current);
                kbdRouter ()
            end
      fun cmdInRouter () = (case recv ci
            of (W.CMD{msg="Delete", ...}) =>
                SyncVar.iPut (quitFlg, ())
             | _ => cmdInRouter()
            (* end case *))
      in
        ignore (spawn controller);
        ignore (spawn kbdRouter);
        ignore (spawn cmdInRouter)
      end
```

Listing 8.12: The window manager

command-in router to signal that the window manager should quit. The controller thread is responsible for managing the client applications and for handling the mouse — it is described in the next section. The keyboard router is implemented by the `kbdRouter` function. It monitors the keyboard channel, and whenever it receives a keyboard message, it forwards it to the current client application. The command-in router is implemented by the `cmdInRouter` function; it monitors the command-in channel for a `"Delete"` message. When it receives one, it writes the unit value into the `quitFlg` I-variable, which signals to the controller that it should shut down the window manager.

Listing 8.12 also includes the code for two helper functions: `highlight` and `sameFrame`, which extend the corresponding frame operations to accept frame options as arguments. These functions are used by the `mouseRouter` and `doMenu` functions in the controller thread.

8.6.3 The controller thread

The bulk of the window manager's code is contained in the `controller` function, which implements the controller thread.   Listing 8.12 shows the code for this function, but omits the bodies of the `mouseRouter` and `doMenu` functions. The code for the former is given in Listing 8.13, and we leave the latter for the next section. The `controller` function starts by allocating the window map that it uses to keep track of the application windows. For each entry in the window map, we record the name of the application that owns the window and the application's frame (as an option). For the root window (*i.e.*, the window manager's window), there is no frame, so we record NONE.

Execution of the controller thread is handled by three mutually recursive functions: `trackMouse`, `mouseRouter`, and `doMenu`.   The `trackMouse` function is called when there is a change in the set of child applications (*e.g.*, when a child is created or terminated). It creates an event value (`childCmdEvt`) that monitors the `co` mailboxes of all of the children, and then calls the `mouseRouter` with the child event as an argument. In the `childCmdEvt` event, when a message is received in one of the child mailboxes, the message is wrapped up with the child's window environment and frame.

The code for the `mouseRouter` function is given in Listing 8.13. It takes two arguments: the first of these (`wasDn`) is a boolean that holds the mouse's button state, and the second (`childCmdEvt`) is the child command event created by `trackMouse`. This function implements a loop that monitors the window manager's mouse channel, the event `childCmdEvt`, and the quit flag. We describe the handling of each of these in turn.

The `mouseRouter` function handles mouse events with the `handleM` function. Each time a mouse message is received, the mouse's position is mapped to the foremost window containing that position. As a side-effect of this mapping process, we also get

```
    fun trackMouse () = ...
    and mouseRouter (wasDn, childCmdEvt) = let
        fun handleM (msg as D.M{btn, pos}) = let
            val (msg', wEnv, {frame = optFr, ...}) =
                WinMap.mapMouse (wMap, msg)
            in
              case (wasDn, btn, SyncVar.mTake curFrame, optFr)
                of (false, true, optFr, NONE) => (
                    highlight(optFr, false);
                    SyncVar.mPut(curFrame, NONE);
                    doMenu pos)
                 | (false, true, optFr, someFr) => (
                    if not(sameFrame(optFr, someFr))
                      then (
                        highlight(optFr, false);
                        highlight(someFr, true))
                      else ();
                    send(W.mouse wEnv, msg');
                    SyncVar.mPut(curFrame, someFr);
                    mouseRouter (true, childCmdEvt))
                 | (_, _, SOME f, _) => (
                    send(W.mouse wEnv, msg');
                    SyncVar.mPut(curFrame, SOME f);
                    mouseRouter (btn, childCmdEvt))
                 | (_, _, NONE, _) => (
                    SyncVar.mPut(curFrame, NONE);
                    mouseRouter (btn, childCmdEvt))
              (* end case *)
            end
        fun handleCI (W.CMD{msg="Delete", ...}, wEnv, fr) = let
            val current = SyncVar.mTake curFrame
            in
              WinMap.delete (wMap, wEnv);
              if (sameFrame(current, SOME fr))
                then SyncVar.mPut(curFrame, NONE)
                else SyncVar.mPut(curFrame, current);
              trackMouse ()
            end
          | handleCI _ = mouseRouter (wasDn, childCmdEvt)
        fun quit () = (
            app ((deleteChild wMap) o #1) (WinMap.listAll wMap);
            MB.send (co, W.CMD{msg="Delete", rect=NONE}))
        in
          select [
            wrap (recvEvt m, handleM),
            wrap (childCmdEvt, handleCI),
            wrap (SyncVar.iGetEvt quitFlg, quit)
          ]
        end
    and doMenu pos = ...
```

Listing 8.13: The window manager mouse router

the mouse message translated to the window's coordinate system and window's frame. In the case that the mouse is not in any application window, then the frame will be NONE. We then do a case analysis of the previous and current mouse-button states (checking for a down transition), the current frame, and the window's frame. There are four cases:

1. There is a down transition, and the mouse is not inside any application window. In this case, we deselect the current application window and invoke the window-manager menu, which is described in the next section.

2. There is a down transition, and the mouse is in an application window. If the mouse is inside the current application window, then we just forward the translated mouse message to it. Otherwise, we need to change the window that contains the mouse cursor be the current window, and we also forward the translated mouse message to the new current application.

3. There is not a down transition, and there is a current application window. In this case, the translated mouse message is forwarded to the current application window.

4. Otherwise, there is not a down transition and there is no current application window. In this case, the mouse message is discarded.

In each of these cases, except the first, the `mouseRouter` function is recursively called.

The `childCmdEvt` event is handled by the `handleCI` function in the `mouse-Router`. If the event is a `"Delete"` request, then the requesting application is removed from the window map. If the deleted application window happens to also be the current window, then we set the current application to be NONE. Finally, since the list of applications has changed, we call the `trackMouse` function, which will recompute the `childCmdEvt` event value.

The last part of the `mouseRouter` handles the `quitFlg` event. When this event is enabled, the `quit` function is called. The `quit` function applies the `deleteChild` function to each of the applications in the window map and then sends a `"Delete"` message on the window manager's command-out mailbox, which completes the termination protocol for the window manager.

Note that the `quitFlg` and `childCmdEvt` events are both *asynchronous*. This means that we can ignore them for a while, while monitoring only the mouse channel (*e.g.*, when handling a menu) and not have to worry about deadlock.

8.6.4 The window manager menu

The last piece of the window manager to describe is the code that puts up its menu and handles the menu actions. As described above, when the user presses the mouse button while the mouse cursor is not inside any application window, the `doMenu` function is called with the mouse's position as its argument. The code for this function is given in Listing 8.14.

The first thing the `doMenu` function does is construct the list of menu items. There are four kinds of menu items, which are represented by the `menu_item` datatype. For each type of client, there is a `NewClient` item that contains the application name, size, and realization function. These items are constructed using the `mkCLientItem` function; note that we increase the size of the client to account for the frame. The menu item list also contains a `Select` item for each application window, and one `Kill` and one `Quit` item. Once the list of items is created, `doMenu` passes it, along with the window manager's environment and the mouse's position, to the `menu` function described in Section 8.5.3. It then does a case analysis on the user's menu selection, and takes the appropriate action. The menu actions require a number of utility functions, which are given in Listing 8.15 and will be described as they are encountered.

If the user selects a `NewClient` item, we need to pick a location for the application window and then create it and realize the application. We start by calling the utility function `whileMouseBtn`, which eats mouse messages until the button state is different than its second argument, and then returns the position of the mouse cursor at this point. In this case, we wait for the button to be depressed, and use the position as the upper-left corner of the client window. Since the client window might not fit at this position, we call the `rectWithin` function from the `Geom` module to adjust its position if necessary. We then call the utility function `createChild` to create the application's window and frame and to start it up. The `createChild` function uses a combination of the `realize` operation from the `WSys` module and the `mkFrame` function to realize the application in its window. It then inserts the application into the window map and returns its frame. The `doMenu` function then takes this frame and makes it the current application window, by highlighting it and storing it in the `curFrame` M-variable (recall that `handleM` previously stored `NONE` in this). Lastly, we eat mouse messages until the user releases the mouse button (recall that `trackMouse` is called with a button state of `false`).

When the user chooses a `Select` item, we make the corresponding application be the current one. We do this by highlighting the selected frame and storing it into the `curFrame` M-variable.

The user can kill an application by selecting the `Kill` item. In this case, we use the `pickWin` utility function to select the victim. This function uses the `whileMouseBtn` function twice: first to wait until the user presses the mouse button and then to wait until the user releases the button. We map both positions to windows and then check to see that they are the same window and are not the root window. In this case, `pickWin` returns

```
fun trackMouse () = ...
and mouseRouter (wasDn, childCmdEvt) = ...
and doMenu pos = let
      datatype menu_item
        = NewClient of (string * G.rect * (WSys.win_env -> unit))
        | Select of F.frame
        | Kill
        | Quit
      val frDelta = G.PT{x=2*F.frameWid, y=2*F.frameWid}
      fun mkClientItem {name, size, realize} = let
          val size = G.rectAdd(size, frDelta)
          in
            ("new "^name, NewClient(name, size, realize))
          end
      fun mkSelItem (wenv, {name, frame}) =
          (name, Select(valOf frame))
      val items =
          (List.map mkClientItem clients) @
            (List.map mkSelItem (WinMap.listAll wMap)) @
              [("Kill", Kill), ("Quit", Quit)]
      in
        case Menu.menu (rootEnv, pos, items)
         of SOME(NewClient(name, rect, realize)) => let
              val pos = whileMouseBtn (m, false)
              val rect = G.rectWithin (W.rect rootEnv, rect)
              val frame = createChild wMap (name, rect, realize)
              in
                F.highlight (frame, true);
                ignore (SyncVar.mSwap (curFrame, SOME frame));
                ignore (whileMouseBtn (m, true))
              end
          | SOME(Select frame) => (
              F.highlight (frame, true);
              ignore (SyncVar.mSwap (curFrame, SOME frame)))
          | (SOME Kill) => (case pickWin(wMap, m)
              of NONE => ()
               | (SOME we) => deleteChild wMap we
              (* end case *))
          | (SOME Quit) => SyncVar.iPut (quitFlg, ())
          | NONE => ()
        (* end case *);
        trackMouse ()
      end
```

Listing 8.14: The window manager menu handler

```
fun whileMouseBtn (m, b) = let
    fun track () = let val D.M{btn, pos} = recv m
        in
            if (btn = b) then track() else pos
        end
    in
      track ()
    end

fun pickWin (wMap, m) = let
    val w1 = #1(WinMap.findByPt (wMap, whileMouseBtn (m, false)))
    val w2 = #1(WinMap.findByPt (wMap, whileMouseBtn (m, true)))
    in
      if (not(W.sameBitmap(w1, #1(WinMap.parent wMap)))
      andalso  W.sameBitmap(w1, w2))
        then SOME w1
        else NONE
    end

fun createChild wMap (name, rect, realize) = let
    val (child, _) =
        W.realize (W.bmap(#1(WinMap.parent wMap)), rect)
          (F.mkFrame realize)
    in
      WinMap.insert (wMap, F.frameEnv child,
        {name = name, frame = SOME child});
      child
    end

fun deleteChild wMap (wEnv as W.WEnv{co, ci, ...}) = let
    fun getAck () = (case MB.recv co
          of W.CMD{msg="delete", ...} => ()
           | _ => getAck()
         (* end case *))
    in
      send (ci, W.CMD{msg="Delete", rect=NONE});
      getAck ();
      WinMap.delete (wMap, wEnv)
    end
```

Listing 8.15: Window manager utilities

the selected window, otherwise it returns NONE. In the case where a window is selected, we call `deleteChild` to execute the deletion protocol on it.

If the user selects the `Quit` item, then we write the unit value into the `quitFlg` I-variable, and call `trackMouse`. When control gets back to the `mouseRouter` function, the quit clause of the `select` will be enabled and termination will occur.

The last case in `doMouse` handles the situation when no item was selected by the user. Once we have handled the user's menu selection, we conclude by calling `trackMouse`, which constructs a new `childCmdEvt` event that reflects any creation or deletion of child applications.

8.7 A sample application

To conclude this chapter, we describe the implementation of a simple texture editor.[6] The texture editor provides the user with two views of the texture being edited: the large view allows the user to set and clear individual pixels in the texture, while the small view shows the actual appearance of the texture on the screen. The texture editor also has a *clear* button for clearing the texture, and a *quit* button.

8.7.1 The editor's architecture

The texture editor consists of four graphical components: the clear and quit buttons, the small view, and the large editable view. In addition, there is a server thread that maintains the current state of the texture. Figure 8.3 shows the communication network of the editor. The most interesting part of this is the interaction between the small and large texture views and the texture state server. The texture state server supports both a client-server style interface for operations on specific pixels, and a notification mechanism (using a multicast channel) to inform views of changes. This architecture allows the views to be decoupled from the state of the texture, which provides a modular framework for multi-view editing. While this application only uses two fixed views of the texture, this architecture allows easy extension to new view types and support for dynamic view creation and deletion.

8.7.2 The `TextureUtil` structure

The texture editor uses a small utility module in its implementation. This module, named `TextureUtil`, has the following interface:

```
val dim : int

val foreachCoord : (int * int -> unit) -> unit
```

The value `dim` is the size of a texture (*i.e.*, 16), and the function `foreachCoord` is an iterator that applies its argument to each coordinate of a texture in *row-major* order.

---

[6]This might more properly be called a *bitmap editor*, but we are following the naming conventions of the display manager.

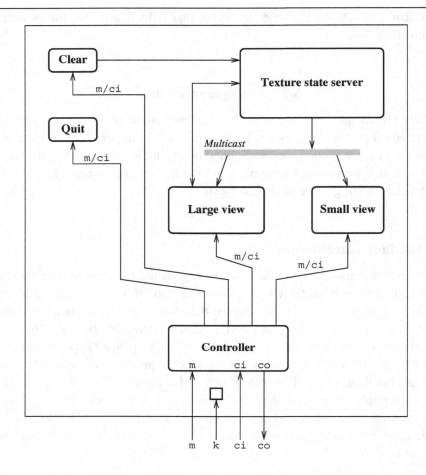

Figure 8.3: The Texture Editor communication network

8.7.3   The texture state server

The current state of the texture is maintained by the *texture state server* thread, which is implemented by the `TextureState` structure. The interface of this structure is given in Listing 8.16. The `newTexture` function creates a new texture state and returns a connection to its server. As can be seen from the communication network diagram in Figure 8.3, the texture state server provides two kinds of interaction. Other threads can modify and query specific cells in the texture using the functions `set`, `clr`, `toggle`, and `get`.   The state server also *publishes* notifications about changes to its state for interested parties. A notification message consists of the coordinates of a cell and its new

```
type texture_state

val newTexture : unit -> texture_state

val viewEvt : texture_state -> (int * int * bool) event

val set    : (texture_state * int * int) -> unit
val clr    : (texture_state * int * int) -> unit
val toggle : (texture_state * int * int) -> unit
val get    : (texture_state * int * int) -> bool
```

Listing 8.16: The texture state interface

value. Threads can *subscribe* to these notifications by calling the `viewEvt` function, which returns an event value for synchronizing on the stream of notifications.

The implementation of the texture state server is typical of servers (see Listing 8.17). The `texture_state` type is a record of a request mailbox and a multicast channel for change notifications. There are request messages to set a texture cell (`SetReq`), to toggle a cell (`ToggleReq`), and to get a cell's value (`GetReq`). The internal representation of the texture is a two-dimensional array of booleans, and the server handles requests by updating, using the `set` function, or reading elements of the array, using the `get` function. In addition to updating the cell, the `set` function also sends out a change notification when the cell's value has been modified.

8.7.4 The small view

The small texture view provides a read-only view of the texture as it would appear on the screen (*i.e.*, each cell in the texture is represented by one pixel). It is implemented by the `SmallView` structure, which has the following signature:

```
val viewRect : Geom.rect

val mkView : TextureState.texture_state
    -> WSys.win_env -> WSys.win_env
```

The `viewRect` value specifies the required size of the small view's window, and the `mkView` function creates the view when given a connection to the texture state server and a window environment. The small view server is a passive component; it ignores the mouse and keyboard, and only reacts to changes in the texture state or `"Delete"` messages.

The implementation of the `SmallView` structure is given in Listing 8.18. The small view's window size is just the dimension of a texture (16 by 16). Much of the `mkView`

```
structure MB = Mailbox
structure MC = Multicast

datatype request_msg
  = SetReq of (int * int * bool)
  | ToggleReq of (int * int)
  | GetReq of (int * int * bool SyncVar.ivar)

datatype texture_state = TS of {
    reqMb : request_msg MB.mbox,
    viewCh : (int * int * bool) MC.mchan
  }

val dim = TextureUtil.dim

fun newTexture () = let
      val reqMb = MB.mailbox()
      val viewCh = MC.mChannel()
      val data = Array2.array (dim, dim, false)
      fun get (i, j) = Array2.sub (data, i, j)
      fun set (i, j, v) = if (Array2.sub (data, i, j) <> v)
          then (
            Array2.update (data, i, j, v);
            MC.multicast (viewCh, (i, j, v)))
          else ()
      fun serverLoop () = (
          case (MB.recv reqMb)
           of (SetReq(i, j, v)) => set(i, j, v)
            | (ToggleReq(i, j)) => set(i, j, not(get(i, j)))
            | (GetReq(i, j, replV)) =>
                SyncVar.iPut(replV, get(i, j))
          (* end case *);
          serverLoop ())
      in
        spawn serverLoop;
        TS{reqMb = reqMb, viewCh = viewCh}
      end

fun viewEvt (TS{viewCh, ...}) = MC.recvEvt(MC.port viewCh)
fun set (TS{reqMb, ...}, i, j) = MB.send(reqMb, SetReq(i, j, true))
fun clr (TS{reqMb, ...}, i, j) = MB.send(reqMb, SetReq(i, j, false))
fun toggle (TS{reqMb, ...}, i, j) = MB.send(reqMb, ToggleReq(i, j))
fun get (TS{reqMb, ...}, i, j) = let
      val replV = SyncVar.iVar ()
      in
        MB.send(reqMb, GetReq(i, j, replV));
        SyncVar.iGet replV
      end
```

Listing 8.17: The texture state server

```
structure A = Array
structure T = TextureState

val dim = TextureUtil.dim

val viewRect = G.RECT{x = 0, y = 0, wid=dim, ht=dim}

fun mkView state (wenv as W.WEnv{win, k, m, ci, co}) = let
      val rawTexture = A.array(dim, 0w0)
      fun mkTexture () = D.TEXTURE(A.foldr (op ::) [] rawTexture)
      fun update (i, j, mode) = let
            val bit = Word.<< (0w1, Word.fromInt(dim - (j+1)))
            val w = A.sub(rawTexture, i)
            in
               A.update (rawTexture, i,
                  if mode
                     then Word.orb(w, bit)
                     else Word.andb(w, Word.notb bit))
            end
      val changeEvt = wrap(T.viewEvt state, update)
      val quitEvt = wrap(recvEvt ci,
            fn (W.CMD{msg="Delete", ...}) => exit()
            | _ => ())
      fun redraw () =
            D.fillRect win (D.SET, mkTexture()) viewRect
      fun server () = (
            redraw();
            select [changeEvt, quitEvt];
            server())
      in
         TextureUtil.foreachCoord
           (fn (i, j) => update(i, j, T.get(state, i, j)));
         W.sink k; W.sink m;
         ignore (spawn server);
         wenv
      end
```

Listing 8.18: The small texture view server

function is concerned with managing a local copy of the texture state, which is represented by an array of words. We choose this representation as it is halfway between the display system's representation of textures (lists of words) and the two-dimensional array of the texture server. The mkTexture function creates a display system texture value from this array. Changing the values of texture cells in the local representation requires some bit twiddling, which is handled by the update function. The small view server loop is simple: each iteration begins by redrawing the texture, and then waiting for either a texture-state change notification or a "Delete" message. In the former case, the local state is updated and the server continues; in the latter case, the server thread exits. Ini-

```
val blockSz = 7
val padSz = 2
val gridWid = 1
val cellSz = gridWid+padSz+blockSz+padSz
val totalSz = TextureUtil.dim*cellSz + gridWid

val viewRect = G.RECT{
        x = 0, y = 0, wid = totalSz, ht = totalSz
      }

fun coordToCell (x, y) = (y div cellSz, x div cellSz)

fun cellToRect (i, j) = G.RECT{
        x = cellSz*j + gridWid + padSz,
        y = cellSz*i + gridWid + padSz,
        wid = blockSz, ht = blockSz
      }

fun drawGrid win = let
      val drawLn = D.drawLine win D.SET
      fun drawLns (mkP1, mkP2) = let
          fun draw z = if (z <= totalSz)
                  then (drawLn (mkP1 z, mkP2 z); draw(z+cellSz))
                  else ()
          in
            draw 0
          end
      in
        drawLns
          (fn z => G.PT{x=0, y=z}, fn z => G.PT{x=totalSz, y=z});
        drawLns
          (fn z => G.PT{x=z, y=0}, fn z => G.PT{x=z, y=totalSz})
      end
```

Listing 8.19: The large texture-view layout

tialization of the local state is done by doing a `get` operation on each cell of the texture (note that the first iteration of the server loop will draw the initial texture).

8.7.5 The large view

The large texture view provides an editable view of the texture. It is implemented by the `LargeView` structure, which has the same signature as the small view above. The implementation of the `LargeView` structure is given in Listings 8.19 and 8.20. The graphical appearance of the large view is as a rectangular grid of square cells separated by grid lines. Each cell consists of a square block, which is drawn white or black depending on the cell's value, and padding around the block. The variables `blockSz`, `padSz`,

```
structure T = TextureState

fun mkView state (wenv as W.WEnv{win, k, m, ci, co}) = let
    fun mouseServer prevBtn = (case (prevBtn, recv m)
        of (false, D.M{btn=true, pos=G.PT{x, y}}) => let
            val (row, col) = coordToCell (x, y)
            in
                T.toggle (state, row, col);
                mouseServer true
            end
        | (_, D.M{btn, ...}) => mouseServer btn
        (* end case *))
    fun drawCell (i, j, mode) = let
        val rect = cellToRect (i, j)
        val rop = if mode then D.SET else D.CLR
        in
            D.fillRect win (rop, D.SOLID) rect
        end
    val changeEvt = wrap(T.viewEvt state, drawCell)
    val quitEvt = wrap(recvEvt ci,
        fn (W.CMD{msg="Delete", ...}) => exit()
        | _ => ())
    fun drawServer () = (
        select [changeEvt, quitEvt];
        drawServer ())
    in
        drawGrid win;
        TextureUtil.foreachCoord (fn (i, j) =>
            drawCell(i, j, T.get(state, i, j)));
        W.sink k;
        ignore (spawn (fn () => mouseServer false));
        ignore (spawn drawServer);
        wenv
    end
```

Listing 8.20: The large texture-view server

and gridWid are the dimensions of these various graphical elements, and together they define the size of a cell (cellSz) and total size of the view (totalSz). The helper function coordToCell maps a point in the view to a cell's row and column. We also need the function cellToRect, which maps a cell's row and column to the rectangle that defines its block. Finally, the drawGrid function draws the grid lines.

The large view actually consists of a pair of threads. The mouse thread (implemented by the mouseServer function) monitors the mouse channel looking for down clicks. When it sees one, it tells the texture state server to toggle the state of the corresponding cell. The other thread (implemented by the drawServer function) waits for texture-state change notifications. When it receives one, it redraws the affected cell. The `drawServer` function also monitors the command-in channel for `"Delete"` events, and exits when it receives one.

8.7.6   Bringing it all together

Now that we have described the individual components, we can show how these are assembled into the texture editor application. This is handled by the following function:

```
val mkEditor : WSys.win_env -> unit
```

which has the appropriate type to be a window-system client. The implementation of the `mkEditor` function is given in Listing 8.21. We start off by creating the texture state server, a window environment for the application (`myEnv`), and a window map. We then create each of the subcomponents and install it in the window map. This is done by applying the `mkWin` function to a list of pairs of realization functions and rectangles. Note that we have omitted the definition of the layout geometry for the components. Finally, we set up a sink on the texture editor's keyboard channel, and on the mouse channel of the `myEnv` environment, and then spawn the editor's controller thread.

The functions `quitAct` and `clearAct` are the actions for the quit and clear buttons. The quit action is to send a `"Delete"` message on the editor's command-in channel; this will cause the controller (described below) to initiate the termination procedure. The clear action clears each of the texture coordinates to the texture state server, which, in turn, causes update messages to be sent to the views. We could avoid this brute force approach by providing a *clear all* operation on the texture state.

The `controller` thread is the central dispatcher for the texture editor. It monitors the mouse and command-in channels (the keyboard channel is ignored by this application). When a mouse message comes in, it calls `handleM`, which maps the mouse location to a window and forwards the translated message to it. Commands are handled by the `handleCI` function. When a `"Delete"` command is received, the command is forwarded to each subwindow and acknowledgement is accepted from each in turn. Note that we do not need to check the format of the acknowledgements, since we know that the subcomponents do not send any other messages on the `co` channels. Once the deletion protocol has been completed with each of the subwindows, the texture editor sends an acknowledgement to its parent and exits. We do not bother deleting the windows of the subcomponents, since they will be deleted by the display system when the texture editor window is deleted.

```
fun mkEditor (env as W.WEnv{win, m, k, ci, co}) = let
    val state = TextureState.newTexture ()
    val myEnv = W.mkEnv win
    val wMap = WinMap.mkWinMap (myEnv, ())
    fun quitAct () =
        send (ci, W.CMD{msg="Delete", rect=NONE})
    fun clearAct () =
        TextureUtil.foreachCoord
            (fn (i, j) => TextureState.clr(state, i, j))
    fun mkSubwin (mkFn, rect) =
        WinMap.insert (wMap, W.realize(win, rect) mkFn, ())
    val envs = List.app mkSubwin [
            (B.mkButton ("Quit", quitAct), quitButRect),
            (B.mkButton ("Clear", clearAct), clearButRect),
            (SmallView.mkView state, smallViewRect),
            (LargeView.mkView state, largeViewRect)
        ]
    fun handleM msg = let
            val (msg', tgt, _) = WinMap.mapMouse (wMap, msg)
            in
                send(W.mouse tgt, msg')
            end
    fun handleCI (msg as W.CMD{msg="Delete", ...}) = let
            fun fwd (W.WEnv{ci, co, ...}, _) = (
                    send(ci, msg);
                    ignore (Mailbox.recv co))
            in
                List.app fwd (WinMap.listAll wMap);
                Mailbox.send(co, msg);
                exit ()
            end
      | handleCI _ = ()
    fun controller () = (
            select [
                wrap (recvEvt m, handleM),
                wrap (recvEvt ci, handleCI)
            ];
            controller ())
    in
      W.sink k;
      W.sink (W.mouse myEnv);
      ignore(spawn controller)
    end
```

Listing 8.21: The texture editor implementation

Notes

In this chapter, we have presented a toy implementation of a window system and simple interactive application that illustrates some of the ways that concurrency can be used to structure user interfaces and interactive applications. The display system API described in Section 8.3 is implemented on top of **eXene** [GR93], which is a multithreaded X Window System toolkit implemented in **CML**.

The argument that user-interface software is most naturally programmed in a concurrent language has been made by a number of people [RG86, Pik89a, Haa90, GR92, GR93].

While the code in this chapter is necessarily simplified, it has the user-input architecture employed by systems such as Pike's **squint** system [Pik89a], Haahr's **Montage** system, and **eXene**. Earlier systems with similar architectures include Cardelli and Pike's language **squeak** [CP85], which was designed for handling user input. This language evolved into **newsqueak** [Pik89b], which is the implementation language of **squint**. The **Pegasus** system [RG86, GR92] was a precursor of **CML** and many of the ideas found in **eXene**. There are other examples of window systems and GUI toolkits that use a concurrent programming model. Schmidtmann et al. describe the design and implementation of a multithreaded version of the **Xlib** library [STW93]. Hauser et al. describe the different ways that threads are used in two large interactive systems [HJT$^+$93]. The **Haggis** toolkit [PF95], which is implemented in **Concurrent Haskell** [PGF96], uses concurrency quite heavily in its implementation, although the model that is presented to the user is sequential. Some toolkits, such as **Trestle** [MN91] and **Java**'s **AWT** library [CL98], are implemented in concurrent languages, but do not exploit this fact in their programming model. If the application programmer wishes components to run in separate threads, she must program this explicitly.

The window system described in this chapter relies on an implementation of overlapping bitmap graphics (Section 8.3.2). Algorithms and data structures for this task have been described by Pike [Pik83] and Myers [Mye86]. The latter technique was used in the **Pegasus** window system [GR92].

One aspect of this chapter that is different from much of the rest of the book is that the example code makes little use of **CML**'s abstraction mechanisms — the multicast channel used in Section 8.7 is the example of a more complicated communication abstraction being used. This is mainly a result of the simplified programming model used in this chapter. In a richer framework, such as **eXene**, there are many places where **CML**'s abstraction mechanisms are useful. A description of some of these can be found in Chapter 9 of [Rep92], and in [GR93].

9

A CML Implementation of Linda

A principal use of concurrent programming is in the implementation of distributed systems. A distributed system consists of processes running in different address spaces on logically different processors. Because the processes are physically disjoint, there are a number of issues that arise in distributed systems that are not present in concurrent programming:

- Communication latency is significantly higher over a network than between threads running in the same address space.

- Processors and network links can go down, and come back up, during the execution of a distributed program.

- Programs running on different nodes may be compiled independently, which means that type security cannot be guaranteed statically.

For these reasons, the synchronous model used in **CML** does not map well to the distributed setting.[1] A different programming model is required for dealing with remote communication.

Although concurrent programming languages, such as **CML**, may not directly provide a notation for distributed programming, they do have an important rôle in implementing distributed systems. A distributed system is made up of individual programs running on different machines, which must communicate with each other. Managing this communication is easier in a concurrent language. Furthermore, multiple threads of control can help hide the latency of network communication. For these reasons, most distributed programming languages and toolkits provide concurrent programming features.

---

[1] Strictly speaking, it is impossible to implement a language like **CML**, which has synchronous channels and both input and output operations in choice contexts, in a distributed system (see Section 6.4).

This chapter explores a distributed implementation of **Linda**-style *tuple spaces* (described in Section 2.6.3). The implementation illustrates several points: first, it shows how **CML** can be used to implement low-level systems services; second, it shows how the **CML** primitives can provide a useful interface to asynchronous distributed programming primitives; and third, it is another extended example of programming in **CML**. The chapter is organized into three parts: first we describe the interface to the **CML-Linda** Library, and present a simple, but classic, programming example. Then we give a high-level description of the implementation, including the major components and protocols. Finally, we explore into the implementation details in all their glory. The implementation details are presented in a bottom-up order, starting with the network interface and ending with the programmer's API. The description of the implementation is quite involved and the casual reader may wish to skip the material after Section 9.4.

9.1   CML-Linda

As discussed in Chapter 2, **Linda** is not a programming language per se, but rather is a small collection of primitives that can be added to an existing language to provide distribution and parallelism. Our **CML** interface to tuple spaces supports the three basic tuple I/O operations: *output*, *input*, and *read*. It does not provide an *eval* operation, since **CML**'s spawn operation provides multiple threads locally, and implementing remote evaluation is beyond the scope of this book.

The programmer's interface to the **CML-Linda** library is provided by the Linda structure, which has the interface given in Listing 9.1. In addition to the tuple-space operations, this interface also includes the concrete representation of tuples and templates, and a mechanism for a program to join a distributed tuple space. For the purposes of this chapter, we choose a fairly restricted class of tuples; it would be straightforward to extend them to richer structures. Tuples and templates have the same internal structure, but differ in the kinds of values found at their leaves: tuples have values, while templates have both values and formal parameters. We use a common parameterized type, tuple_rep, to represent the internal structure. The datatype val_atom is a tagged union of the values found at the leaves of a tuple (integers, strings and booleans). This type is also used to represent the *tag* of a tuple or template, which is the first element of a tuple_rep value. The leaves of a template are represented by the pat_atom type, and include tagged values, typed formals, and a *wildcard* that matches any value of any type. The out operation puts a tuple into the specified tuple space. Since the input operations inEvt and rdEvt may block, they are given an event-value return type. These input operations take a template as an argument and return a list of values, which are the bindings for the formals in the matched template. The rules for template/tuple matching are defined in Table 9.1.

```
signature LINDA =
  sig

    datatype val_atom
      = IVal of int
      | SVal of string
      | BVal of bool

    datatype pat_atom
      = IPat of int
      | SPat of string
      | BPat of bool
      | IFormal
      | SFormal
      | BFormal
      | Wild

    datatype 'a tuple_rep = T of (val_atom * 'a list)

    type tuple = val_atom tuple_rep
    type template = pat_atom tuple_rep

    type tuple_space

    val joinTupleSpace : {
          localPort  : int option,
          remoteHosts : string list
        } -> tuple_space

    val out   : (tuple_space * tuple) -> unit
    val inEvt : (tuple_space * template) -> val_atom list event
    val rdEvt : (tuple_space * template) -> val_atom list event

  end;
```

Listing 9.1: The **CML-Linda** interface

The `joinTupleSpace` operation provides a mechanism for a distributed tuple space to be established in an incremental fashion. Suppose, for example, that we want to have three processors (*A*, *B*, and *C*) share a tuple space. Then, we start by executing the code

```
Linda.joinTupleSpace{localPort = NONE, remoteHosts = []}
```

on processor *A*, which creates the initial tuple space on *A*. Then *B* joins the tuple space by executing

```
Linda.joinTupleSpace{localPort = NONE, remoteHosts = ["A"]}
```

Table 9.1: Template matching semantics

Pattern	Matching tuple
IPat i	IVal i
SPat s	SVal s
BPat b	BVal b
IFormal	IVal i
SFormal	SVal s
BFormal	BVal b
Wild	*any value*

Lastly, *C* joins by executing

```
Linda.joinTupleSpace{localPort = NONE, remoteHosts = ["A", "B"]}
```

Since the `joinTupleSpace` operation is designed for joining an existing tuple space (as defined by the list of remote hosts), the order in which these commands get executed is important.[2]

As an example of programming in **CML-Linda**, we consider a solution to the classic *Dining Philosophers* problem. The program is a simulation of n philosophers sitting at a round table with a bowl of noodles in the center. The philosophers alternate between thinking and eating. To eat, a philosopher must have two chopsticks, but there are only n chopsticks at the table (one between each pair of adjacent philosophers). The philosophers represent processes in a concurrent system, and the chopsticks are resources. The problem is that if each philosopher acquires a single chopstick, then no philosopher can make progress (*i.e.*, eat) and the system is deadlocked. Our solution to this problem is to introduce *tickets* that must be acquired by a philosopher before chopsticks are acquired. By limiting the number of tickets to $n-1$, we guarantee that at least one philosopher will be able to eat. The **CML-Linda** implementation of this scheduling policy can be found in Listing 9.2. Each philosopher is assigned to a processor in the system; the chopsticks and tickets are represented by tuples in the tuple space. Since a philosopher may only use the chopsticks that are next to him, the chopsticks are labeled with their position, and we use the tuple-space pattern matching to match a philosopher with the correct chopsticks. The function `philosopher` is called to start a philosopher; it takes the total number of philosophers and list of remote hosts to join as arguments. It joins the tuple space, and then starts executing the philsopher's actions. Since a different list of hosts will be

---

[2]A more sophisticated implementation could remove this restriction.

```
structure L = Linda

val tagCHOPSTICK = L.SVal "chopstick"
val tagTICKET = L.SVal "ticket"

fun initTS (ts, 0) = L.out (ts, L.T(tagCHOPSTICK, [L.IVal 0]))
  | initTS (ts, i) = (
        L.out (ts, L.T(tagCHOPSTICK, [L.IVal i]));
        L.out (ts, L.T(tagTICKET, [])))

fun philosopher (numPhils, hosts) = let
        val ts = L.joinTupleSpace {
                localPort   = NONE,
                remoteHosts = hosts
                }
        val philId = length hosts
        fun input x = sync(L.inEvt (ts, x))
        val left = philId and right = (philId+1) mod numPhils
        fun loop () = (
                think philId;
                input (L.T(tagTICKET, []));
                input (L.T(tagCHOPSTICK, [L.IPat left]));
                input (L.T(tagCHOPSTICK, [L.IPat right]));
                eat philId;
                L.out (ts, L.T(tagCHOPSTICK, [L.IVal left]));
                L.out (ts, L.T(tagCHOPSTICK, [L.IVal right]));
                L.out (ts, L.T(tagTICKET, []));
                loop ())
        in
          initTS(ts, philId);
          loop()
        end
```

Listing 9.2: Dining philosophers in **CML-Linda**

used on each machine (as in the example above), we can use the length of the host list to assign philosopher IDs. Note that the initialization of the tuple space is handled in a distributed fashion.

9.2 An implementation overview

A **CML-Linda** program consists of one, or more, **CML** programs running on one, or more, machines in a network. These programs communicate via shared tuple spaces, where a tuple-space representation is distributed among the **CML** programs that have joined the space. Without loss of generality, we assume a one-to-one correspondence between the **CML** programs in the system and the machines they run on. And we use the term "processor" to mean either the program or the machine. To simplify the implementation, we ignore the problems related to failure (*i.e.*, what happens when one of the machines or programs crashes).

In the remainder of this section, we describe the architecture of the system and give an overview of the major system components.

9.2.1   Distribution of tuple space

The main design issue is how to distribute the tuples of a tuple space over the processors in a system. There are two basic ways to implement a distributed tuple space:

- *Read-all, write-one:* where each tuple is located at a single processor. A write operation adds a tuple to some processor, while a read operation must query all the processors in the system for a match.

- *Read-one, write-all:* where each processor has a copy of every tuple. A write operation must add the tuple to all processors, while a read operation need only query the local processor's copy of tuple space. Note, however, that a successful input operation must communicate with all of the other processors to remove the tuple from their copies of the tuple space. This means that both the `inEvt` and `out` (but not `rdEvt`) operations involve communicating with all other processors in the system.

For our implementation, we use the first organization. Each processor has a thread, called the *tuple server*, that maintains a *tuple store*, which is the processor's portion of the tuple space.

With a read-all, write-one distribution, the implementation of the `out` operation is straightforward. When a tuple is written, some decision must be made as to where the tuple should be placed, and then a message is sent to the appropriate processor. Simple policies for tuple placement include always placing tuples locally, and round-robin placement. More sophisticated schemes might use static analysis or dynamic information for better placement. In our implementation, each processor has a thread, called the *output server*, that implements the distribution policy for output operations.

The `inEvt` and `rdEvt` operations require that a client communicate with all of the tuple servers in the system. To provide a uniform interface to the tuple servers, each processor has a *tuple-server proxy* for each tuple server in the system (including its own). Client threads in the system communicate with the proxies, which in turn communicate with the tuple servers.

Figure 9.1 shows how these various servers are interconnected in a two-processor tuple space. The solid lines represent local communications (using **CML** operations), while the dotted lines are remote communications (using network operations). A **CML** application

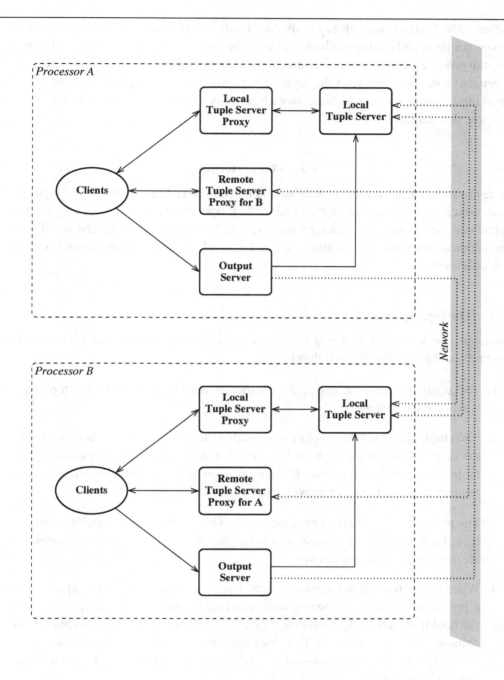

Figure 9.1: The communication network for a two-processor tuple space

that uses the **CML-Linda** library (called a *client*) communicates with the tuple-server proxies for input and read operations, and with the output server for output operations. In turn, the proxies must communication with their corresponding tuple servers. The output server also communicates with the tuple servers when distributing tuples. Note that the actual implementation has additional threads, such as network-buffer threads, that are not shown in this diagram.

9.3   The protocols

There are three basic protocols implemented by the **CML-Linda** library: the input protocol, which implements the `inEvt` and `rdEvt` operations; the protocol for outputing tuples; and the protocol for joining a tuple space. To understand better the detailed implementation description that follows, we first give a high-level description of how these protocols work.

9.3.1   The input protocol

The input operations (`inEvt` and `rdEvt`) require a fairly complicated protocol. The basic protocol for `inEvt` is as follows:

1. The reading processor, call it P, broadcasts the template to all the tuple-space servers in the system.

2. Each tuple-space server checks for a match. If it finds one, then it places a *hold* on the tuple and sends the tuple to P; otherwise, it remembers the input request in a table of outstanding requests. If some subsequent output tuple matches the input request, then the tuple server will send the matching tuple to P.

3. The processor P waits for a matching tuple. Once P receives a matching tuple, say from Q, it sends Q a message acknowledging the tuple, and sends a *cancellation* message to the other processors.

4. When Q receives the acknowledgement, it removes the tuple from its space. When a processor that has a matching tuple receives a cancellation message, it cancels the hold it placed on the matching tuple, which allows it to be used to match other requests. When a processor that does not have a matching tuple receives a cancellation message, it removes the record of the original request from its table of outstanding requests.

The protocol for `rdEvt` is similar; the main difference is that the tuple is not removed in step 4.

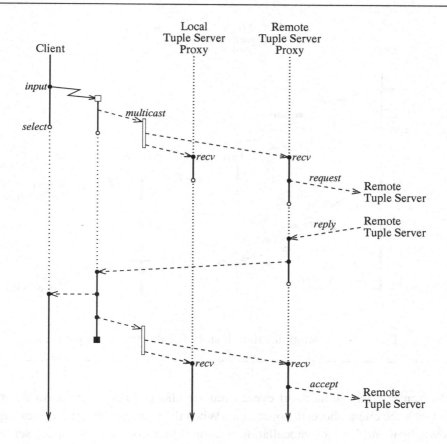

Figure 9.2: Communication history for successful read operation

For each `input` (or `read`) request, we spawn a new thread to manage the operation. This thread broadcasts the template to be matched to the tuple servers, and coordinates the replies. Furthermore, its thread ID serves as a locally unique ID for the transaction.[3] Once a matching tuple has been found, it is communicated to the reading thread, and the cancellation messages are sent out to the other processors. Figure 9.2 shows the message traffic for such a situation. Since the `inEvt` and `rdEvt` operations are event-valued, there is the added complication that these operations can be used in a selection context, where they might be aborted. We use negative acknowledgements to handle this situation. Once the manager thread has broadcast the read request, it waits for either

---

[3]The thread ID is mapped to an integer ID by the proxy and this integer is paired with the tuple-space ID to give a system-wide unique ID for the transaction.

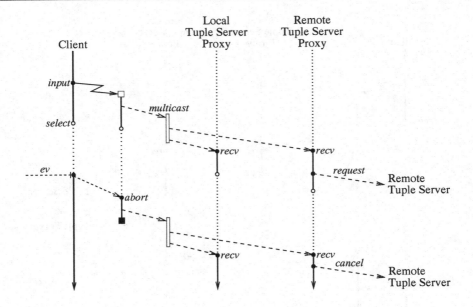

Figure 9.3: Communication history for aborted read operation

a reply from a proxy or an abort event from the client. Figure 9.3 shows the message traffic when the client aborts the operation. When the manager thread receives a negative acknowledgement, it sends cancellation messages to all of the tuple-space servers. We also take care not to send the acknowledgement message until we are sure that the tuple has been accepted. We do this by synchronizing on the choice of sending the matching tuple on the reply channel and receiving the negative acknowledgement. The semantics of **CML** channels guarantee that only one of these can occur.

9.3.2 The output protocol

The out operation protocol is trivial. For this implementation, we choose a round-robin distribution policy for tuples, which is implemented by the local output server.

9.3.3 The join protocol

The join protocol provides a mechanism for a process to join an already existing tuple space. When an application calls joinTupleSpace, it supplies a list of remote hosts. Implementing this operation requires creating a local proxy for each remote host and establishing a connection between the proxy and the remote host. These connections are also used by the output server to place tuples in the remote parts of the tuple space. At each remote host, a proxy for the new member of the tuple space must be created, and the new member must be added to output server's list. Since our implementation is based on TCP/IP sockets, which provide bidirectional communication, the remote hosts do not have to establish a network connection back to the new member. One tricky point about the join protocol is that once it is completed, the new member should have a view of the tuple-space state that is consistent with the rest of the members, including any outstanding input operations. Without this information, tuples at the new member cannot be used to satisfy outstanding requests that were made prior to when it joined. To address this problem, we employ a *log server*, which keeps a log of outstanding requests that were issued by its local clients. When a new member joins, each existing member sends the new member a list of outstanding requests, which results in a consistent global state.

9.4 The major components

Before diving into a detailed description of the implementation, it is useful to survey the major components. The system is implemented in seven distinct modules, which are logically organized into three layers — client, server, and network — as follows:

Client layer

> The client layer is implemented by the `Linda` structure, which has the interface given in Listing 9.1. It includes the implementation of the threads that are spawned to manage input operations.

Server layer

> The server layer contains the bulk of the system. It includes the output server, which implements the output mapping policy for tuples; the tuple server proxies, which provide a uniform interface between the client operations and the tuple servers; and the tuple server itself, which maintains the local portion of the distributed tuple space. It consists of the following modules:

> **structure** `TupleServer : TUPLE_SERVER`
>> This structure implements the local tuple server, the tuple-server proxies, and the log server.

> **structure** `TupleStore : TUPLE_STORE`
>> This structure implements the storage mechanism for the local portion of tuple space.

> **structure** `OutputServer`
>> This structure implements the output server thread, including the policy for distributing tuples.

Network layer

The network layer provides an abstract interface to distributed communication over some communication fabric.[4] It consists of the following modules:

structure Network : NETWORK

This structure provides the network layer API to the server layer. It includes operations for sending/receiving messages to/from specific remote hosts.

structure NetMessage

This structure defines the basic message types used by the network communication and provides operations to read and write messages over the network.

structure DataRep

This structure implements operations for marshalling and unmarshalling tuple and template data.

In addition, there is the Tuple structure, which defines the tuple and template types. Since these have already been described above (see Listing 9.1), we do not discuss this structure any further. The remainder of this chapter examines each of these layers in detail, starting from the bottom (network interface).

9.5   The network layer

At the lowest level, the servers that implement the distributed tuple space must communicate over some sort of network. There are many different kinds of network communication, so it is useful to isolate the implementation details in an abstraction of the required network services. The implementation of this abstraction layer must address several issues: establishing and managing connections to the other tuple servers in the tuple space; routing messages from the network connections to the appropriate threads; and encoding and decoding messages.

There are a number of ways that we might implement this layer, including a single address space implementation on top of **CML** primitives. For the purpose of this chapter, we choose an implementation on top of TCP/IP streams, which provide ordered reliable communication between processors. While it would be more efficient to use UDP datagrams, it would require additional complexity for handling lost and out-of-order messages, and so we leave it as an exercise for the reader.

For any TCP/IP connection, one process is called the *client* and the other is the *server*. This asymmetry is reflected in the way that the connection is established. For a connection between a tuple server on processor A and a tuple-server proxy for A on processor B, we designate A as the server and B as the client.

---

[4]We use TCP/IP for network communication, but other mechanisms could be used without affecting the other layers of the system.

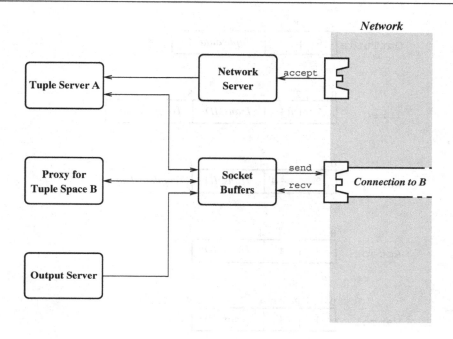

Figure 9.4: The communication topology for the network layer

Figure 9.4 gives the local communication topology for the network layer in a two-processor tuple space. The network layer consists of the *network server* thread and a *socket buffer* thread for each remote connection. The network server thread is responsible for accepting new connections and creating socket buffer threads. The socket buffer threads handle socket I/O and marshalling and unmarshalling of messages.

9.5.1 Message representation

The first issue that must be addressed is how the various requests and replies are represented when communicated between processors. When designing such a representation, we must be aware that different processors in a common tuple space may have different internal representations of **ML** values. For the purpose of this system, we assume a basic machine size of 32 bits,[5] so we only have to worry about endianess. We choose a big-endian representation for this implementation (*i.e.*, the most significant byte has the lower address). Figure 9.5 gives a pictorial view of the message representation. All

---

[5] As of this writing, **SML/NJ** only has 32-bit implementations, although 64-bit versions may appear in the future.

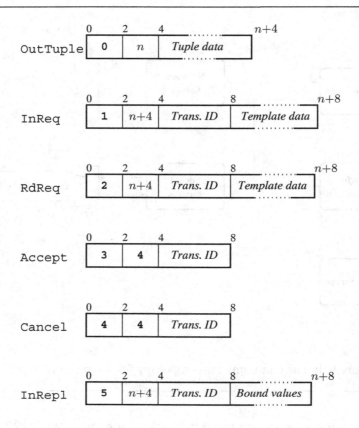

Figure 9.5: The network message representation

messages have a standard 4-byte header consisting of a 16-bit message kind and a 16-bit message length. The message length specifies the number of bytes following the header. For all message kinds except OutTuple, the first element of the message body is the *transaction ID*, which is a 4-byte integer.

We also use a simple encoding scheme for tuples, templates, and bound values. Table 9.2 gives the encoding scheme for the fields of a template; values are encoded in the same format, except that there are no formals or wildcards. A template, tuple, or sequence of bound values is represented as a sequence of the field encodings, terminated by a semicolon.

The encoding and decoding of messages is implemented across two modules: the message header and transaction ID is handled in the NetMessage structure, which is described in the next section; and the encoding of tuples, templates, and value sequences

Table 9.2: Template field encoding

Encoding	Field	
$i\,b_1\,b_2\,b_3\,b_4$	IPat k	*where* $k = 2^24 \cdot b_1 + 2^16 \cdot b_2 + 2^8 \cdot b_3 + b_4$
t	BPat true	
f	BPat false	
$s\,b_1\,b_2\,b_3\,b_4\,c_1 \ldots c_k$	SPat "$c_1 \cdots c_k$"	*where* $k = 2^24 \cdot b_1 + 2^16 \cdot b_2 + 2^8 \cdot b_3 + b_4$
I	IFormal	
B	BFormal	
S	SFormal	
–	Wild	

is implemented by the `DataRep` structure, whose interface is given in Listing 9.3. This structure also provides functions for computing the size of tuples, templates, and value sequences. The decoding functions take a vector of bytes and an index into the vector, and return the decoded value and next index. Similarly, the encoding functions take a value, an array of bytes, and a starting index in the array, and return the index of the first byte after the encoded value. Returning the next index allows multiple values to be included in a message; while our implementation does not use this feature, a more optimized network layer might want to piggyback multiple messages in a single network message. We do not include the implementation of the `DataRep` structure here, since it is straightforward.

```
type vector = Word8Vector.vector
val decodeTuple    : (vector * int) -> (Tuple.tuple * int)
val decodeTemplate : (vector * int) -> (Tuple.template * int)
val decodeValues   : (vector * int) -> (Tuple.val_atom list * int)

type array = Word8Array.array
val encodeTuple    : (Tuple.tuple * array * int) -> int
val encodeTemplate : (Tuple.template * array * int) -> int
val encodeValues   : (Tuple.val_atom list * array * int) -> int

val tupleSz    : Tuple.tuple -> int
val templateSz : Tuple.template -> int
val valuesSz   : Tuple.val_atom list -> int
```

Listing 9.3: The `DataRep` interface

```
datatype message
  = OutTuple of Tuple.tuple
  | InReq of {
      transId : int,
      pat : Tuple.template
    }
  | RdReq of {
      transId : int,
      pat : Tuple.template
    }
  | Accept of { transId : int }
  | Cancel of { transId : int }
  | InReply of {
      transId : int,
      vals : Tuple.val_atom list
    }

type 'a sock = ('a, Socket.active Socket.stream) Socket.sock

val recvMessage : 'a sock -> message
val sendMessage : ('a sock * message) -> unit
```

Listing 9.4: The `NetMessage` interface

9.5.2   Network communication

The reading and writing of messages on a socket is implemented in the `NetMessage` structure; its interface is given in Listing 9.4. In addition to handling socket I/O, the functions `recvMessage` and `sendMessage` also manage the conversion between the `message` datatype and the wire representation of messages. Listing 9.5 gives the implementation of the `recvMessage` function. This function first reads the 4-byte header and unpacks the message kind and length (notice we use the big-endian unpacking operations).[6] We then read the rest of the message data, then decode it based on the message's kind (using the `DataRep` structure to decode the **Linda** values carried in a message). We do not present the code for the `sendMessage` function here, but it is similar.

9.5.3   Network interface

The `Network` structure provides the interface to the network layer; its interface, the `NETWORK` signature, is given in Listing 9.6. The abstract `network` type is used as a handle for the collection of network threads; its only use is as an argument to the

---

[6]We use the utility function, `recvVec`, from the **SML/NJ** Library to read a specific number of bytes from a socket.

```
structure DR = DataRep

fun recvMessage sock = let
      val hdr = SockUtil.recvVec (sock, 4)
      val kind = Pack16Big.subVec(hdr, 0)
      val len = LargeWord.toInt(Pack16Big.subVec(hdr, 1))
      val data = SockUtil.recvVec (sock, len)
      fun getId () = LargeWord.toInt(Pack32Big.subVec(data, 0))
      fun getTuple () = #1 (DR.decodeTuple (data, 0))
      fun getPat () = #1 (DR.decodeTemplate (data, 4))
      fun getVals () = #1 (DR.decodeValues (data, 4))
      in
        case kind
         of 0w0 => OutTuple(getTuple ())
          | 0w1 => InReq{transId=getId(), pat=getPat()}
          | 0w2 => RdReq{transId=getId(), pat=getPat()}
          | 0w3 => Accept{transId=getId()}
          | 0w4 => Cancel{transId=getId()}
          | 0w5 => InReply{transId=getId(), vals=getVals()}
          | _ => error "recvMessage: bogus message kind"
        (* end case *)
      end
```

Listing 9.5: The implementation of `recvMessage`

shutdown function.[7] The abstract `server_conn` type is an abstraction of the connection to a remote server. It is used to send requests, receive replies, and to acknowledge replies. Tuple-server IDs are represented by the `ts_id` type. The network layer assigns these IDs when creating connections to remote members of the tuple space. The `reply` type represents a reply to an input operation. It is a record of a transaction ID (generated by the remote server) and a list of the values bound to the free variables of input operation's template. Requests from remote clients are represented by the `client_req` datatype. Note that each of the client request constructors corresponds to a send operation on a server connection. The `InReq` constructor deserves additional comment: the `remove` field is used to distinguish between input requests generated from **in** and those from **rd** operations; in the former case, the `remove` flag will be `true`, and the tuple should be removed when successfully read. The `reply` field is a function that is used to send a reply to the appropriate remote client (via the corresponding socket buffer thread). The last type defined in the `Network` structure is `remote_server_info`, which is a record of information about a remote server (name, ID, and the server connection).

The function `initNetwork` is used to establish the network server thread and ini-

---

[7]In this implementation, the `shutdown` is just a stub. Implementing a shutdown protocol is left as an exercise for the reader.

```
signature NETWORK =
  sig
    type network
    type server_conn
    eqtype ts_id

    type reply = {transId : int, vals : Tuple.val_atom list}

    datatype client_req
      = OutTuple of Tuple.tuple
      | InReq of {
          from : ts_id,
          transId : int,
          remove : bool,
          pat : Tuple.template,
          reply : reply -> unit
        }
      | Accept of {from : ts_id, transId : int}
      | Cancel of {from : ts_id, transId : int}

    type remote_server_info = {
          name : string,
          id : ts_id,
          conn : server_conn
        }

    val initNetwork : {
          port    : int option,
          remote  : string list,
          tsReqMb : client_req Mailbox.mbox,
          addTS   : remote_server_info -> unit
        } -> {
          myId    : ts_id,
          network : network,
          servers : remote_server_info list
        }

    val sendOutTuple : server_conn -> Tuple.tuple -> unit
    val sendInReq : server_conn -> {
          transId : int,
          remove : bool,
          pat : Tuple.template
        } -> unit
    val sendAccept    : server_conn -> {transId : int} -> unit
    val sendCancel    : server_conn -> {transId : int} -> unit
    val replyEvt      : server_conn -> reply event

    val shutdown : network -> unit

  end (* NETWORK *)
```

Listing 9.6: The abstract network interface

tial remote connections. It takes as arguments an optional port number,[8] a list of remote servers, a mailbox for communicating with the local tuple server thread, and a function to notify the server level that a new member has joined the tuple space. The `initNetwork` function returns the tuple-server ID assigned to the local server, the network handle, and information about each of the remote servers. Listing 9.7 gives the implementation of `initNetwork`. We start by parsing the list of remote server names into host name, address, and port records, which is done by mapping the `parseHost` function over the list of remote hosts. We then spawn the network server with a call to `spawnNetServer`. The network server is responsible for assigning tuple-server IDs to members that join after initialization. Internally, we use integers for the tuple-server IDs (type `ts_id`). We assign 0 to the local server, and 1 through n for the initial n remote hosts. We pass the first ID after that $(n + 1)$ to `spawnNetServer`. The remote server information is created by folding the `mkServer` function over the list of hosts. This function connects a fresh socket to the remote hosts and calls `spawnBuffers` to spawn the socket buffer threads. The `spawnBuffers` function (described below) returns the client connection for the remote host.

The `parseHost` function is responsible for translating a host name into uniform address information. A hostname consists of a *host part* and an optional *port part*, separated by a colon. The *host part* may be a numeric IP address, or a symbolic name. Likewise, the port may be specified by an integer port number, or by the name of a service. We use a couple of functions from the `SockUtil` structure provided by the **SML/NJ** Library to handle the parsing of the host information. The `scanAddr` function is first used to parse the hostname into the host and port parts, and to classify the parts as symbolic or numeric. Then we use the `resolveAddr` function to resolve symbolic addresses. If the port is not specified, we use the default of `7001`.

The last piece of the network initialization code is the `spawnNetServer` function, which creates a new socket and thread for listening for new connections. Each time a new connection is accepted, we spawn new socket buffer threads for the connection, figure out the name of the connecting host,[9] and pass this information to the `addTS` function, which handles adding the new connection at the server level (see Section 9.7.1). The `spawnNetServer` function also creates the network object, which has the following representation:

```
datatype network = NETWORK of {shutdown : unit SyncVar.ivar}
```

Note that the `shutdown` field is not being used in this implementation.

---

[8]The full "address" of a socket consists of the machine that it is on and its port number. The **CML-Linda** library uses port `7001` as its default port, but the `port` argument allows this to be overridden.

[9]The hostname is not strictly necessary, but it is useful to have this information when debugging higher levels of the implementation.

```
fun parseHost h = (case (StringCvt.scanString SockUtil.scanAddr h)
        of NONE => error "bad hostname format"
         | (SOME info) => (case SockUtil.resolveAddr info
            of {host, addr, port = NONE} =>
                    {host = host, addr = addr, port = 7001}
             | {host, addr, port = SOME p} =>
                    {host = host, addr = addr, port = p}
          (* end case *))
            handle (SockUtil.BadAddr msg) => error msg
      (* end case *))

fun spawnNetServer (myPort, startId, tsMb, addTS) = let
      val mySock = INetSock.TCP.socket()
      fun loop nextId = let
            val (newSock, addr) = Socket.accept mySock
            val proxyConn = spawnBuffers (nextId, newSock, tsMb)
            val (host, port) = INetSock.fromAddr addr
            val name = (case NetHostDB.getByAddr host
                    of (SOME ent) => NetHostDB.name ent
                     | NONE => "??"
                  (* end case *))
            in
                addTS {name = name, id = nextId, conn = proxyConn};
                loop (nextId+1)
            end
      val port = getOpt(myPort, 7001)
      in
        Socket.bind (mySock, INetSock.any port);
        Socket.listen (mySock, 5);
        spawn (fn () => loop startId);
        NETWORK{shutdown = SyncVar.iVar()}
      end

fun initNetwork {port, remote, tsReqMb, addTS} = let
      val hosts = List.map parseHost remote
      val startId = length hosts + 1
      val network = spawnNetServer (port, startId, tsReqMb, addTS)
      fun mkServer ({host, addr, port}, (id, l)) = let
            val sock = INetSock.TCP.socket()
            val sockAddr = INetSock.toAddr(addr, port)
            val _ = Socket.connect (sock, sockAddr)
            val conn = spawnBuffers (id, sock, tsReqMb)
            in
                (id+1, {name = host, id = id, conn = conn}::l)
            end
      in
        { myId = 0, network = network,
          servers = #2 (List.foldl mkServer (1, []) hosts)
        }
      end
```

Listing 9.7: Initializing the network interface

```
datatype server_conn = CONN of {
    out : Msg.message -> unit,
    replyEvt : reply event
  }

fun spawnBuffers (id, sock, tsMb) = let
      val outMb = Mailbox.mailbox()
      fun outLoop () = (
          Msg.sendMessage (sock, Mailbox.recv outMb);
          outLoop())
      val inMb = Mailbox.mailbox()
      fun reply r = Mailbox.send(outMb, Msg.InReply r)
      fun inLoop () = (
          case Msg.recvMessage sock
           of (Msg.OutTuple t) => Mailbox.send(tsMb, OutTuple t)
            | (Msg.InReq{transId, pat}) =>
              Mailbox.send(tsMb, InReq{
                  from=id, transId=transId,
                  remove = true, pat=pat, reply=reply
                })
            | (Msg.RdReq{transId, pat}) =>
              Mailbox.send(tsMb, InReq{
                  from=id, transId=transId,
                  remove = false, pat=pat, reply=reply
                })
            | (Msg.Accept{transId}) =>
                Mailbox.send(tsMb, Accept{from=id, transId=transId})
            | (Msg.Cancel{transId}) =>
                Mailbox.send(tsMb, Cancel{from=id, transId=transId})
            | (Msg.InReply repl) => Mailbox.send(inMb, repl)
          (* end case *);
          inLoop ())
      in
        spawn outLoop; spawn inLoop;
        CONN{
            out = fn req => Mailbox.send(outMb, req),
            replyEvt = Mailbox.recvEvt inMb
          }
      end
```

Listing 9.8: Creating the socket buffer threads

The `spawnBuffers` function (see Listing 9.8) is responsible for creating the socket buffer threads. The output buffer thread is quite simple: it repeatedly gets a message from a mailbox and uses `sendMessage` to send it out on the network connection. The input buffer thread is more complicated. When it receives a message from the socket, it examines the message type and routes it to the appropriate target: to the tuple server's mailbox (`tsMb`) for output operations and requests from a remote client, and to the client connection mailbox (`inMb`) for replies to requests from local clients. The request mes-

```
signature TUPLE_SERVER =
  sig
    type ts_id = Network.ts_id

    datatype ts_msg
      = IN of {
            tid : thread_id,
            remove : bool,
            pat : Tuple.template,
            replFn : (Tuple.val_atom list * ts_id) -> unit
          }
      | CANCEL of thread_id
      | ACCEPT of (thread_id * ts_id)

    val mkLogServer : ts_msg Multicast.port
          -> unit -> (ts_msg Multicast.port * ts_msg list)
    val mkTupleServer :
          (ts_id * Network.client_req Mailbox.mbox * ts_msg event)
            -> unit
    val mkProxyServer :
          (ts_id * Network.server_conn * ts_msg event * ts_msg list)
            -> unit

  end
```

Listing 9.9: The `TupleServer` interface

sages passed to the tuple server are tagged with the ID of the connection. In the case of input or read requests, the input buffer also adds the reply function to the message. The reply function routes the reply to the output buffer's mailbox. With the use of this reply function and the tuple-server mailbox, the tuple server is isolated from having to know about the individual remote connections.

9.6   The server layer

The server layer is the meat of the **CML-Linda** system. It consists of four kinds of threads: a set of tuple-server proxies, which provide a uniform interface between the client level and the tuple servers (both remote and local); the local tuple server, which maintains the local portion of the tuple space; the log server, which maintains a log of the current outstanding requests; and the output server, which manages the distribution of locally generated tuples. The first three of these are implemented in the `TupleServer` structure, which has the signature given in Listing 9.9. The local tuple server is built on top of the tuple storage mechanism provided by the `TupleStore` structure. The output server thread is implemented in the `OutputServer` structure. We examine each of these threads, as well as the tuple storage mechanism, in turn.

```
structure TransTbl = Hash2TableFn (
    structure Key1 = struct
        type hash_key = thread_id
        val hashVal = hashTid
        val sameKey = sameTid
    end
    structure Key2 = struct
        type hash_key = int
        val hashVal = Word.fromInt
        val sameKey = (op = : (int * int) -> bool)
    end)
```

Listing 9.10: The transaction table structure

9.6.1 The tuple-server proxies

The tuple server proxies provide an abstraction layer between the transaction manager threads that implement the input operations, and the tuple servers. This abstraction layer hides the location of the particular tuple server represented by a given proxy.

A tuple-server proxy must maintain the set of outstanding transactions, and be able to locate a transaction based on the local ID, which is the thread ID of the transaction manager, and the remote ID. To accomplish this, we use the double-keyed hash table functor from the **SML/NJ** Library to implement transaction tables (see Listing 9.10). The items that we store in these tables have the following record type:

```
type trans_info = {
    id : int,
    replFn : (T.val_atom list * ts_id) -> unit
}
```

The `id` field is the transaction ID that is assigned to the transaction by the proxy server and is forwarded to the remote tuple servers,[10] and the `replFn` field is used to send a matching tuple to the thread that is managing the transaction.

The actual implementation of a proxy server is contained in the `proxyServer` function, which is given in Listing 9.11. This function is used to create proxy servers for both remote tuple servers and the local tuple server, so it is necessary to use an abstraction of the connection to the tuple server. We use a record of functions for this interface (the `conn_ops` record type). The body of the proxy server is a simple message handling loop. Requests from local clients are handled by `handleMsg`, while `handleReply` deals with replies from the tuple server. The set of outstanding transactions is kept in a double-keyed hash table, as described above. When an `IN` message is received from the client, a new transaction ID is generated (using the function `nextId`), the request

---

[10]We do not use the transaction manager's thread ID for this because there is no easy way to send it to a remote system.

```
type conn_ops = {
    sendInReq  : {
        transId : int, remove : bool, pat : T.template
      } -> unit,
    sendAccept : {transId : int} -> unit,
    sendCancel : {transId : int} -> unit,
    replyEvt   : Net.reply event
  }

fun proxyServer (myId, conn : conn_ops, reqEvt, initInReqs) = let
    val tbl = TransTbl.mkTable (32, Fail "TransTbl")
    val nextId = let val cnt = ref 0
          in
            fn () => let val id = !cnt in cnt := id+1; id end
          end
    fun handleMsg (IN{tid, remove, pat, replFn}) = let
          val id = nextId()
          val req = {transId = id, remove = remove, pat = pat}
          in
            TransTbl.insert tbl (tid, id, {id=id, replFn=replFn});
            #sendInReq conn req
          end
      | handleMsg (CANCEL tid) = let
          val {id, ...} = TransTbl.remove1 tbl tid
          in
            #sendCancel conn {transId=id}
          end
      | handleMsg (ACCEPT(tid, tsId)) = let
          val {id, ...} = TransTbl.remove1 tbl tid
          in
            if (tsId = myId)
              then #sendAccept conn {transId=id}
              else #sendCancel conn {transId=id}
          end
    fun handleReply {transId, vals} = (
          case TransTbl.find2 tbl transId
           of NONE => ()
            | (SOME{id, replFn}) => replFn (vals, myId)
          (* end case *))
    fun loop () = (
          select [
              wrap (reqEvt, handleMsg),
              wrap (#replyEvt conn, handleReply)
            ];
          loop ())
    in
      List.app handleMsg initInReqs;
      ignore (spawn loop)
    end
```

Listing 9.11: The implementation of proxyServer

```
fun mkProxyServer (myId, conn, reqEvt, initInList) = let
    val conn = {
            sendInReq  = Net.sendInReq conn,
            sendAccept = Net.sendAccept conn,
            sendCancel = Net.sendCancel conn,
            replyEvt   = Net.replyEvt conn
        }
    in
      proxyServer (myId, conn, reqEvt, initInList)
    end
```

Listing 9.12: The implementation of `mkProxyServer`

is recorded in the table, and the request is forwarded to the tuple server with the generated ID as the transaction ID. When a CANCEL or ACCEPT message is received, the corresponding entry is removed from the table and the transaction ID is retrieved. Then the message is tagged with the transaction ID, and forwarded to the tuple server. Replies from the tuple server are a bit easier to deal with, since there is only one kind of message involved. When a reply comes in, we use the transaction ID to find the corresponding item in the table, and use the item's `replFn` field to forward the reply back to the transaction manager in the client level. Note that there is a race between a cancel message being received by the remote server, and the remote server offering a matching tuple. To avoid any problems caused by this race condition, the `handleReply` function detects the situation where the transaction has already been removed from the table and ignores the reply.

A proxy server for a remote tuple server is created by the function `mkProxyServer`, which is shown in Listing 9.12. This function is a wrapper on `proxyServer`; its only work is to package up the server connection provided by the network layer (see Listing 9.6) as a `conn_ops` record.

9.6.2 The tuple store

The `TupleStore` structure implements the storage mechanism for the local piece of the distributed tuple space (*i.e.*, the part managed by the local tuple server). Listing 9.13 gives the interface of this structure. The abstract `tuple_store` type contains the tuples in the local part of the tuple space (including those that are held), as well as a record of outstanding input requests. The `id` type is used to tag input requests. It consists of the tuple server ID that generated the request and a unique transaction ID (which is an integer). The `match` type constructor is used to represent information about input requests. It is a record consisting of the ID of the input request, a function for replying

```
signature TUPLE_STORE =
  sig

    type tuple_store
    type id = (Network.ts_id * int)
    type 'a match = {
        id    : id,
        reply : Network.reply -> unit,
        ext   : 'a
      }
    type bindings = Tuple.val_atom list

    val newStore : unit -> tuple_store

    val add : (tuple_store * Tuple.tuple) -> bindings match option
    val input : (tuple_store * Tuple.template match) -> bindings option
    val cancel : (tuple_store * id) -> bindings match option
    val remove : (tuple_store * id) -> unit

  end
```

Listing 9.13: The TUPLE_STORE signature

to the request, and an extension field with additional information. Depending on the context, the extension field of a match is either a template or set of variable bindings (the bindings type is a list of values that are bound to the free variables of a template).

The TupleStore structure also provides operations that correspond to the messages that a tuple server must handle (see Section 9.6.3). The add operation is used to add new tuples to the store (*i.e.*, because of an output operation). Since the new tuple may match some outstanding input request, the add operation returns optional match information. The input operation is used to query the store for possible matches to an input request. If the request cannot be satisfied immediately, it is recorded in the store. Lastly, the cancel and remove operations are used to complete the transaction initiated by an input request: cancel removes the hold on a tuple (which frees the tuple to match another outstanding request), and remove removes the tuple from the store.

The type declarations for the data structures used to represent the tuple store are given in Listing 9.14. The tuple_store type is actually represented by a pair of hash tables. The *tuple table* maps the key portion of a tuple or template to a *bucket*, where the bucket for a given key is a record of the list of outstanding input requests with that key and the list of tuples with that key. The other hash table in a tuple_store is the *hold table*, which is used to keep track of those tuples that are being held pending acceptance or cancellation of a matching input operation.

One important operation used in the implementation of the tuple store is matching

```
structure T = Tuple

type id = (Network.ts_id * int)

type 'a match = {
    id    : id,
    reply : Network.reply -> unit,
    ext   : 'a
}
type bindings = T.val_atom list

type bucket = {
    waiting : T.template match list ref,
    holds   : (id * T.tuple) list ref,
    items   : T.tuple list ref
}

structure TupleTbl = HashTableFn (struct
        type hash_key = T.val_atom
        fun hashVal (T.BVal false) = 0w0
          | hashVal (T.BVal true) = 0w1
          | hashVal (T.IVal n) = Word.fromInt n
          | hashVal (T.SVal s) = HashString.hashString s
        fun sameKey (k1 : T.val_atom, k2) = (k1 = k2)
      end)

structure QueryTbl = HashTableFn (struct
      type hash_key = id
      fun hashVal (_, id) = Word.fromInt id
      fun sameKey ((tsId1, id1), (tsId2, id2) : hash_key) =
          ((tsId1 = tsId2) andalso (id1 = id2))
    end)

datatype query_status = Held | Waiting

datatype tuple_store = TS of {
    queries : (query_status * bucket) QueryTbl.hash_table,
    tuples : bucket TupleTbl.hash_table
}
```

Listing 9.14: The various types used in the tuple-store representation

a template to a tuple. This is done by the match function given in Listing 9.15. This function takes a template and tuple as arguments and returns NONE if there is no match or some bindings if there is a match. The match function is only called in contexts where the keys have already been matched (by the hash table lookup), so only the rest of the template and tuple are compared. The implementation is straightforward: the mFields function iterates over the field list accumulating bindings, while the mField function checks a pattern field against a value field using the rules in Table 9.1.

```
fun match (T.T(_, rest1), T.T(_, rest2)) = let
      fun mFields ([], [], binds) = SOME binds
        | mFields (f1::r1, f2::r2, binds) = (
            case mField(f1, f2, binds)
             of (SOME binds) => mFields(r1, r2, binds)
              | NONE => NONE
            (* end case *))
        | mFields _ = NONE
      and mField (T.IPat a, T.IVal b, binds) =
            if (a = b) then SOME binds else NONE
        | mField (T.BPat a, T.BVal b, binds) =
            if (a = b) then SOME binds else NONE
        | mField (T.SPat a, T.SVal b, binds) =
            if (a = b) then SOME binds else NONE
        | mField (T.IFormal, x as (T.IVal _), binds) =
            SOME(x::binds)
        | mField (T.BFormal, x as (T.BVal _), binds) =
            SOME(x::binds)
        | mField (T.SFormal, x as (T.SVal _), binds) =
            SOME(x::binds)
        | mField (T.Wild, _, binds) = SOME binds
        | mField _ = NONE
    in
      mFields (rest1, rest2, [])
    end
```

Listing 9.15: Matching a template and tuple

The implementation of the add function is given in Listing 9.16. The add function takes a tuple store and tuple to be added and returns a match option. We first do a lookup in the tuple table using the tuple's key. The simple case is where there is no bucket with this key in the table, in which case, we insert a new bucket with the tuple as its only item into the tuple table and return NONE. In the case where there is already a bucket for the tuple's key, we must scan the list of outstanding input requests for a possible match. If we find such a match, we put the tuple in the hold table (instead of in the tuple table), and return the match information. If there is no match, then we add the tuple to the list of tuples in the bucket and return NONE.

The code for the remaining tuple-store operations is presented in Listings 9.17 and 9.18. The input operation searches the tuple store for a tuple that matches the given template. We start by using the template's key to do a lookup in the tuple table. If there is no bucket with the given key, then we insert a new bucket with no items and the input request information in the waiting list, and return NONE. When the tuple table already contains a bucket with the given key, we need to scan the item list for a matching tuple. If we find a matching tuple, then we remove it from the item list and put it into the hold table, and we return the bindings from the match. If the matching tuple is the only tuple in the bucket,

```
fun add (TS{tuples, queries}, tuple as T.T(key, _)) = (
    case (TupleTbl.find tuples key)
      of NONE => (
          TupleTbl.insert tuples (key, {
              items = ref [tuple],
              waiting = ref[],
              holds = ref[]
          });
          NONE)
       | (SOME(bucket as {items, waiting, holds})) => let
          fun scan ([], _) = (items := tuple :: !items; NONE)
            | scan ((x as {reply, id, ext})::r, wl) = (
                case match(ext, tuple)
                  of NONE => scan(r, x::wl)
                   | (SOME binds) => (
                       waiting := List.revAppend(wl, r);
                       holds := (id, tuple) :: !holds;
                       QueryTbl.insert queries (id, (Held, bucket));
                       SOME{reply=reply, id=id, ext=binds})
                 (* end case *))
          in
            scan (!waiting, [])
          end
    (* end case *))
```

Listing 9.16: Adding a tuple to the tuple store

then we also remove the bucket from the tuple table. When there is no matching tuple, we add input request information to the waiting list, and return NONE.

The `cancel` and `remove` operations are quite simple. They just remove the specified held tuple from the hold table; in the case of `cancel`, this tuple is then added to the tuple table, while in the case of `remove`, the tuple is discarded.

9.6.3 The local tuple server

The tuple server thread manages a tuple store in response to request messages. As seen in Figure 9.1, these messages come from the local output server, from remote output servers and proxies (via the socket buffer), and from the local proxy server. All of the sources that send `client_req` messages use the same mailbox to communicate with the tuple server, which greatly simplifies the implementation.[11] Listing 9.19 gives the code for the tuple server. The body of the server is the `handleReq` function, which maps each `client_req` message (see Listing 9.6) onto a tuple-store operation. In the

---

[11]This is why input request messages carry a reply operation; it frees the tuple server from having to know the source of the message when sending a reply.

```
fun input (TS{tuples, queries}, {reply, ext as T.T(key, _), id}) = (
    case (TupleTbl.find tuples key)
      of NONE => let
          val bucket = {
                  waiting = ref[{reply=reply, id=id, ext=ext}],
                  holds = ref[],
                  items = ref[]
              }
        in
          TupleTbl.insert tuples (key, bucket);
          QueryTbl.insert queries (id, (Waiting, bucket));
          NONE
        end
      | (SOME(bucket as {items, waiting, holds})) => let
          fun look (_, []) = (
                  waiting := !waiting @
                    [{reply=reply, id=id, ext=ext}];
                  QueryTbl.insert queries (id, (Waiting, bucket));
                  NONE)
            | look (prefix, item :: r) = (
                  case match(ext, item)
                    of NONE => look (item::prefix, r)
                     | (SOME binds) => (
                          items := List.revAppend(prefix, r);
                          holds := (id, item) :: !holds;
                          QueryTbl.insert queries (id, (Held, bucket));
                          SOME binds)
                  (* end case *))
        in
          look ([], !items)
        end
    (* end case *))
```

Listing 9.17: The tuple-store `input` operation

case of adding a tuple or cancelling a hold, we may have to reply to an outstanding input request. The `replyIfMatch` function takes care of this. Likewise, an input request may be immediately satisfied, in which case we send a reply.

The function `mkTupleServer` is actually responsible for creating the tuple server and local proxy, and for hooking them together. Listing 9.20 gives the code for this function. Most of the code is involved in implementing the `conn_ops` record for the proxy connection. Once this is built, we spawn off the tuple server and its proxy server.

9.6.4 The log server

The log server keeps track of outstanding input requests, so that when a new member joins the tuple space, it can be told about them. The log server is created by the function

```
fun cancel (tbl as TS{tuples, queries}, id) = (
      case (QueryTbl.remove queries id)
       of (Waiting, {items, waiting, holds}) => (
            case (removeFromList (fn t => (#id t = id)) (! waiting))
             of ({ext, ...}, []) =>
                  if (null(! items) andalso null(! holds))
                     then ignore(TupleTbl.remove tuples (T.key ext))
                     else waiting := []
              | (_, 1) => waiting := 1
            (* end case *);
            NONE)
        | (Held, {items, waiting, holds}) => let
            val ((_, tuple), 1) =
                  removeFromList (fn (id', _) => (id' = id)) (! holds)
            in
              holds := 1;
              add (tbl, tuple)
            end
      (* end case *))

fun remove (tbl as TS{tuples, queries}, id) = let
      val (_, {items, waiting, holds}) = QueryTbl.remove queries id
      val ((_, tuple), 1) =
            removeFromList (fn (id', _) => (id' = id)) (! holds)
      in
        if (null 1 andalso null(! items) andalso null(! waiting))
           then ignore(TupleTbl.remove tuples (T.key tuple))
           else holds := 1
      end
```

Listing 9.18: Other tuple-store operations

mkLogServer, which is shown in Listing 9.21. This function takes a port on the client request multicast channel, and returns a function to get a new port on the multicast channel plus a list of outstanding input requests. The list of outstanding requests is a compressed prefix of the local client request stream, which reflects the local contribution to the global state of the distributed tuple space.

The implementation of the log server is a simple message handling loop that accepts requests from the client-request multicast channel, and requests for a new port. It maintains a hash table of outstanding input transactions: IN requests are added to the table, while ACCEPT and CANCEL messages cause the corresponding IN requests to be removed. When a new port is needed for the proxy of some new member, we copy the

```
fun tupleServer tsMb = let
      val tupleTbl = TupleStore.newStore()
      fun replyIfMatch NONE = ()
        | replyIfMatch (SOME{reply, id = (_, transId), ext}) =
            reply{transId = transId, vals = ext}
      fun handleReq (Net.OutTuple t) =
            replyIfMatch (TupleStore.add (tupleTbl, t))
        | handleReq (Net.InReq{from, transId, remove, pat, reply}) =
            let
            val match = {
                    reply = reply,
                    id = (from, transId),
                    ext = pat
                  }
            in
              case TupleStore.input (tupleTbl, match)
               of (SOME binds) => reply {transId=transId, vals=binds}
                | NONE => ()
              (* end case *)
            end
        | handleReq (Net.Accept{from, transId}) =
            TupleStore.remove (tupleTbl, (from, transId))
        | handleReq (Net.Cancel{from, transId}) =
            replyIfMatch(TupleStore.cancel(tupleTbl, (from, transId)))
      fun serverLoop () = (
            handleReq(Mailbox.recv tsMb);
            serverLoop ())
      in
        spawn serverLoop
      end
```

Listing 9.19: The implementation of the local tuple server

master port[12] and get the current list of outstanding requests. This request/reply interaction is packaged up as a simple RPC using the mkRPC function from the *CML Library*.

9.6.5 The output server

The output server is responsible for the distribution of tuples to tuple servers according to some policy. For our system, we use a simple round-robin scheme. The output server is implemented in the OutputServer structure, which is given in Listing 9.22. The output server, which is created by the function spawnServer, maintains a list of tuple servers (represented by output functions) and distributes tuples to them in a round-robin fashion. The spawnServer takes the local server connection as an argument, and

---

[12]The Multicast.copy operation produces a new port that will give exactly the same stream of messages as the port being copied.

```
fun mkTupleServer (myId, tsMb, reqEvt) = let
    val replyToProxyCh = channel()
    fun sendInReq {transId, remove, pat} =
        Mailbox.send (tsMb, Net.InReq{
            from = myId, transId = transId,
            remove = remove, pat = pat,
            reply = fn repl => send(replyToProxyCh, repl)
        })
    fun sendAccept {transId} =
        Mailbox.send (tsMb, Net.Accept{
            from = myId, transId = transId
        })
    fun sendCancel {transId} =
        Mailbox.send (tsMb, Net.Cancel{
            from = myId, transId = transId
        })
    val conn = {
            sendInReq = sendInReq,
            sendAccept = sendAccept,
            sendCancel = sendCancel,
            replyEvt = recvEvt replyToProxyCh
        }
    in
      tupleServer tsMb;
      proxyServer (myId, conn, reqEvt, [])
    end
```

Listing 9.20: The implementation of `mkTupleServer`

returns a record of two operations: `output` for outputing a tuple, and `addTS` for adding a new tuple server to the list. We use a function abstraction to represent the connection to the tuple servers; in the local case, this sends the tuple to the local tuple server's mailbox, and in the remote case, this sends the tuple to the appropriate output buffer thread (see `sendOutTuple` in Listing 9.6). As we will see, the `addTS` operation is used during initialization and as part of the join protocol.

9.7 The client layer

The programmer's interface to **CML-Linda** is provided by the `Linda` structure, which has the interface given above in Listing 9.1. The implementation of this structure collects together bindings from other structures. The type definitions for tuples and templates are defined in the `Tuple` structure. The definition of the `tuple_space` type and the client-side implementation of the tuple-space operations is provided by the `Linda` structure. We also open the `Tuple` structure inside the `Linda` structure to inherit its components.

```
structure TidTbl = HashTableFn (struct
    type hash_key = thread_id
    val hashVal = hashTid
    val sameKey = sameTid
  end)

fun mkLogServer masterPort = let
      val log = TidTbl.mkTable (16, Fail "TransactionLog")
      fun handleTrans (trans as IN{tid, ...}) =
            TidTbl.insert log (tid, trans)
        | handleTrans (CANCEL tid) =
            ignore(TidTbl.remove log tid)
        | handleTrans (ACCEPT(tid, _)) =
            ignore(TidTbl.remove log tid)
      val transEvt =
            CML.wrap(Multicast.recvEvt masterPort, handleTrans)
      fun handleGetLog () =
            (Multicast.copy masterPort, TidTbl.listItems log)
      val {call, entryEvt} = SimpleRPC.mkRPC handleGetLog
      fun serverLoop () = (
            select [entryEvt, transEvt]; serverLoop())
    in
      spawn serverLoop;
      call
    end
```

Listing 9.21: The implementation of the log server

Since the `Tuple` structure consists solely of the type definitions, we do not give its source here.

As noted above, the representation of the `tuple_space` type is defined in the `Linda` structure. A tuple space is represented by a record of two functions:

```
datatype tuple_space = TS of {
    request : TupleServer.ts_msg -> unit,
    output : Tuple.tuple -> unit
  }
```

The `request` function multicasts a request to the tuple-server proxies, and the output function sends a tuple to the output server. The `Linda` structure also holds the client-side implementation of the tuple-space operations, which we describe in the remainder of this section.

9.7.1 The `joinTupleSpace` operation

The implementation of the `joinTupleSpace` operation in the Linda structure is given in Listing 9.23. This function brings together the various pieces that we have

```
structure OutputServer : sig

    val spawnServer : (Tuple.tuple -> unit) -> {
            output : Tuple.tuple -> unit,
            addTS : (Tuple.tuple -> unit) -> unit
        }

  end = struct
    structure MB = Mailbox

    fun spawnServer localServer = let
          datatype msg
            = OUT of Tuple.tuple
            | ADD of (Tuple.tuple -> unit)
          val mbox = MB.mailbox()
          fun server tupleServers = let
              fun loop [] = loop tupleServers
                | loop (next::r) = (case MB.recv mbox
                    of (OUT t) => (next t; loop r)
                     | (ADD f) => server (f::tupleServers)
                    (* end case *))
              in
                loop tupleServers
              end
          in
            spawn (fn () => server [localServer]);
            { output = fn tuple => MB.send (mbox, OUT tuple),
              addTS = fn f => MB.send (mbox, ADD f)
            }
          end

  end (* OutputServer *)
```

Listing 9.22: The output server creation function

described above. It starts by creating the multicast channel (reqMCh) that is used to communicate to the tuple-server proxies, and the request mailbox (tsReqBox) used to send requests to the local tuple server. It then spawns the output server (see Section 9.6.5), passing in a function (out) for outputing a tuple to the local tuple server. The function newRemoteTS is defined for handling a new remote tuple server. It notifies the output server about the remote server and creates a new tuple server proxy. With this function defined, the network layer is initialized by a call to initNetwork (see Section 9.5.2). Once the network is initialized, we can create the local tuple server and the proxies for the remote tuple servers. Lastly, the representation of the tuple space is created and returned.

```
structure MChan = Multicast
structure SRV = TupleServer
structure Net = Network

fun joinTupleSpace {localPort, remoteHosts} = let
    val reqMCh = MChan.mChannel()
    val tsReqMb = Mailbox.mailbox()
    fun out tuple = Mailbox.send(tsReqMb, Net.OutTuple tuple)
    val {output, addTS} = OutputServer.spawnServer out
    val getInReqLog = SRV.mkLogServer (MChan.port reqMCh)
    fun newRemoteTS {name, id, conn} = let
        val (port, initInReqs) = getInReqLog()
        in
          addTS (Net.sendOutTuple conn);
          SRV.mkProxyServer (
            id, conn, MChan.recvEvt port, initInReqs)
        end
    val {myId, network, servers} = Net.initNetwork{
        port    = localPort,
        remote  = remoteHosts,
        tsReqMb = tsReqMb,
        addTS   = newRemoteTS
      }
    in
      SRV.mkTupleServer (
        myId, tsReqMb, MChan.recvEvt(MChan.port reqMCh));
      List.app newRemoteTS servers;
      TS{
          request = fn msg => MChan.multicast(reqMCh, msg),
          output = output
        }
    end
```

Listing 9.23: The implementation of `joinTupleSpace`

9.7.2 The tuple-space operations

The implementation of the `inEvt`, `rdEvt`, and `out` operations is given in Listing 9.24. Recall from the discussion of the input protocols (Section 9.3.1) that we need negative acknowledgements to abort the operation when another event is chosen. Thus, we use `withNack` to implement the `inEvt` and `rdEvt` operations. The `doInputOp` function (also given in Listing 9.24) implements the actual operation for both operations. The only difference between the two is the value of the `remove` flag sent in the input request (recall that `inEvt` removes the tuple, while `rdEvt` does not).

The `doInputOp` works by allocating a fresh reply channel and spawning the transaction manager for the request; it returns the event of receiving a reply, which is what the client will synchronize upon. Most of the details are in the implementation of this thread.

```
fun doInputOp (TS{request, ...}, template, removeFlg) nack = let
      val replCh = channel ()
      fun transactionMngr () = let
            val tid = getTid()
            val replMB = Mailbox.mailbox()
            fun handleNack () = request(SRV.CANCEL tid)
            fun handleRepl (msg, tsId) = select [
                  wrap (nack, handleNack),
                  wrap (sendEvt(replCh, msg),
                      fn () => request(SRV.ACCEPT(tid, tsId)))
                  ]
            in
              request (SRV.IN{
                  tid = tid,
                  remove = removeFlg,
                  pat = template,
                  replFn = fn x => Mailbox.send(replMB, x)
                  });
              select [
                  wrap (nack, handleNack),
                  wrap (Mailbox.recvEvt replMB, handleRepl)
                  ]
            end
      in
        spawn transactionMngr;
        recvEvt replCh
      end

fun inEvt (ts, template) = withNack (doInputOp (ts, template, true))
fun rdEvt (ts, template) = withNack (doInputOp (ts, template, false))

fun out (TS{output, ...}, tuple) = output tuple
```

Listing 9.24: The client-side implementation of **CML-Linda** input operations

After creating a reply mailbox, the transaction manager thread multicasts an IN request to all of the tuple-server proxies in the system. This request includes the transaction manager's thread ID, which serves as the local transaction ID, the remove flag, the template to be matched, and a function for sending replies to the reply mailbox. We might have considered using an I-variable for the reply, but that would not work in the situation where we get multiple replies. Once the request has been sent, the transaction manager waits for a reply or for the nackEvt to be enabled. If the manager thread receives a negative acknowledgement, then it sends cancellation messages to all of the tuple-space servers. We also take care not to send the acknowledgement message until we are sure that the tuple has been accepted. We do this by synchronizing on the choice of sending the matching tuple on the replyCh and receiving the negative acknowledgement. The semantics of **CML** guarantee that only one of these can occur.

Lastly, the user-level out operation is trivial; it is implemented by sending the argument tuple to the tuple space's output server.

Notes

A discussion of the **Linda** programming model can be found in Chapter 2, and further information can be found in a survey article by Carriero and Gelernter [CG89a], or in their book on parallel programming [CG90]. The implementation of the Dining Philosophers problem is adapted from another article by Carriero and Gelernter [CG89b].

This chapter was inspired by Siegel and Cooper's implementation of **Linda** in **SML** done at Carnegie Mellon University [SC91]. The protocol we use for implementing input requests is adopted from their implementation. One can also find a discussion of tuple-space distribution in a technical report by Bjornson et al [BCGL87]. Harkavy and Stone have also implemented a distributed version of **Linda** using **CML**.[13]

The implementation presented in this chapter can be extended and improved in a number of ways. At the user level, we can extend the tuple and template types to support structured data and we can add an operation for leaving the tuple space. The efficiency of the implementation can be improved by reimplementing the network layer on top of the UDP protocol and by using more sophisticated tuple distribution techniques.

Another example of distributed systems programming using **CML** is the **Distributed ML (DML)** system, developed by Krumvieda and Cooper at Cornell [Kru91, CK92, Kru92, Kru93]. **DML** is based on the reliable multicast primitives of **Isis** [BJ87, Bv93], and uses the **CML** events to provide a synchronous interface to a collection of distributed programming abstractions.

There are many books about low-level network programming in general, and specifically programming with sockets. Stevens provides a comprehensive description of UNIX network programming [Ste90], while Hall et al. describe sockets programming on Microsoft Windows [HTA+93]. The **SML** sockets API is part of the **SML** Basis Library [GR04]. This chapter also used additional functions from the **SML/NJ** Library, which are described in the accompanying documentation.

---

[13]Chris Stone, personal communication, March 1995.

10

Implementing Concurrency in SML/NJ

The main focus of this book is concurrent programming, but in this chapter, we examine the related topic of using the features of **SML/NJ** to implement concurrency libraries (including the basic ideas used in the implementation of **CML**). The compiler technology used in the **SML/NJ** system makes it an excellent basis for the implementation of concurrency primitives. Most importantly, **SML/NJ** provides constant-time *first-class continuations* as an extension. Continuations capture the essence of the process abstraction. Because they are first class in **SML/NJ**, it is possible to implement process scheduling mechanisms directly in **SML** without any special run-time support.

10.1 First-class continuations

Continuations are a semantic concept that captures the meaning of the "rest of the program." They have a wide and varied rôle in programming language design, implementation, and semantics. Our main interest here, however, is the provision of first-class continuations in programming languages. At any given point in the execution of a program, there is a notion of "what to do next." For example, consider the expression " (x+y) +z," at the point that x and y are added, the next thing to do is to take the result of "x+y" and add z to it. In a higher-order language such as **SML**, we can explicitly represent the notion of "what to do next" by using functions

$$\text{(fn k => k(x+y)) (fn v => v+z)}$$

Here, the variable k is bound to a function that represents the next thing to do following the addition of x and y; this function is an example of a *continuation*. We could further transform this program to represent the continuation of the whole expression explicitly:

$$\text{fn k' => (fn k => k(x+y)) (fn v => k'(v+z))}$$

where this is applied to a continuation representing the next thing to do after computing the sum. The result of this transformation is called *continuation-passing style* (CPS), since the continuation of a function call is explicitly passed as an argument to the call. The CPS representation has the property that all functions end in a call, and that all calls are tail calls. Because of these properties of CPS, the program's control flow is represented explicitly. This means that it is easy to capture the current thread of computation (it is just the continuation value that represents the rest of the program), which provides sufficient support for process abstraction. CPS is an awkward programming style, however, so using it as the notational base of a concurrent language is unreasonable. Fortunately, some languages provide a mechanism for programs to capture the current continuation explicitly when necessary. In the case where the compiler uses CPS as an internal representation, capturing these continuations can be extremely cheap.

The **SML/NJ** system uses CPS as its internal representation in its optimization phases. As a result, it can provide language-level access to first-class continuations. Continuations are represented as an abstract type with two operations:

```
type 'a cont
val callcc : '(a cont -> 'a) -> 'a
val throw  : 'a cont -> 'a -> 'b
```

The function `callcc` (*call with current continuation*) calls a function with the current continuation (which is the function's return continuation) as an argument. The function `throw` is used to transfer control to a continuation; notice that the application `throw` does not return, and thus its return type is polymorphic. These operations are defined in the `SMLofNJ` structure, but we assume that they have been rebound at top-level in this chapter, so as to reduce clutter.

First-class continuations can be used to implement loops, back-tracking, exceptions, and various concurrency mechanisms. For example, the following is a continuation-based version of a function that computes the product of a list of integers:

```
fun product l = callcc (
      fn exit => let
        fun loop ([], n) = n
          | loop (0::_, _) = throw exit 0
          | loop (i::r, n) = loop (r, i*n)
      in
        loop (l, 1)
      end)
```

This function uses the continuation `exit` to short-circuit the evaluation if any element in the argument list is 0.

A more complicated example is a function that prepends a function onto a continuation:

```
val prepend : ('a -> 'b) -> 'b cont -> 'a cont
```

```
signature COROUTINES =
  sig
    val yield : unit -> unit
    val fork : (unit -> unit) -> unit
    val exit : unit -> 'a
  end (* COROUTINES *)
```

Listing 10.1: Coroutine operations

When applied to a function and a continuation, it returns a new continuation that will evaluate the function and throw the result to the continuation. The implementation is somewhat tricky:

```
fun prepend f k = callcc (
    fn k1 => throw k (f (callcc (fn k2 => throw k1 k2))))
```

The continuation bound to k2 will pass its argument to f; we use the the continuation bound to k1 to pass k2 out as the result of prepend. One important point about this example is what happens if f raises an exception. A continuation in **SML/NJ** includes the exception handler context of the point at which it was bound. Thus, if evaluation of f raises an exception, control will be passed to the handler that was in effect when prepend was defined.

10.2 Coroutines

To begin our examination of implementing concurrency in **SML/NJ**, we consider the problem of introducing multiple threads of control.

The simplest example is the implementation of a *coroutine* package that supports creation of threads with explicit context switching. There are three operations: yield relinquishes the processor allowing another thread to run, fork creates a new thread, and exit terminates the current thread. Listing 10.1 gives the signature of this interface.

The implementation of multiple threads of control is quite straightforward, and is based on the observation that a suspended thread of control can be represented directly as a continuation. Listing 10.2 gives the implementation of the coroutine interface. The main data structure is a queue of threads that are ready to run, called the *ready queue*, which is represented by the top-level variable rdyQ. We use the Queue structure from the **SML/NJ** Library to implement this queue. A thread is represented as a unit continuation. The dispatch function is a utility function that removes the next thread in the queue, which is a continuation, and resumes executing the thread by throwing the unit value to it. If the ready queue is empty, which is symptomatic of deadlock, then the dispatch operation will fail (the dequeue function raises an exception).

```
structure Coroutines : COROUTINES =
  struct

    structure Q = Queue

    val rdyQ : unit cont Q.queue = Q.mkQueue ()

    fun dispatch () = throw (Q.dequeue rdyQ) ()

    fun yield () = callcc (fn k => (
          Q.enqueue (rdyQ, k);
          dispatch ()))

    fun exit () = dispatch ()

    fun fork f = callcc (fn parentK => (
          Q.enqueue (rdyQ, parentK);
          (f ()) handle _ => ();
          exit ()))

  end; (* Coroutines *)
```

Listing 10.2: The implementation of coroutines

The `yield` operation saves the current thread's state and then dispatches another thread. Grabbing the current thread's state is just a matter of capturing its current continuation (*i.e.*, `callcc`). The current continuation k is added to the ready queue, and then the next thread is dispatched. The `exit` operation is similar to `yield`, except that the current thread's continuation is not saved, which means that the thread is terminated.

In the implementation of `fork`, we grab the parent's continuation and put it into the ready queue, and start executing the newly created child thread immediately. In effect, the parent's thread of control *becomes* the child, and the newly created thread of control becomes the parent. We must ensure that when the child thread terminates, it does not return from the `fork` call, so after executing the child's body (the function f), we call `exit`. Note also, that the evaluation of the thread's body is wrapped in an exception handler.

This implementation of `fork` defines a scheduling policy that favors the child over the parent (*i.e.*, the parent is suspended, while the child is dispatched immediately). In some cases, it might be preferable to insert the newly created child into the ready queue, and continue executing the parent. This scheduling policy requires a bit of trickery to implement, as shown in Listing 10.3. We need to create a continuation that will execute the body of the new thread (*i.e.*, the application of the function f), and store the continuation in the ready queue. We do this by using an outer `callcc` to avoid having to execute

```
fun fork f = let
      val newThread = callcc (fn k1 => (
            callcc (fn k2 => (throw k1 k2));
            (f ()) handle _ => ();
            exit ())))
      in
        Q.enqueue (rdyQ, newThread)
      end
```

Listing 10.3: An alternative implementation of `fork`

the continuation of the inner `callcc`. In Listing 10.3, the continuation bound to `k2` is
bound to the initial representation of the new thread, and the continuation bound to `k1` is
used to escape the inner `callcc` without returning, that is, without executing the calls
to `f` and `exit`. Throwing the `k2` continuation to `k1` results in `k2` being bound to the
variable `newThread`. The `fork` operation then enqueues `newThread` in the ready
queue.

An implementation of threads by itself is not very interesting; we need mechanisms
for the threads to communicate and synchronize. In the remainder of this chapter, we
look at extending this implementation with various different synchronization and communication mechanisms.

10.3 Shared-memory concurrency

In this section, we extend the coroutine implementation with simple shared-memory
synchronization primitives. Listing 10.4 gives the signature of our coroutine package
extended with mutex locks and condition variables (see Section 2.4.2). The functions
`mutex` and `condition` create new locks and condition variables, respectively. Note
that condition variables are created with respect to a specific lock. The operation `withLock`
is used to protect the execution of a critical region; the critical region is encapsulated as
a function. When in a critical region, a thread may use the `wait` operation for condition synchronization. The `wait` operation automatically releases the associated mutex
lock and then blocks the thread on the condition. The `signal` operation releases one of
the threads waiting on a condition, while the `broadcast` operation releases all threads
waiting on a condition. When a waiting thread is signaled, it must first reacquire the
mutex lock before it can proceed; if the mutex lock is held by some other thread, then the
signaled thread must wait until the mutex is available.

```
signature MUTEX =
  sig
    val yield : unit -> unit
    val fork : (unit -> unit) -> unit
    val exit : unit -> 'a

    type mutex
    type condition

    val mutex : unit -> mutex
    val condition : mutex -> condition
    val withLock : mutex -> ('a -> 'b) -> 'a -> 'b
    val signal : condition -> unit
    val broadcast : condition -> unit
    val wait : condition -> unit (* implicit mutex lock *)
  end; (* MUTEX *)
```

Listing 10.4: Shared-memory synchronization primitives

10.3.1 Implementing mutex locks

First we examine the implementation of mutex locks, which is given in Listing 10.5. A mutex lock consists of a boolean flag, which is `true` when the lock is held by some thread, and a queue of threads that are waiting for the lock. Initially, the lock is unheld and the queue is empty. We use two low-level operations, `acquire` and `release`, to handle locks. The `acquire` operation checks to see if the mutex is locked; if it is, then the current thread is added to the blocked thread queue, and a new thread is dispatched. Otherwise, the `acquire` function acquires the lock for the calling thread by setting the flag to `true`. The `release` function is used to unlock the mutex, but there is some subtlety in how this is accomplished. It first checks to see if there are any waiting threads; if not, then `release` sets the `lock` flag to `false`. But if there are blocked threads, `release` puts the current thread on the ready queue and dispatches the next waiting thread without changing the `lock` flag. In effect, this passes control of the lock from the releasing thread to the first thread blocked waiting to acquire the lock, which is why the `acquire` function does not have to set the flag when it resumes.

Using these basic operations, the implementation of `withLock` is straightforward; the only subtlety is in handling the case in which the critical region raises an exception. This situation is handled by catching the exception, releasing the lock, and then reraising the exception.

```
structure Mutex : MUTEX =
  struct

    structure Q = Queue

    ...

    datatype mutex = M of {
        locked  : bool ref,
        blocked : unit cont Q.queue
      }

    fun mutex () = M{locked = ref false, blocked = Q.mkQueue()}

    fun acquire (mu as M{locked, blocked}) =
        if (! locked)
          then callcc (fn k => (
            Q.enqueue (blocked, k);
            dispatch()))
          else locked := true

    fun release (M{locked, blocked}) =
        if (Q.isEmpty blocked)
          then locked := false
          else callcc (fn k => (
            Q.enqueue (rdyQ, k);
            throw (Q.dequeue blocked) ()))

    fun withLock mu f x = (
        acquire mu;
          ((f x) handle ex => (release mu; raise ex))
        before release mu)

    ...

  end (* Mutex *)
```

Listing 10.5: The implementation of mutex locks

10.3.2 Implementing conditions

The Mutex structure is completed by the implementation of conditions, which is given in Listing 10.6. A condition is represented as a record consisting of the associated mutex lock and a queue of waiting threads. The wait operation releases the associated mutex and suspends the thread until it is signaled, at which point the thread reacquires the lock. This is accomplished by capturing a continuation (bound to k) that will reacquire the lock and adding it to the queue of treads blocked on the condition. The wait function then releases the lock and dispatches another thread. Note that the code for releasing the lock is a specialized version of the release function implementation from Listing 10.5.

```
structure Mutex : MUTEX =
  struct

    structure Q = Queue

    . . .

    datatype condition = COND of {
        lock    : mutex,
        waiting : unit cont Q.queue
      }

    fun condition mu = COND{lock = mu, waiting = Q.mkQueue()}

    fun wait (COND{lock as M{locked, blocked}, waiting}) = (
        callcc (fn k => (
          Q.enqueue (waiting, k);
          if (Q.isEmpty blocked)
            then (locked := false; dispatch())
            else throw (Q.dequeue blocked) ()));
        acquire lock)

    fun signal (COND{waiting, ...}) =
        if (Q.isEmpty waiting)
          then ()
          else (Q.enqueue (rdyQ, Q.dequeue waiting))

    fun broadcast (COND{waiting, ...}) = let
        fun clearQ () = if (Q.isEmpty waiting)
              then ()
              else (
                Q.enqueue (rdyQ, Q.dequeue waiting);
                clearQ())
      in
        clearQ ()
      end

  end (* Mutex *)
```

Listing 10.6: The implementation of conditions

A waiting thread is signaled by removing it from the waiting queue and adding it to the ready queue. In the case of `signal`, this is done once (assuming the queue is not empty), while in the case of `broadcast`, this is done until all the waiting threads have been signaled.

The semantics of conditions requires that a thread holds the associated mutex lock before waiting on a condition. This implementation does not check that this requirement

```
signature CRXW =
  sig
    type crxw_lock

    val crxwLock    : unit -> crxw_lock
    val readAccess  : crxw_lock -> (unit -> 'a) -> 'a
    val writeAccess : crxw_lock -> (unit -> 'a) -> 'a
  end
```

Listing 10.7: Concurrent-read, exclusive-write locks

is met in the implementation of `wait`; to do so would require introducing some form of thread identity.

10.3.3 Concurrent-read, Exclusive-write locks

Given the implementation of simple mutex locks and condition variables, one can implement higher-level mechanisms, such as the producer/consumer buffer in Section 2.4.2. In this section, we illustrate this with the implementation of a more sophisticated locking mechanism using the simple mutex locks and condition variables.

Often, a shared data object can support access by multiple, concurrent readers, but require that write access be exclusive. We can use a *concurrent-read, exclusive-write* (CRXW) lock to provide concurrency control for such objects. Listing 10.7 gives the signature of this mechanism. The function `crxwLock` creates a new CRXW lock. The two functions `readAccess` and `writeAccess` are similar to the `withLock` operation: `readAccess` is used by readers, and allows concurrent access, while `writeAccess` is used by writers, and ensures exclusive access.

Listing 10.8 gives the implementation of the CRXW locks. A CRXW lock has three basic states: `IDLE`, when the no threads are accessing the shared object; `READ`, when one, or more, threads has read access to the object; and `WRITE`, when exactly one thread has write access to the object. The representation of a CRXW lock consists of its state, a mutex lock to protect access to its state, and a condition variable for signaling when the state becomes idle. Creating a new CRXW lock (`crxwLock`) requires creating a mutex lock and associated condition variable, and initializing the state.

The access functions have a common structure: wait until access is legal; then execute the operation; and finally reset the state. The `readAccess` and `writeAccess` functions are defined in terms of the higher-order `access` function, which takes the mutex lock and functions to wait for access and finish access as arguments.

The `readAccess` wait function loops until there are no writers (*i.e.*, the state is either

```
structure CRXW : CRXW =
  struct

    datatype lock_state = IDLE | WRITE | READ of int

    datatype crxw_lock = LOCK of {
        state : lock_state ref,
        lock  : Mutex.mutex,
        cond  : Mutex.condition
      }

    fun crxwLock () = let val mu = Mutex.mutex()
        in
          LOCK{
              state = ref IDLE,
              lock  = mu,
              cond  = Mutex.condition mu
            }
        end

    fun access (lock, wait, finish) f = (
        Mutex.withLock lock wait;
          f () before
        Mutex.withLock lock finish)

    fun readAccess (LOCK{state, lock, cond}) = let
        fun wait () = (case (! state)
              of WRITE => (Mutex.wait cond; wait())
               | IDLE => state := READ 1
               | (READ n) => state := READ(n+1)
             (* end case *))
        fun finish () = (case (! state)
              of (READ 1) => (state := IDLE; Mutex.signal cond)
               | (READ n) => state := READ(n-1)
             (* end case *))
        in
          access (lock, wait, finish)
        end

    fun writeAccess (LOCK{state, lock, cond}) = let
        fun wait () = (case (! state)
              of IDLE => state := WRITE
               | _ => (Mutex.wait cond; wait())
             (* end case *))
        fun finish () = (state := IDLE; Mutex.broadcast cond)
        in
          access (lock, wait, finish)
        end

  end;
```

Listing 10.8: Concurrent-read, exclusive-write lock implementation

```
signature CHAN =
  sig
    val yield : unit -> unit
    val fork : (unit -> unit) -> unit
    val exit : unit -> 'a

    type 'a chan
    val channel : unit -> 'a chan
    val send : ('a chan * 'a) -> unit
    val recv : 'a chan -> 'a
  end; (* CHAN *)
```

Listing 10.9: Simple message-passing operations

idle or reading). When a reader finishes access, it decrements the number of readers; if the number falls to zero, then the state becomes IDLE, and the condition is signaled. Note that at this point, only writers can be waiting for the lock, since concurrent readers are allowed. This is why the condition is signaled, instead of being broadcast.

The writeAccess wait function must wait until the state is idle, since exclusive access is required. When the writer finishes access, the state is reset to IDLE, and the condition is broadcast. We use broadcast here, since there may be multiple readers waiting for access.

10.4 Simple message passing

Using the shared-memory primitives of the previous section, one can implement higher-level concurrency mechanisms, such as message-passing primitives. It is more efficient, however, to implement them directly, in much the same way that we implemented mutex locks and conditions. Listing 10.9 gives the interface of a simple set of message-passing operations on typed channels.

The message-passing interface does not specify whether the send operation is blocking or non-bocking, so we present implementations for both versions. Both implementations represent channels as a pair of queues: one for pending sends and one for pending receives.

10.4.1 Asynchronous message passing

We start with the asynchronous implementation of channels, which is given in Listing 10.10. As noted above, a channel is represented by two queues; the channel function creates a channel by allocating two new queues. The sendQ queue contains

```
structure AsyncChan : CHAN =
struct

    structure Q = Queue

    . . .

    datatype 'a chan = CH of {
        sendQ : 'a Q.queue,
        recvQ : 'a cont Q.queue
      }

    fun channel () = CH{
            sendQ = Q.mkQueue (),
            recvQ = Q.mkQueue ()
          }

    fun send (CH{sendQ, recvQ}, msg) =
            if (Q.isEmpty recvQ)
            then Q.enqueue(sendQ, msg)
            else callcc (fn k => (
              Q.enqueue(rdyQ, k);
              throw (Q.dequeue recvQ) msg))

    fun recv (CH{sendQ, recvQ}) =
            if (Q.isEmpty sendQ)
            then callcc (fn k => (
              Q.enqueue(recvQ, k); dispatch()))
            else Q.dequeue sendQ

end; (* AsyncChan *)
```

Listing 10.10: An implementation of asynchronous message passing

messages that have been sent, but not received. The recvQ queue contains the continuations of threads waiting for messages. The channel representation has the invariant that
at most one of the queues is non-empty.

The implementation of the asynchronous send operation first checks to see if recvQ
is empty; if this is the case, then the message is added to sendQ and the sender continues
its execution. If recvQ is non-empty, then the send function throws the message to the
next continuation in recvQ. But before doing this, it grabs the sender's continuation
and puts it into the queue of ready threads. It would be possible to implement a different
scheduling policy, where the receiver is added to the ready queue and the sender continues
execution (*i.e.*, giving higher priority to the sender), but it would require some callcc
gymnastics.

The recv operation first checks to see if the sendQ holds any pending messages.

When the sendQ is empty, it uses `callcc` to capture the receiving thread's continuation, which it adds to the `recvQ` and then it dispatches another thread. In the case that there is already a message waiting for the receiver, `recv` just dequeues the message and returns it.

There is a problem with this implementation in that if a thread rapidly executes a loop containing a `send` operation, the `sendQ` can grow without bound. To avoid this, we can rewrite the `send` operation to force a context switch whenever it is executed:

```
fun send (CH{sendQ, recvQ}, msg) = callcc (fn k => (
        if (Q.isEmpty recvQ)
          then (
            Q.enqueue(rdyQ, k);
            Q.enqueue(sendQ, msg);
            dispatch())
          else (
            Q.enqueue(rdyQ, k);
            throw (Q.dequeue recvQ) msg)))
```

Note that the converse situation is not a problem, since the `recv` operation is blocking.

10.4.2 Synchronous message passing

The simple channel interface can also be implemented with a blocking `send` operation. The synchronous version requires a modification of the representation of channels, since the `sendQ` now must contain both the message being sent, as well as the continuation of the blocked sending thread. It also requires minor modifications to the message-passing operations. The implementation is given in Listing 10.11; we have omitted the `channel` function, since it is identical to the asynchronous case.

The synchronous `send` operation differs from the second asynchronous version only in the case where the channel's `recvQ` is empty. In this situation, it enqueues the pair of the message and the sender's continuation in the `sendQ`. The only difference in the `recv` operation is when the channel's `sendQ` is non-empty. In this case, both the message and sender's continuation are dequeued, and the sender is added to the queue of ready threads.

10.4.3 Supporting simple selective communication

It is fairly easy to extend either of the message passing implementations described above with support for a restricted form of selective communication. We extend the CHAN interface, given in Listing 10.9, with the operation

```
val select : ('a chan * ('a -> 'b)) list -> 'b
```

```
    structure SyncChan : CHAN =
  struct

    structure Q = Queue

    ...

    datatype 'a chan = CH of {
        sendQ : ('a * unit cont) Q.queue,
        recvQ : 'a cont Q.queue
      }

    fun channel () = ...

    fun send (CH{sendQ, recvQ}, msg) = callcc (fn k => (
        if (Q.isEmpty recvQ)
          then (Q.enqueue(sendQ, (msg, k)); dispatch())
          else (
            Q.enqueue(rdyQ, k);
            throw (Q.dequeue recvQ) msg)))

    fun recv (CH{sendQ, recvQ}) =
        if (Q.isEmpty sendQ)
          then callcc (fn k => (
          Q.enqueue(recvQ, k); dispatch()))
          else let val (msg, senderK) = Q.dequeue sendQ
          in
            Q.enqueue(rdyQ, senderK);
            msg
          end

  end; (* SyncChan *)
```

Listing 10.11: An implementation of synchronous message passing

which is an input-only, first-order, selective communication operation. This operation takes a list of input clauses; each of which consists of an input channel and an associated action. The `select` operation blocks the calling thread until there is input on one of the channels, at which time it invokes the associated action. Note that all the channels (and actions) must have the same type.

As mentioned above, this operation fits into both the asynchronous and synchronous models; for purposes of this section, we implement the asynchronous version. The implementation of the synchronous version is similar.

The main difficulty in implementing this simple form of `select` is bookkeeping. When a thread attempts to read from several empty channels, its continuation will be enqueued in each channel's `recvQ`, but only one of these continuations is actually used.

Therefore, we need a mechanism to remove the unused continuations, once one of the clauses has been selected. To manage this bookkeeping, we associate a *unique ID* with each blocked input operation.[1] The unique IDs are represented as reference cells (recall that two reference cells are equal only if they are the same cell). Since the contents of the cell are unimportant, we use unit references. This requires modifying the type of the recvQ in the representation of channels:

```
datatype 'a chan = CH of {
    sendQ : 'a Q.queue,
    recvQ : (unit ref * (unit ref * 'a) cont) Q.queue
}
```

We add a unique ID to each element of recvQ, and add an ID as an argument to the continuations of threads waiting for input. In the case of the basic message-passing operations, the unique ID is mostly ignored. When resuming a blocked thread from the recvQ, the send operation passes both the message and the unique ID to the receiver, while the recv operation allocates a dummy ID, which it ignores. Listing 10.12 gives the code for these as operations.

The select operation is structured into three phases: first it *polls* for available input; if all of the channels are empty, then it *waits* for input; and when resumed, it *removes* the unused input continuations. Listing 10.13 gives the code for this.

The polling phase is implemented as a linear search over the list of channels. The first non-empty channel is selected, and the associated action is applied to the enqueued message. Such an implementation is quite unfair, which could result in problems for the user. It could be improved by randomizing the search, or by associating an "age" with outstanding messages and selecting the oldest available (we discuss this further in Section 10.5.6).

If the polling phase fails to find a non-empty channel, then the thread must wait for a message. First a list of unique IDs is generated, one for each clause in the select. Then callcc is used to capture the thread's continuation; this continuation, along with the corresponding ID, is added to each channel's recvQ. The enqueueing of continuations is done by the wait function, which dispatches another thread when it is done. The blocked thread is resumed by some other thread sending a message on one of the channels. When this is done, the unique tag is also passed to the blocked thread's resumption continuation. The tag of the selected input operation is used when deleting the now defunct pending I/O operations from the channel recvQs. In addition, the action associated with the selected channel is extracted and returned by the remove function. Finally, the returned action is applied to the message which computes the result of the select operation.

---

[1] As shown in the next section, there are other techniques for managing this bookkeeping.

```
structure AsyncSelectChan : CHAN =
  struct

    structure Q = Queue

    . . .

    fun send (CH{sendQ, recvQ}, msg) = callcc (fn k => (
            if (Q.isEmpty recvQ)
              then (
                Q.enqueue(rdyQ, k);
                Q.enqueue(sendQ, msg);
                dispatch())
              else let
                val (id, recvK) = Q.dequeue recvQ
                in
                  Q.enqueue(rdyQ, k);
                  throw recvK (id, msg)
                end))
    fun recv (CH{sendQ, recvQ}) =
            if (Q.isEmpty sendQ)
              then let
                val (_, msg) = callcc (fn k => (
                        Q.enqueue(recvQ, (ref(), k));
                        dispatch()))
                in
                  msg
                end
              else Q.dequeue sendQ

    . . .

  end; (* AsyncSelectChan *)
```

Listing 10.12: Channel I/O operations with simple selective communication

10.5   First-class synchronous operations

In the previous section, we examined one approach to implementing simple selective communication. While this approach could be extended to handle generalized selective communication, it suffers from the serious limitation that all of the channels must have the same type. First-class synchronous operations, on the other hand, provide a much more general mechanism. In this section, we extend the simple synchronous message-passing operations with event values and event combinators; Listing 10.14 gives the interface of this extension.

The implementation of first-class synchronous operations is fairly complex, so before diving into the details, it is useful to first consider a very simple subset of events without

```
structure AsyncSelectChan : CHAN =
  struct

    structure Q = Queue

    ...

    fun select choices = let
        fun pollCh (CH{sendQ, ...}, _) = not(Q.isEmpty sendQ)
        fun wait ids k = let
            fun blk (id, (CH{recvQ, ...}, _)) =
                Q.enqueue (recvQ, (id, k))
          in
            ListPair.app blk (ids, choices);
            dispatch()
          end
        fun remove (id, ids) = let
            fun del (id'::r1, (CH{recvQ, ...}, act)::r2) =
                if (id = id')
                  then (del (r1, r2); act)
                  else (
                    Q.delete (recvQ,
                      fn (id'', _) => (id' = id''));
                    del (r1, r2))
          in
            del (ids, choices)
          end
      in
        case (List.find pollCh choices)
          of (SOME(CH{sendQ, ...}, act)) =>
               act(Q.dequeue sendQ)
           | NONE => let
               val ids = List.map (fn _ => ref()) choices
               val (id, msg) = callcc (wait ids)
             in
               remove (id, ids) msg
             end
        (* end case *)
      end

  end; (* AsyncSelectChan *)
```

Listing 10.13: Implementing simple selective communication

```
signature EVENTS =
  sig
    val yield : unit -> unit
    val fork : (unit -> unit) -> unit
    val exit : unit -> 'a

    type 'a chan
    type 'a event

    val channel : unit -> 'a chan
    val sendEvt : ('a chan * 'a) -> unit event
    val recvEvt : 'a chan -> 'a event
    val wrap : ('a event * ('a -> 'b)) -> 'b event
    val choose : 'a event list -> 'a event
    val sync : 'a event -> 'a
  end; (* EVENTS *)
```

Listing 10.14: Simple event operations

choice. In particular, consider the asynchronous `recv` operation from Listing 10.10. For pedagogical purposes, we rewrite it as follows:

```
fun recv (CH{sendQ, recvQ}) = let
      fun body k = if (Q.isEmpty sendQ)
            then (Q.enqueue(recvQ, k); dispatch())
            else Q.dequeue sendQ
    in
      callcc body
    end
```

Notice that the resumption continuation of the calling process, denoted by the variable k, is a free variable in the body of the operation. This observation, which holds for all synchronous operations, is the key to the implementation of first-class synchronous operations. In this simple setting, it means that an event value can be represented as a function that abstracts over the resumption continuation

```
type 'a event = ('a cont -> 'a)
```

Using this representation, the event-valued version of `recv` is

```
fun recvEvt (CH{sendQ, recvQ}) = let
      fun body k = if (Q.isEmpty sendQ)
            then (Q.enqueue(recvQ, k); dispatch())
            else Q.dequeue sendQ
    in
      body
    end
```

It follows that `sync` is implemented directly by `callcc`. The implementation of `wrap` must feed the value produced by synchronizing on its first argument to its second argument, which can be done as follows:

```
fun wrap (evt, f) = fn k => (throw k (f (callcc evt)))
```

The continuation that applies f to its argument is passed to the event value being wrapped; the result of evaluating f is then thrown to the continuation that is the argument to the event value constructed by `wrap`. Note that this is just a convoluted form of function composition.

10.5.1   Representing event values

Unfortunately, this simple representation of events is unable to support selective communication. As we observed in Section 10.4.3, implementing choice requires a multi-phase operation. For the richer collection of operations given in Listing 10.14, the act of synchronizing on an event value has four distinct phases:

Polling. The first step is to poll the base events to see if any of them are satisfiable immediately.

Selection. If one or more of the base events is satisfiable immediately, then one of these is selected and executed.

Logging. If there are no immediately satisfiable base events, then the synchronizing thread must be added to the waiting queues of the base events.

Unlogging. Once one of the base events is satisfied, the thread must be removed from the other base events' waiting queues, and the chosen event's wrappers must be applied.

This organization is slightly different from that in Section 10.4.3, because the implementation of choice is distributed over several different event operations.

The representation of base-event values reflects the phases of a selective communication. A base-event value is represented as a triple of functions: the `pollFn` tests an event to see if it is enabled, the `doFn` is used to execute an enabled event immediately, and the `blockFn` is used to log an event value. To support choice, we represent an event as a list, with one item per base event. Listing 10.15 gives the datatype declarations for this representation of event values. The `bool ref` argument to the `blockFn` is used to support unlogging in a lazy fashion, and is discussed below.

```
datatype 'a base_evt = BEVT of {
    pollFn  : unit -> bool,
    doFn    : unit -> 'a,
    blockFn : (bool ref * 'a cont) -> unit
  }

and 'a event = EVT of 'a base_evt list
```

Listing 10.15: The representation of event values

10.5.2   The `sync` operator

The `sync` operator's rôle is to manage the synchronization; the heavy lifting is done
by the three functions that comprise the base-event values. The code for `sync` is given
in Listing 10.16. The basic structure is not much different from the simple selective
communication operation in Section 10.4.3. First, the list of base events is polled until
an enabled event is found, or all of the events have been polled. If there is an enabled
event, then its `doFn` is invoked and the `sync` operation is done. Otherwise, each event is
logged by calling its `blockFn`, and then some other thread is dispatched. Note that each
successful synchronization involves one thread executing a `blockFn` followed by another thread executing the `doFn` of a matching event (at least for the case of synchronous
message passing).

This implementation of events uses a lazy unlogging scheme. As we saw in Listing 10.16, each instance of a blocking `sync` operation has a unique boolean flag associated with it, which is called its *dirty* flag. When the `sync` operation is completed, the
dirty flag is set to `true` by the `doFn` that completes the synchronization. The `pollFns`

```
fun sync (EVT evts) = let
      fun poll (BEVT{pollFn, ...}) = pollFn()
    in
      case (List.find poll evts)
        of (SOME(BEVT{doFn, ...}))) => doFn()
         | NONE => callcc (fn k => let
            val dirtyFlg = ref false
            fun block (BEVT{blockFn, ...}) = blockFn(dirtyFlg, k)
            in
              app block evts; dispatch()
            end)
      (* end case *)
    end
```

Listing 10.16: The implementation of `sync`

of base events are responsible for removing any dirty entries in the underlying queues. To support this lazy unlogging of events, we again modify the representation of channels:

```
datatype 'a chan = CH of {
    sendQ : (bool ref * ('a * unit cont)) Q.queue,
    recvQ : (bool ref * 'a cont) Q.queue
}
```

We also define a function that discards dirty elements while checking for a non-empty channel queue:

```
fun pollQ q = if (Q.isEmpty q)
    then false
    else (case (Q.head q)
        of (ref true, _) => (Q.dequeue q; pollQ q)
         | (ref false, _) => true
        (* end case *))
```

In effect, this approach uses one ID per synchronization, whereas the simple select implementation of Section 10.4.3 used one ID per communication.

10.5.3 Implementing base-event constructors

The implementation of the base-event constructors `sendEvt` and `recvEvt` is mostly a reorganization of the implementations of `send` and `recv` in Listing 10.11. The test for an empty queue becomes the `pollFn`, the non-empty case becomes the `doFn`, and the empty case becomes the `blockFn`. Listing 10.17 gives the code for these base-event constructors. Note that the `doFn`s set the dirty flag of the dequeued item.

10.5.4 Implementing event combinators

The implementation of the event combinators `wrap` and `choose` must maintain the representation of event values in Listing 10.15. This is, in effect, a rewriting of the event values into a "canonical" representation. To illustrate, consider the example event value from page 55:

```
val ev = choose [
        wrap (bev₁, w₁),
        wrap (choose [
            wrap (bev₂, w₂),
            wrap (bev₃, w₃),
        ], w₄)
    ]
```

This has the tree representation given in Figure 10.1(a). To map this to the canonical representation, shown in Figure 10.1(b), requires composing the wrapper functions and flattening the lists of choices. The implementation does this rewriting incrementally as each event combinator application is evaluated.

```
fun sendEvt (CH{sendQ, recvQ}, msg) = let
      fun pollFn () = pollQ recvQ
      fun doFn () = callcc (fn k => let
          val (flg, recvK) = Q.dequeue recvQ
          in
            flg := true;
            Q.enqueue(rdyQ, k);
            throw recvK msg
          end)
      fun blockFn (flg, k) = Q.enqueue(sendQ, (flg, (msg, k)))
      in
        EVT[BEVT{pollFn = pollFn, doFn = doFn, blockFn = blockFn}]
      end

fun recvEvt (CH{sendQ, recvQ}) = let
      fun pollFn () = pollQ sendQ
      fun doFn () = let val (flg, (msg, senderK)) = Q.dequeue sendQ
          in
            flg := true;
            Q.enqueue(rdyQ, senderK);
            msg
          end
      fun blockFn (flg, k) = Q.enqueue(recvQ, (flg, k))
      in
        EVT[BEVT{pollFn = pollFn, doFn = doFn, blockFn = blockFn}]
      end
```

Listing 10.17: The implementation of `sendEvt` and `recvEvt`

The implementation of the event combinators is given in Listing 10.18. The `wrap` operation must compose its second argument with each of the wrappers of its first argument's base events. In the canonical representation, a base event's wrapper is folded into both the `doFn` and `blockFn` functions. For the `doFn`, the composition of wrappers is implemented directly using function composition, but in the case of the `blockFn`, we need a tricky use of `callcc` to implement function composition. The implementation of `choose` is a straightforward flattening of lists of lists, with the proper wrapping and unwrapping of the EVT constructor to get the types right.

10.5.5   Preserving tail recursion

One important, but subtle, aspect of the implementation of `sync` is the preservation of tail recursion. We have seen many examples of the form

```
fun loop state = sync (choose [
        wrap (recvEvt ch1, fn x => loop (f (state, x))),
        wrap (recvEvt ch2, fn x => loop (h (state, x)))
      ])
```

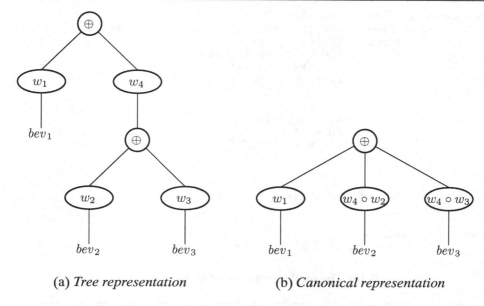

(a) *Tree representation*   (b) *Canonical representation*

Figure 10.1: An example of event-value representations

where a synchronous operation is wrapped with a tail-recursive call. If the implementation of sync (and select) does not preserve the tail recursion, these kinds of loops will cause the program to exhaust the available memory.

Unfortunately, it turns out that the above implementation of sync does not preserve tail recursion, because of the semantics of callcc. In **SML**, the current thread of control is actually comprised of two continuations: the regular continuation, and the *exception handler continuation*. The callcc binds both continuations into a cont value. This means that an application of callcc in a tail-call position is not tail recursive (much the same way that an exception handler wrapped around a tail-recursive call makes it non-tail recursive). Because callcc is not tail-recursive, sync is not tail recursive. The implementation of **CML** avoids this problem by using a special version of callcc that does not save and restore the exception handler continuation.

10.5.6 Fairness

Another implementation issue is ensuring the *fairness* of the synchronization primitives (see Section 2.3). The implementation of sync in Listing 10.16 is not fair. For example, if a thread repeatedly synchronizes on the choice of two events, where the first one is always available, then the second one will never be selected. There are several ways to

```
fun wrap (EVT bevs, f) = let
      fun wrapBEvt (BEVT{pollFn, doFn, blockFn}) = let
          fun blockFn' (flg, k) =
                  throw k (f (callcc (fn k' => (
                    blockFn (flg, k');
                      raise Fail "never get here")))))
          in
            BEVT{
                pollFn = pollFn,
                doFn = (f o doFn),
                blockFn = blockFn'
              }
          end
      in
        EVT(map wrapBEvt bevs)
      end

fun choose evts =
      EVT(foldr (fn (EVT bevs', bevs) => bevs' @ bevs) [] evts)
```

Listing 10.18: The implementation of <code>wrap</code> and <code>choose</code>

avoid this problem. One simple approach is to poll all of the events, and when there is more than one enabled, to select one randomly. This gives a probabilistic guarantee of fairness that should be sufficient in practice. A more complicated scheme is to associate priorities with channels, based on how many times they have been enabled in a choice without being selected. In this scheme, the `pollFn` returns a priority, and the highest priority base event is selected.

10.6   Scheduling issues

In order to prevent a thread that is executing a long (or infinite) computation from monopolizing the processor, **CML** uses preemptive thread scheduling. This is done in a straightforward manner using an interval timer provided by the operating system, and the **SML/NJ** signal mechanism. The interval timer is set to generate an *alarm* signal every n milliseconds (n is typically in the range from 10 to 50). **CML** installs a signal handler that forces a context switch on each alarm.

Preemption introduces some complexity to the implementation, since there can now be interference between threads accessing the same channel data structures, and between the threads and the signal handler when accessing the `readyQ`. We could implement mutex locks to protect these critical regions, but since we are executing on a uniprocessor, a much simpler technique will work.

We define a global flag that is used to mark when execution is in a critical region:

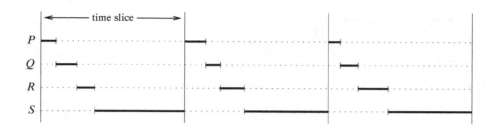

Figure 10.2: Simple round-robin scheduling

```
datatype atomic_state = NonAtomic | Atomic | SignalPending
val atomicState : atomic_state ref
```

and two operations for bracketing critical regions:

```
val atomicBegin : unit -> unit
val atomicEnd   : unit -> unit
```

The function `atomicBegin`, which sets the `atomicState` flag to `Atomic`, is called just prior to entering a critical region, and the function `atomicEnd`, which resets the flag to `NonAtomic`, is called on exit. If a signal occurs while `atomic_state` is `Atomic`, then the signal handler does not force a context switch; instead it sets `atomic_state` to `SignalPending` and returns. The function `atomicEnd` checks the flag before resetting it; if it is `SignalPending`, then a context switch is performed.[2] Note that this mechanism is internal to the implementation of **CML**; users have no access to these operations.

Another scheduling issue is insuring that computationally intensive threads do not monopolize the processor.[3] The basic round-robin scheduling that we use in this chapter does not prevent this. Consider the scenario where we have a single computationally intensive thread and several threads that are communicating frequently (so-called *interactive* threads). Figure 10.2 illustrates what three successive time slices might look like in such a case; here, the threads *P*, *Q*, and *R* are interactive, and the thread *S* is computationally intensive. This figure shows that the interactive threads only get to run once per time-slice; if there were two computationally intensive threads the interactive threads would only get to run once per two slices. For any application that is sensitive to real-time constraints, this scheduling results in unacceptable performance. One obvious way

---

[2]The reader may recognize that there is a potential race when exiting a critical region between the time of the test for a pending signal and the resetting of the flag. The implementation of signals in **SML/NJ**, however, ensures that this race cannot happen.

[3]A *computationally intensive* thread is one that computes with little or no communication.

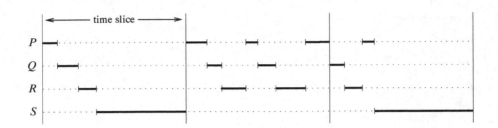

Figure 10.3: Two-level round-robin scheduling

to address this problem is to use finer grain time slices, but many operating systems do not support granularities finer than 10 ms. granularity, which is not fine enough. Furthermore, using finer slices does not scale to large numbers of computationally intensive threads.

The implementation of **CML** uses a two-level scheduling queue; interactive threads are scheduled out of the primary queue, while computationally intensive threads are scheduled out of the secondary queue. A simple hueristic is used to catalogue threads. Each thread has an associated boolean flag, called `doneComm`, which is set to `true` whenever it voluntarily yields the processor during a concurrency operation. The flag is set to `false` whenever the thread is preempted. If a thread is preempted and its `doneComm` flag is `false`, then it is classified as a computationally intensive thread and is placed into the secondary queue. If an interactive thread is preempted, then one thread from the secondary queue is promoted to the primary queue.[4] This has the effect of allowing a computationally intensive thread to run once every other time slice, which means that interactive threads get at least 50% of the processor. Figure 10.3 illustrates this policy for our example.

Notes

Continuations are one of the fundamental ideas in computer science, and appear in many contexts. The idea of first-class continuations dates back to Landin's **J** operator [Lan65, Fel87], although other researchers also discovered the concept independently. A paper by Reynolds provides an interesting history of these multiple discoveries of continuations [Rey93]. Continuation-passing style has been used in lazy languages to program I/O [HS88], including Holmström's concurrent extension of **ML**

---

[4] A thread can also be promoted if there are no threads available in the primary queue.

called **PFL** [Hol83a]. Continuations have also been important in the understanding of the semantics of control [Gor79]. The use of continuation-passing style in the **SML/NJ** compiler is described in Appel's book [App92].

SML/NJ's `callcc` function was inspired by the language **Scheme** [RC86]. Most of the work on using continuations to implement concurrency has been done in the context of **Scheme**. The basic technique dates back to Wand's seminal paper in which he described the implementation of coroutines using **Scheme**'s continuations [Wan80]. This work was refined further by Haynes, Friedman, and Wand [HFW84]. Dybvig and Hieb have shown how to implement "engines," which are an abstraction of time slices, using continuations [DH89]. Most recently, Shivers has explored the connections between threads and continuations in the context of operating system software [Shi97].

It is interesting to note that the representation of wrapped base events as functions is required by the type system. With a richer type system, it would be possible to represent event values as a datatype with constructors for the different combinators, and implement `sync` as an interpreter of the datatype. As noted in the text, our implementation of first-class synchronous operations omitted important implementation details, such as preserving tail recursion, ensuring fairness, preemptive scheduling, and the full set of **CML** event combinators. The event rewriting discussed in Section 10.5.4, was used as an informal specification of the semantics of **PML** [Rep88]. Ferreira, Hennessy, and Jeffrey have proved that this transformation is semantics preserving for the **PML** subset of **CML** [FHJ96].

In addition to **CML**, there have been several other implementations of concurrency features using **SML/NJ**'s first-class continuations. The dirty flag technique described in Section 10.5.2 was invented by Ramsey in his implementation of **PML**-like primitives [Ram90]. The shared-memory primitives of Section 10.3 are a subset of those implemented by Cooper and Morrisett [CM90]. Morrisett and Tolmach implemented a multi-processor version of low-level thread primitives [MT93].

Another approach to implementing concurrency is to provide primitives in the run-time system that support the concurrency operations. **PML** was implemented this way, as was Pike's language **newsqueak** [Pik90], and Cardelli described an implementation model for **Amber** in terms of an abstract machine [Car84].

This chapter describes a uniprocessor implementation of selective communication, which takes advantage of the fact that there is only one active thread of control at any point in time in its implementation of concurrency control. Implementing selective communication on a multiprocessor is significantly more difficult. Various researchers, such as Buckley and Silberschatz [BS83], Bornat [Bor86], and Bagrodia [Bag89], have described such implementations. The basic strategy in these implementations is to first make *tentative* offers of communication; when two tentative offers match, one thread must freeze its state until the other thread either commits or rejects the communication.

The choice of which thread will fix its state is based upon the order of the threads' IDs; this avoids the possibility of cyclic dependencies and deadlock. Generalized selective communication cannot be implemented in a distributed setting because of the possibility of failures and communication delays. If one assumes a reliable network, however, it is possible to design distributed protocols for choice, as was done by Knabe for the implementation of **Facile** [Kna92].

Appendix A
A CML Reference

This appendix provides a reference for the **CML** features used in this book. It is excerpted from *The Concurrent ML Reference Manual*, which is included in the **CML** distribution, and can also be found on the Web at the following URL:

```
http://cml.cs.uchicago.edu/index.html
```

The full manual contains information about additional libraries, as well as instructions on compiling and running **CML** programs. The remainder of this appendix contains descriptions of most of the modules in the **CML** system. In order of their appearance, these are as follows:

structure `CML : CML`
> This module contains the basic types and operations used by **CML**.

structure `SyncVar : SYNC_VAR`
> This module defines *synchronous memory* in the form of I-variables and M-variables and their operations.

structure `Mailbox : MAILBOX`
> This module defines buffered asynchronous channels, which are called mailboxes.

structure `Result : RESULT`
> This module provides a way of communicating both values and exceptions as results.

structure `OS : CML_OS`
> This module is an extension of the `OS` structure defined in the **SML** Basis Library.

signature `CML_TEXT_STREAM_IO`
  This module is an extension of the `TEXT_STREAM_IO` signature defined in the **SML** Basis Library.

structure `TextIO : CML_TEXT_IO`
  This module is an extension of the `TextIO` structure defined in the **SML** Basis Library.

structure `Multicast : MULTICAST`
  This module defines asynchronous multicast channels.

structure `SimpleRPC : SIMPLE_RPC`
  This module provides some help in implementing simple servers.

The first four of these are core **CML** modules, the next three are **CML** specific versions of **SML** Basis Library modules,[1] and the last two are **CML** library modules. Note that while we do not include the documentation for **CML**'s version of the *binary I/O* interfaces here, the extensions are similar to those provided for text I/O.

---

[1] We assume that the reader is familiar with the **SML** Basis Library specification.

The CML structure

The CML structure provides the basic operations for thread creation, synchronous channels, and the event type constructor and combinators.

Synopsis

```
signature CML
structure CML : CML
```

Interface

```
type thread_id
type 'a event
type 'a chan

val version : {system : string, version_id : int list, date : string}
val banner : string

val spawnc : ('a -> unit) -> 'a -> thread_id
val spawn  : (unit -> unit) -> thread_id
val yield : unit -> unit
val exit : unit -> 'a

val wrap        : ('a event * ('a -> 'b)) -> 'b event
val wrapHandler : ('a event * (exn -> 'a)) -> 'a event
val guard       : (unit -> 'a event) -> 'a event
val withNack : (unit event -> 'a event) -> 'a event
val choose : 'a event list -> 'a event
val sync : 'a event -> 'a
val select : 'a event list -> 'a
val never       : 'a event
val alwaysEvt : 'a -> 'a event

val channel : unit -> 'a chan
val sameChannel : ('a chan * 'a chan) -> bool
val send : ('a chan * 'a) -> unit
val recv : 'a chan -> 'a
val sendEvt  : ('a chan * 'a) -> unit event
val recvEvt  : 'a chan -> 'a event
val sendPoll : ('a chan * 'a) -> bool
val recvPoll : 'a chan -> 'a option

val getTid : unit -> thread_id
val sameTid    : (thread_id * thread_id) -> bool
val compareTid : (thread_id * thread_id) -> order
val hashTid    : thread_id -> word
val tidToString : thread_id -> string
val joinEvt : thread_id -> unit event

val timeOutEvt : Time.time -> unit event
val atTimeEvt : Time.time -> unit event
```

Description

type thread_id

> Each thread in a **CML** execution has a unique thread ID. These IDs are in an unspecified total order that can be used to break cyclic dependencies (see compareTid).

type 'a event

> Event values are abstract representations of synchronous operations (so-called *first-class synchronous operations*).

type 'a chan

> This type constructor generates the types for synchronous channels, where the parameter specifies the types of values carried on the channel.

val version : {system : string, version_id : int list, date : string}
val banner : string

> These specify which version of **CML** is implemented by this structure (banner is a string representation of the version value).

val spawnc : ('a -> unit) -> 'a -> thread_id

> spawnc f x spawns a new thread, which evaluates the application of f to x. The thread ID of the new thread is returned.

val spawn : (unit -> unit) -> thread_id

> spawn f is equivalent to the expression spawnc f ().

val yield : unit -> unit

> This function can be used to implement an explicit context switch. Since **CML** is preemptively scheduled, it should never be necessary for user programs to call this function. It is mainly used for performance measurements.

val exit : unit -> 'a

> This function terminates the calling thread.

val wrap : ('a event * ('a -> 'b)) -> 'b event

> wrap (ev, f) wraps the post-synchronization action f around the event value ev.

```
val wrapHandler : ('a event * (exn -> 'a)) -> 'a event
```

wrapHandler (*ev*, *h*) wraps the exception handler function *h* around the event value *ev*. If, during execution of some post-synchronization action in *ev*, an exception is raised, it will be caught and passed to *h*. Nesting of handlers works as would be expected: the innermost handler is the first one invoked. Note that exceptions raised in the pre-synchronization actions in *ev* (*i.e.*, actions defined by guard and withNack) are not handled by *h*.

```
val guard : (unit -> 'a event) -> 'a event
```

guard *g* creates a *delayed* event value from the function *g*. When the resulting event value is synchronized on, the function *g* will be evaluated and the resulting event value will be used in the synchronization. This combinator provides a mechanism for implementing pre-synchronization actions, such as sending a request to a server.

```
val withNack : (unit event -> 'a event) -> 'a event
```

withNack *g* creates a *delayed* event value from the function *g*. As in the case of guard, the function *g* will be evaluated at synchronization time and the resulting event value will be used in the synchronization. Furthermore, when *g* is evaluated, it is passed a *negative acknowledgement* event as an argument. This negative acknowledgement event is enabled in the case where some other event involved in the synchronization is chosen instead of the one produced by *g*. The withNack combinator provides a mechanism for informing servers that a client has aborted a transaction.

```
val choose : 'a event list -> 'a event
```

choose *evs* constructs an event value that represents the non-deterministic choice of the events in the list *evs*.

```
val sync : 'a event -> 'a
```

sync *ev* synchronizes the calling thread on the event *ev*.

```
val select : 'a event list -> 'a
```

select *evs* synchronizes on the non-deterministic choice of the events in the list evs. It is semantically equivalent to the expression sync (choose *evs*) but is more efficient.

```
val never : 'a event
```

This event value is one that is never enabled for synchronization. It is semantically equivalent to the expression choose[].

val alwaysEvt : 'a -> 'a event

alwaysEvt *x* creates an event value that is always enabled, and that returns the value *x* upon synchronization. A thread that synchronizes on a choice of events, which includes an event created by alwaysEvt, is guaranteed not to block, but there is no guarantee that the event created by alwaysEvt will be chosen, since there may be some other enabled event (*i.e.*, there is no priority on enabled events in a choice).

val channel : unit -> 'a chan

This function creates a new synchronous channel.

val sameChannel : ('a chan * 'a chan) -> bool

This function returns true, if its two arguments are the same channel.

val send : ('a chan * 'a) -> unit

send (*ch*, *msg*) sends the message *msg* on the synchronous channel *ch*. This operation blocks the calling thread until there is another thread attempting to receive a message from the channel *ch*, at which point the receiving thread gets the message and both threads continue execution.

val recv : 'a chan -> 'a

recv *ch* receives a message from the channel *ch*. This operation blocks the calling thread until there is another thread attempting to send a message on the channel *ch*, at which point both threads continue execution.

val sendEvt : ('a chan * 'a) -> unit event
val recvEvt : 'a chan -> 'a event

These functions create event values that represent the send and recv operations, respectively.

val sendPoll : ('a chan * 'a) -> bool

sendPoll (*ch*, *msg*) attempts to send the message *msg* on the synchronous channel *ch*. If this operation can complete without blocking the calling thread, then the message is sent and true is returned. Otherwise, no communication is performed and false is returned. This function is not recommended for general use; it is provided as an efficiency aid for certain kinds of protocols.

val recvPoll : 'a chan -> 'a option

> recvPoll *ch* attempts to receive a message from the channel *ch*. If there is no other thread offering to send a message on *ch*, then this returns NONE. Otherwise it returns *SOME* wrapped around the message. This function is not recommended for general use; it is provided as an efficiency aid for certain kinds of protocols.

val getTid : unit -> thread_id

> This function returns the thread ID of the calling thread.

val sameTid : (thread_id * thread_id) -> bool

> This function returns true if its two arguments are the same thread ID, and otherwise returns false.

val compareTid : (thread_id * thread_id) -> order

> This function compares the two thread IDs and returns their order in the total ordering of thread IDs. The precise semantics of this ordering is left unspecified, other than to say it is a total order.

val hashTid : thread_id -> word

> This function returns a word value that can be used as a hash key for the thread ID. Note that it is possible that two different thread IDs will have the same hash value.

val tidToString : thread_id -> string

> This function returns a string representation of the thread ID.

val joinEvt : thread_id -> unit event

> joinEvt *tid* creates an event value for synchronizing on the termination of the thread with the ID *tid*. There are three ways that a thread may terminate: the function that was passed to spawn (or spawnc) may return; it may call the *exit* function; or it may have an uncaught exception. Note that joinEvt does not distinguish between these cases; it also does not become enabled if the named thread deadlocks (even if it is garbage collected).

val timeOutEvt : Time.time -> unit event

> timeOutEvt *t* creates an event value that becomes enabled at the time interval *t* after synchronization. For example, the expression
>
> sync (timeOutEvt (Time.fromSeconds 1))
>
> will delay the calling thread for one second. Note that the specified time interval is actually a minimum waiting time, and the delay may be longer.

val atTimeEvt : Time.time -> unit event

atTimeEvt t   creates an event value that becomes enabled at the specified time t. For example, the expression

```
sync (atTimeEvt (Date.toTime (Date.date {
      year = 2000, month = Date.Jan, day = 0,
      hour = 0, minute = 0, second = 0,
      offset = NONE
   }))))
```

blocks the calling thread until the beginning of the year 2000.

The `SyncVar` structure

The `SyncVar` structure provides **Id**-style synchronous variables (or memory cells). These variables have two states: *empty* and *full*. An attempt to read a value from an empty variable blocks the calling thread until there is a value available. An attempt to put a value into a variable that is full results in the `Put` exception being raised. There are two kinds of synchronous variables: I-variables are write-once, while M-variables are mutable.

Synopsis

```
signature SYNC_VAR
structure SyncVar : SYNC_VAR
```

Interface

```
exception Put

type 'a ivar

val iVar     : unit -> 'a ivar
val iPut     : ('a ivar * 'a) -> unit
val iGet     : 'a ivar -> 'a
val iGetEvt  : 'a ivar -> 'a CML.event
val iGetPoll : 'a ivar -> 'a option
val sameIVar : ('a ivar * 'a ivar) -> bool

type 'a mvar

val mVar      : unit -> 'a mvar
val mVarInit  : 'a -> 'a mvar
val mPut      : ('a mvar * 'a) -> unit
val mTake     : 'a mvar -> 'a
val mTakeEvt  : 'a mvar -> 'a CML.event
val mTakePoll : 'a mvar -> 'a option
val mGet      : 'a mvar -> 'a
val mGetEvt   : 'a mvar -> 'a CML.event
val mGetPoll  : 'a mvar -> 'a option
val mSwap     : ('a mvar * 'a) -> 'a
val mSwapEvt  : ('a mvar * 'a) -> 'a CML.event
val sameMVar  : ('a mvar * 'a mvar) -> bool
```

Description

```
exception Put
```

This exception is raised when an attempt is made to put a value into a variable that is already full (see `iPut` and `mPut`).

```
type 'a ivar
```

This type constructor generates the types for I-variables, where the parameter specifies the types of values stored in the variable I-structured variables are write-once variables that provide synchronization on read operations. They are especially useful for one-shot communications, such as reply messages in client/server protocols, and can also be used to implement shared *incremental* data structures.

val iVar : unit -> 'a ivar

This function creates a new empty I-variable.

val iPut : ('a ivar * 'a) -> unit

iPut (*iv*, *x*)   fills the I-variable *iv* with the value *x*. Any threads that are blocked on *iv* will be resumed. If *iv* already has a value in it, then the Put exception is raised.

val iGet : 'a ivar -> 'a

iGet *iv*   returns the contents of the I-variable *iv*. If the variable is empty, then the calling thread blocks until the variable becomes full.

val iGetEvt : 'a ivar -> 'a CML.event

iGetEvt *iv*   returns an event value that represents the iGet operation on *iv*.

val iGetPoll : 'a ivar -> 'a option

This function is a non-blocking version of iGet. If the corresponding blocking form would block, then it returns NONE; otherwise it returns SOME of the variable's contents.

val sameIVar : ('a ivar * 'a ivar) -> bool

sameIVar (*iv1*, *iv2*)   returns true, if *iv1* and *iv2* are the same I-variable.

type 'a mvar

This type constructor generates the types for M-variables, where the parameter specifies the types of values stored in the variable. Unlike ivar values, M-structured variables may be updated multiple times. Like I-variables, however, they may only be written if they are empty.

val mVar : unit -> 'a mvar

mVar ()   creates a new empty M-variable.

val mVarInit : 'a -> 'a mvar

mVarInit *x*   creates a new M-variable initialized to *x*.

val mPut : ('a mvar * 'a) -> unit

> mPut (*mv*, *x*) fills the M-variable *mv* with the value *x*. Any threads that are blocked on *mv* will be resumed. If *mv* already has a value in it, then the Put exception is raised.

val mTake : 'a mvar -> 'a

> mTake *mv* removes and returns the contents of the M-variable *mv* making it empty. If the variable is already empty, then the calling thread is blocked until a value is available.

val mTakeEvt : 'a mvar -> 'a CML.event

> mTakeEvt *mv* returns an event value that represents the mTake operation on *mv*.

val mGet : 'a mvar -> 'a

> mGet *mv* returns the contents of the M-variable *mv* without emptying the variable; if the variable is empty, then the thread blocks until a value is available. It is equivalent to the atomic execution of the following expression:
>
> > **let val** x = mTake *mv* **in** mPut(*mv*, x); x **end**

val mGetEvt : 'a mvar -> 'a CML.event

> mGetEvt *mv* returns an event value that represents the mGet operation on *mv*.

val mTakePoll : 'a mvar -> 'a option
val mGetPoll : 'a mvar -> 'a option

> These are non-blocking versions of mTake and mGet, respectively. If the corresponding blocking form would block, then they return NONE; otherwise they return SOME of the variable's contents.

val mSwap : ('a mvar * 'a) -> 'a

> mSwap (*mv*, *newV*) puts the value *newV* into the M-variable *mv* and returns the previous contents. If the variable is empty, then the thread blocks until a value is available. It is equivalent to the atomic execution of the following expression:
>
> > **let val** x = mTake *mv* **in** mPut(*mv*, *newV*); x **end**

val mSwapEvt : ('a mvar * 'a) -> 'a CML.event

> mSwapEvt (*mv*, *newV*) returns an event value that represents the mSwap operation on *mv* and *newV*.

val sameMVar : ('a mvar * 'a mvar) -> bool

> sameMVar (*mv1*, *mv2*) returns true, if *mv1* and *mv2* are the same M-variable.

The `Mailbox` structure

The `Mailbox` structure provides support for buffered asynchronous communication, via *mailboxes*. Mailbox buffers are unbounded and preserve the order that messages are sent (e.g., FIFO ordering).

Synopsis

```
signature MAILBOX
structure Mailbox : MAILBOX
```

Interface

```
type 'a mbox

val mailbox    : unit -> 'a mbox
val sameMailbox : ('a mbox * 'a mbox) -> bool
val send       : ('a mbox * 'a) -> unit
val recv       : 'a mbox -> 'a
val recvEvt    : 'a mbox -> 'a CML.event
val recvPoll   : 'a mbox -> 'a option
```

Description

`type` `'a mbox`

This type constructor generates the types for mailboxes, where the parameter specifies the types of values that can be sent to the mailbox. A mailbox is a communication channel with unbounded buffering.

`val` `mailbox : unit -> 'a mbox`

This function creates a new mailbox.

`val` `sameMailbox : ('a mbox * 'a mbox) -> bool`

`sameMailbox` (*mb1*, *mb2*) returns `true`, if *mb1* and *mb2* are the same mailbox.

`val` `send : ('a mbox * 'a) -> unit`

`send` (*mb*, *msg*) sends the message *msg* to the mailbox *mb*. Note that unlike the `CML.send` operation, sending a message on a mailbox will never block the sending thread.

`val` `recv : 'a mbox -> 'a`

`recv` *mb* receives the next message from the mailbox *mb*. If *mb* is empty, then this blocks the calling thread until there is a message available.

val recvEvt : 'a mbox -> 'a CML.event

recvEvt *mb* returns the event value that represents the recv operation on *mb*.

val recvPoll : 'a mbox -> 'a option

This function is the non-blocking version of *recv*. If the corresponding blocking form would block (because the mailbox is empty), then this returns NONE. Otherwise it returns SOME of the received message.

Discussion

Note that mailbox buffers are unbounded, which means that there is no flow control to prevent a producer from greatly outstripping a consumer, and thus exhausting memory. In situations where there is no natural limit to the rate of send operations, it is recommended that the synchronous channels from the CML structure be used instead.

The `Result` structure

The `Result` structure provides support for communicating results. A *result variable* is a write-once memory cell that can contain either a value or an exception.

Synopsis

```
signature RESULT
structure Result : RESULT
```

Interface

```
type 'a result

val result : unit -> 'a result
val put    : ('a result * 'a) -> unit
val putExn : ('a result * exn) -> unit
val get    : 'a result -> 'a
val getEvt : 'a result -> 'a CML.event
```

Description

`type 'a result`

This type constructor generates the types for result variables, where the parameter specifies the types of values stored in the variable A `result` value has essentially the same semantics as an `ivar`, except that it can contain either a value or an exception packet to raise.

`val result : unit -> 'a result`

This function creates a new `result` variable.

`val put : ('a result * 'a) -> unit`

`put (r, v)` puts the value `v` into the result variable `r`. If the result variable `r` already holds a result, then the `SyncVar.Put` exception is raised.

`val putExn : ('a result * exn) -> unit`

`putExn (r, exn)` puts the exception packet `exn` into the result variable `r`. If the result variable `r` already holds a result, then the `SyncVar.Put` exception is raised.

`val get : 'a result -> 'a`

`get r` gets the contents of the result variable `r`. If `r` is empty, then the calling thread blocks until another thread puts a value into `r` (using `put` or `putExn`). If `r` holds an exception packet, then that exception is raised; otherwise the value that `r` holds is returned.

```
val getEvt : 'a result -> 'a CML.event
```

This function constructs an event value that represents the `get` operation.

The `OS` structure

CML extends the `OS` structure, which is part of the **SML** Basis Library, by adding event-value constructors for low-level system events.

Synopsis

```
signature CML_OS
structure OS : CML_OS
```

Interface

```
include OS

structure Process : sig
    include OS_PROCESS
    val systemEvt : string -> status Event.event
  end

structure IO : sig
    include OS_IO
    val pollEvt : poll_desc list -> poll_info list Event.event
  end
```

Description

```
structure Process : sig ... end
```

The `Process` substructure extends the `OS.Process` structure from the **SML** Basis Library by adding an event constructor for the `system` function.

```
val systemEvt : string -> status Event.event
```

> `systemEvt` *cmd* asks the operating system to execute the command *cmd*, and returns an event value that can be used to synchronize on the termination of the command's execution. This function will raise `OS.SysErr`, if the command cannot be executed for some reason.
>
> Note that, although this function is independent of the operating system, the interpretation of the string *cmd* depends very much on the underlying operating system and shell.

```
structure IO : sig ... end
```

The `IO` substructure extends the `OS.IO` structure from the **SML** Basis Library by adding an event constructor for the `poll` function.

```
val pollEvt : poll_desc list -> poll_info list Event.event
```

> `pollEvt` *l* returns an event value that synchronizes on one or more of a collection of I/O devices satisfying the conditions specified by the list of poll descriptors *l*. Successful synchronization will return a non-empty list of `poll_info` values

corresponding to those descriptors in `l` whose conditions are enabled. The returned list respects the order of the argument list, and a value in the returned list will reflect a (nonempty) subset of the conditions specified in the corresponding argument descriptor. The `pollEvt` function will raise `OS.SysErr` if, for example, one of the file descriptors refers to a closed file.

Note that unlike the `poll` function, there is no timeout argument. A non-zero timeout can be provided by putting the polling event in a choice with a timeout event.

Discussion

Note that the interface as given is not a valid **SML** signature, since it redefines the `Process` and `IO` substructures.

The `CML_TEXT_STREAM_IO` signature

The `CML_TEXT_STREAM_IO` signature defines the interface of the *Stream I/O* layer in **CML**'s text I/O stack. It provides input streams, which are treated in the lazy functional style, and output streams, which are treated more conventionally. This signature is an enrichment of the `TEXT_STREAM_IO` signature from the **SML** Basis Library. In addition to the operations provided by the Basis Library, it adds event-value constructors for the various input operations. For more information see the descriptions of the `STREAM_IO` and `TEXT_STREAM_IO` signatures in the **SML** Basis Library documentation.

Synopsis

signature `CML_TEXT_STREAM_IO`

Interface

include `TEXT_STREAM_IO`

```
val input1Evt   : instream -> (elem * instream) option CML.event
val inputNEvt   : (instream * int) -> (string * instream) CML.event
val inputEvt    : instream -> (string * instream) CML.event
val inputAllEvt : instream -> (string * instream) CML.event
val inputLineEvt : instream -> (string * instream) CML.event
```

Description

val `inputEvt : instream -> (string * instream) CML.event`

    `inputEvt` *instrm*   returns an event value that represents the `input` operation on the instream *instrm*. More precisely, the returned event value can be used to synchronize on there either being input available or an end-of-stream being detected. In the former case, the result of synchronization is the available input and the continuation of the stream, while in the latter case the empty string and stream continuation are returned. While `inputEvt` does not raise any exceptions itself, synchronizing on the returned event value will raise the `Io` exception when there is an error in the underlying system calls.

val `input1Evt : instream -> (elem * instream) option CML.event`

    `input1Evt` *instrm*   returns an event value that represents the `input1` operation on the instream *instrm*. Synchronizing on the resulting event will produce a character and the rest of the stream, or else `NONE` when the end of stream is reached. While `input1Evt` does not raise any exceptions itself, synchronizing on the returned event value will raise the `Io` exception when there is an error in the underlying system calls.

val `inputNEvt : (instream * int) -> (string * instream) CML.event`

    `inputNEvt (`*instrm*`, `*n*`)`   returns an event value that represents the `inputN` operation. This function raises the `Size` exception when *n* is either less than zero or larger than the maximum length string. Furthermore, synchronizing on the resulting event value will raise the Io exception when there is an error in the underlying system calls.

val `inputAllEvt : instream -> (string * instream) CML.event`

> `inputAllEvt` *instrm*   returns an event value that represents the `inputAll` operation on the instream *instrm*. While `inputAllEvt` does not raise any exceptions itself, synchronizing on the returned event value will raise the Io exception when there is an error in the underlying system calls, and will raise Size when if the number of elements to be returned is greater than the maximum string length.

val `inputLineEvt : instream -> (string * instream) CML.event`

> `inputLineEvt` *instrm*   returns an event value that represents the `inputLine` operation on the instream *instrm*. While `inputLineEvt` does not raise any exceptions itself, synchronizing on the returned event value will raise the Io exception when there is an error in the underlying system calls, and will raise Size when if the number of elements to be returned is greater than the maximum string length.

Discussion

> One point that may not be obvious from the above descriptions is that these functions construct event values with respect to a specific input stream value. Thus, each time one synchronizes on an input event one gets the same result.

The `TextIO` structure

The `TextIO` structure defines the interface of the *imperative I/O* layer in the text I/O stack. This layer provides buffered I/O using mutable streams, and the ability to rebind imperative-level streams dynamically to different stream-level streams. The **CML** implementation of imperative input streams serializes access to the underlying functional stream. Thus, if a thread is blocked attempting to read from a stream *strm,* any other thread that attempts an operation on *strm* will have to wait until the first thread's operation completes (even if the second thread is attempting a non-blocking operation like `endOfStream`).

Synopsis
```
signature CML_TEXT_IO
structure TextIO : CML_TEXT_IO
```

Interface
```
include TEXT_IO

structure StreamIO : CML_TEXT_STREAM_IO
  where type reader = TextPrimIO.reader
  where type writer = TextPrimIO.writer
  where type pos = TextPrimIO.pos
  where type vector = string
  where type elem = char

val input1Evt   : instream -> elem option CML.event
val inputNEvt   : (instream * int) -> string CML.event
val inputEvt    : instream -> string CML.event
val inputAllEvt : instream -> string CML.event

val openChanIn  : string CML.chan -> instream
val openChanOut : string CML.chan -> outstream
```

Description

```
structure StreamIO : CML_TEXT_STREAM_IO
```

This substructure implements the Stream I/O layer of the text I/O stack. Note that it has the enriched **CML** specific signature.

```
val input1Evt : instream -> elem option CML.event
val inputNEvt : (instream * int) -> string CML.event
val inputEvt : instream -> string CML.event
val inputAllEvt : instream -> string CML.event
```

These operations are event-value constructors for the standard input operations on input streams.

val openChanIn : string CML.chan -> instream

> openChanIn *ch*   returns an input stream that is connected to the output end of the channel *ch*. Strings sent on the channel *ch* can be read by using any of the input operations on the stream. Note that sending a message on *ch* may block the sending thread until some other thread performs an input operation on the stream.

val openChanOut : string CML.chan -> outstream

> openChanOut *ch*   returns an output stream that is connected to the input end of the channel *ch*. Data written to the output stream is buffered, and may be read from the channel.

Discussion

Note that the interface as given is not a valid **SML** signature, since it redefines the StreamIO substructure.

The `Multicast` structure

Multicast channels provide a mechanism for broadcasting a stream of messages to a collection of threads. Threads receive multicast messages via an *output port*; each port receives each message sent since the port was created. Multicast channels are particularly useful for communicating with a dynamically varying group of threads, since the sender does not need to know how many threads are listening.

Synopsis

```
signature MULTICAST
structure Multicast : MULTICAST
```

Interface

```
type 'a mchan
type 'a port
type 'a event = 'a CML.event

val mChannel : unit -> 'a mchan
val port : 'a mchan -> 'a port
val copy : 'a port -> 'a port
val recv : 'a port -> 'a
val recvEvt : 'a port -> 'a event
val multicast : ('a mchan * 'a) -> unit
```

Description

```
type 'a mchan
```

The type constructor for multicast channels.

```
type 'a port
```

The type constructor for output ports on multicast channels.

```
val mChannel : unit -> 'a mchan
```

This function creates a new multicast channel.

```
val port : 'a mchan -> 'a port
```

port *mc*   creates a new output port on the multicast channel *mc*.

```
val copy : 'a port -> 'a port
```

copy *p*   creates a new output port that has the same state as the port *p*; *i.e.*, the stream of messages seen on the two ports will be identical. This function is useful when two threads need to see exactly the same stream of messages.

val recv : 'a port -> 'a

> recv *p*   receives the next message from the port *p*. The calling thread is blocked until there is a message available.

val recvEvt : 'a port -> 'a event

> recvEvt *p*   creates an event value that represents the recv operation on the port *p*.

val multicast : ('a mchan * 'a) -> unit

> multicast (*mc*, *v*)   multicasts the value *v* on the channel *mc*. It is a nonblocking operation.

The `SimpleRPC` structure

The `SimpleRPC` structure provides higher-order functions for implementing a simple RPC (*remote procedure call*) protocol. The protocol is one where the client's call blocks until a reply is received from the server, and the server's entry event is enabled whenever there is a client attempting a call. These functions take a server action as an argument and return the client call function and server entry as results.

Synopsis

```
signature SIMPLE_RPC
structure SimpleRPC : SIMPLE_RPC
```

Interface

```
type 'a event = 'a CML.event

val mkRPC : ('a -> 'b) -> {
        call      : 'a -> 'b,
        entryEvt : unit event
      }

val mkRPC_In : (('a * 'c) -> 'b) -> {
        call      : 'a -> 'b,
        entryEvt : 'c -> unit event
      }

val mkRPC_Out : ('a -> ('b * 'c)) -> {
        call      : 'a -> 'b,
        entryEvt : 'c event
      }

val mkRPC_InOut : (('a * 'c) -> ('b * 'd)) -> {
        call      : 'a -> 'b,
        entryEvt : 'c -> 'd event
      }
```

Description

```
val mkRPC : ('a -> 'b) -> {
        call : 'a -> 'b,
        entryEvt : unit event
      }
```

`mkRPC` *action* packages the action function *action* in a simple RPC protocol, where the client operation is a blocking function and the server entry is an event that is enabled whenever a client request is made. The `mkRPC` function is the least general of the functions in this structure; there are no additional arguments or results to the action function. Any state that is local to the server must be included in the action's closure. For example, the following code shows how `mkRPC` can be used to implement access to shared state:

```
fun mkServer init = let
      val r = ref init
      val {call=get, entryEvt=getEvt} = mkRPC(fn () => !r)
      val {call=put, entryEvt=putEvt} = mkRPC(fn x => r := x)
      fun server () = (select[getEvt, putEvt]; server())
      in
         ignore (spawn server);
         {get = get, put = put}
      end
```

```
val mkRPC_In : (('a * 'c) -> 'b) -> {
      call : 'a -> 'b,
      entryEvt : 'c -> unit event
   }
```

The mkRPC_In function supports an action function that takes an additional argument. This argument is supplied by the server when creating the entry event value. For example, we can modify the reference cell example to use mkRPC_In for the get action

```
fun mkServer init = let
      val r = ref init
      val {call=get, entryEvt=getEvt} = mkRPC_In(fn (_, x) => x)
      val {call=put, entryEvt=putEvt} = mkRPC(fn x => r := x)
      fun server () = (select[getEvt(!r), putEvt]; server())
      in
         ignore (spawn server);
         {get = get, put = put}
      end
```

```
val mkRPC_Out : ('a -> ('b * 'c)) -> {
      call : 'a -> 'b,
      entryEvt : 'c event
   }
```

The mkRPC_Out function supports an action function that returns an additional result. This argument is supplied by the server when creating the entry event value. Using mkRPC_In for the get operation and mkRPC_Out for the put operation results in the following implementation of the shared cell:

```
fun mkServer init = let
      val {call=get, entryEvt=getEvt} = mkRPC_In(fn (_, x) => x)
      val {call=put, entryEvt=putEvt} = mkRPC_Out(fn x => ((), x))
      fun server v = server(select[getEvt v, putEvt])
      in
         ignore (spawnc server init);
         {get = get, put = put}
      end
```

```
val mkRPC_InOut : (('a * 'c) -> ('b * 'd)) -> {
      call : 'a -> 'b,
      entryEvt : 'c -> 'd event
   }
```

The mkRPC_InOut function provides for both additional arguments and results to the action function.

Discussion

Note that these functions do not support communicating server-side exceptions back to the client; in fact, they are written under the assumption that the action functions never produce uncaught exceptions.

Appendix B

The Semantics of CML

One of the attractive properties of **SML** is that it has a formal definition, which serves as both a guide to implementors and users. Following this tradition, a semantics of "Mini-**CML**" has been developed, and some basic properties of the semantics have been proven. In this appendix, we present both the dynamic and static semantics of Mini-**CML**, and state some theorems relating the two. Mini-**CML** is based on a purely functional subset of **SML** without datatypes, pattern matching, modules, or exceptions.[1] This sequential base is extended with the complete set of **CML** event combinators, as well as threads and channels. While we have necessarily restricted ourselves to a subset of **CML**, the full range of **CML** concurrency primitives is covered by this semantics. This appendix is not meant to be a theoretical treatise, but rather an aid to understanding the language.

B.1 Notation

Before diving into the semantics of Mini-**CML**, it is necessary to review notation.

If A and B are sets, then $A \cup B$ is their union, $A \cap B$ is their intersection, and $A \setminus B$ is their difference. The notation $A \xrightarrow{\text{fin}} B$ denotes the set of *finite maps* from A to B (*i.e.*, partial functions with finite domains). If f is a map, then the *domain* and *range* of f are defined as

$$\begin{aligned} \text{dom}(f) &= \{x \mid f(x) \text{ is defined}\} \\ \text{rng}(f) &= \{f(x) \mid x \in \text{dom}(f)\} \end{aligned}$$

The notation $\{a_1 \mapsto b_1, \ldots, a_n \mapsto b_n\}$ denotes a finite map with domain $\{a_1, \ldots, a_n\}$, such that a_i is mapped to b_i; we write $\{\}$ for the map with the empty domain. If $A' \subset A$,

---

[1] Of these features, exceptions are the only feature that would require significant reworking of the dynamic semantics. This is because exception names are global over all processes in the system, which requires extra bookkeeping in the semantic rules.

A' is finite and $b \in B$, then $\{A' \mapsto b\} \in A \xrightarrow{\text{fin}} B$ is the finite map that maps each $a \in A'$ to B. If f and g are maps, then $f \circ g$ is their *composition*, and $f \pm g$, called f *modified by* g, is a map with domain $\text{dom}(f) \cup \text{dom}(g)$, such that

$$(f \pm g)(x) = \left\{ \begin{array}{ll} g(x) & \text{if } x \in \text{dom}(g) \\ f(x) & \text{otherwise} \end{array} \right.$$

The symbol $\pm$ is used because something is added and something is take away (when $\text{dom}(g) \cap \text{dom}(f) \neq \emptyset$). We often find it useful to view finite maps as sets of ordered pairs and write $f \subseteq g$, if $\text{dom}(f) \subseteq \text{dom}(g)$ and for $x \in \text{dom}(f)$, $f(x) = g(x)$. In this case, g is called an *extension* of f. We write $e[x' \mapsto e']$ for the capture-free substitution of the term e' for the variable x' in the term e.

B.2　Syntax

We first present the *surface syntax* of Mini-**CML**.[2] As is usual, we assume the existence of countable sets of *variables* and *constants*:

$$
\begin{array}{lll}
x & \in & \text{VAR} \qquad\qquad\qquad\qquad\qquad\qquad\qquad \text{variables} \\
b & \in & \text{CONST} = \text{BCONST} \cup \text{FCONST} \qquad\qquad \text{constants} \\
& & \text{BCONST} = \{\,(), \texttt{true}, \texttt{false}, 0, 1, \ldots\} \qquad \text{base constants} \\
& & \text{FCONST} = \{\texttt{+}, \texttt{-}, \texttt{fst}, \texttt{snd}, \ldots\} \qquad \text{function constants}
\end{array}
$$

The set of function constants, FCONST, includes the following symbols for the concurrency primitives: `alwaysEvt`, `channel`, `choose`, `guard`, `neverEvt`, `recvEvt`, `sendEvt`, `wrap`, and `withNack`.

The surface syntax of Mini-**CML** expressions is defined by the following grammar:

$$
\begin{array}{rll}
e & ::= \quad x & \text{variables} \\
& | \quad b & \text{constants} \\
& | \quad (e_1, e_2) & \text{pairs} \\
& | \quad \textbf{fn } x \texttt{=>} e & \text{function abstraction} \\
& | \quad (e_1 \ e_2) & \text{function application} \\
& | \quad \textbf{let } x \texttt{=} e_1 \textbf{ in } e_2 & \text{let binding} \\
& | \quad \textbf{spawn } e & \text{process creation} \\
& | \quad \textbf{sync } e & \text{synchronization}
\end{array}
$$

The dynamic semantics of Mini-**CML** are defined in terms of an *internal syntax*, which is the surface syntax extended with special syntactic forms used to represent semantic

---

[2]That is, the syntax used by programmers and accepted by compilers.

objects. We need two additional sets of names for channels and conditions, which are distinct from the variables and constants:

$$\kappa \;\in\; \text{CH} \qquad \text{channel names}$$
$$\gamma \;\in\; \text{COND} \qquad \text{condition names}$$

We then extend the surface syntax with the following grammar productions:

$$
\begin{array}{lll}
e & ::= & \ldots \\[2pt]
& \mid & \kappa & \text{channel names} \\
& \mid & \gamma & \text{condition event} \\
& \mid & e? & \text{receive event} \\
& \mid & e_1!e_2 & \text{send event} \\
& \mid & e_1 \Rightarrow e_2 & \text{wrap event} \\
& \mid & \mathbf{N}\, e & \text{guarded event function with nack} \\
& \mid & (e_1 \oplus e_2) & \text{event choice} \\
& \mid & (e_1 \mid e_2) & \text{abort wrapper} \\
& \mid & \Lambda & \text{never event}
\end{array}
$$

Note that we use $\mathbf{N}\, e$ to represent the product of both `guard` and `withNack`.

It is useful to distinguish two subsets of expressions: *values* (denoted v) and *event values* (denoted ev). These are defined as the least subsets of expressions satisfying the following grammars:

$$
\begin{array}{lll}
v & ::= & b \\
& \mid & \kappa \\
& \mid & (v_1, v_2) \\
& \mid & \mathbf{fn}\; x \texttt{=>} e \\
& \mid & \mathbf{N}\, v \\
& \mid & ev
\end{array}
\qquad\qquad
\begin{array}{lll}
ev & ::= & \kappa? \\
& \mid & \kappa!v \\
& \mid & \gamma \\
& \mid & ev \Rightarrow v \\
& \mid & (ev_1 \oplus ev_2) \\
& \mid & (ev \mid v) \\
& \mid & \Lambda
\end{array}
$$

Variables are not included in the set of values, because our dynamic semantics is substitution based, instead of environment based. Thus, there are three syntactic classes of terms in Mini-**CML**:

$$
\begin{array}{lll}
e & \in & \text{EXP} \qquad\qquad \text{expressions} \\
v & \in & \text{VAL} \subset \text{EXP} \qquad \text{values} \\
ev & \in & \text{EVENT} \subset \text{VAL} \quad \text{event values}
\end{array}
$$

B.3   Dynamic semantics

Specifying the dynamic semantics requires some additional notation. We use $\mathcal{K} \subset \text{CH}$ to denote finite sets of channels, and $\mathcal{C} \in \text{COND} \xrightarrow{\text{fin}} \{\textbf{true}, \textbf{false}\}$ to denote the state of a collection of conditions. Each Mini-**CML** process has a unique *process identifier* $\pi \in \text{PROCID}$. We use $\mathcal{P} \in \text{PROCID} \xrightarrow{\text{fin}} \text{EXP}$ to denote the state of a set of processes. With this notation, the state of a Mini-**CML** computation is defined as a *configuration* $\mathcal{C}, \mathcal{K}, \mathcal{P}$, where $\mathcal{C}$ is the *condition state*, $\mathcal{K}$ is the set of *allocated* channel names, and $\mathcal{P}$ is the *process state*. We say that a configuration $\mathcal{C}, \mathcal{K}, \mathcal{P}$ is *well formed*, if for any γ in the terms of $\mathcal{P}$ we have $\gamma \in \mathcal{C}$, and if for any κ in the terms of $\mathcal{P}$ we have $\kappa \in \mathcal{K}$.

The dynamic semantic of Mini-**CML** is organized around four reduction relations. *Concurrent evaluation* defines how configurations evolve:

$$\mathcal{C}, \mathcal{K}, \mathcal{P} \Rightarrow \mathcal{C}', \mathcal{K}', \mathcal{P}'$$

The *rendezvous projection* relation describes how a collection of processes can execute a rendezvous:

$$\mathcal{C}, \mathcal{P} \mapsto (\mathcal{P}', \mathcal{P}'')/\mathcal{A}$$

where $\mathcal{A}$ is the set of *negative acknowledgement conditions* (NACK conditions) of the rendezvous. The primitive notions of synchronization and communication are captured by a family of *event-matching* relations

$$\mathcal{C} \vdash (ev_1, \ldots, ev_k) \rightsquigarrow_k (e_1, \ldots, e_k)/\mathcal{A}$$

where $\mathcal{A} \subset \text{COND}$ is the set of NACK conditions of the match. A *sequential configuration* is a triple $\mathcal{C}, \mathcal{K}, e$. The sequential evaluation of individual processes is defined by the *sequential evaluation* relation on sequential configurations

$$\mathcal{C}, \mathcal{K}, e \hookrightarrow \mathcal{C}', \mathcal{K}', e'$$

Each of these is defined in detail in the sequel. While it would be possible to collapse these into two relations (concurrent evaluation and event matching), we prefer this organization because it separates the concept of concurrent evaluation from sequential evaluation.

Our semantics is given as a transition system, and we use Felleisen's notion of an evaluation context to define the concurrent and sequential evaluation relations. An *evaluation context* is a single-hole context where the hole marks the next redex (or is at the top if the term is irreducible). The evaluation of Mini-**CML** is call-by-value and left-to-right, which leads to the following grammar for the evaluation contexts:

$$
\begin{aligned}
E \quad ::= \quad & [\,] \mid (E\ e) \mid (v\ E) \mid (E, e) \mid (v, E) \\
& \mid\ \textbf{let}\ x = E\ \textbf{in}\ e \mid \textbf{spawn}\ E \mid \textbf{sync}\ E \\
& \mid\ (E \mid \gamma)
\end{aligned}
$$

The last of these deserves some comment. As shown below, it is necessary to evaluate on the left-hand side of an abort expression to properly describe the semantics of negative acknowledgements (`withNack`).

B.3.1 Concurrent evaluation

The concurrent evaluation relation is defined by three simple rules. The first describes a single sequential step by one of the processes in the configuration

$$\frac{\mathcal{C}, \mathcal{K}, e \hookrightarrow \mathcal{C}', \mathcal{K}', e' \quad \pi \notin \mathrm{dom}(\mathcal{P})}{\mathcal{C}, \mathcal{K}, \mathcal{P} \cup \{\langle \pi, e \rangle\} \Rightarrow \mathcal{C}', \mathcal{K}', \mathcal{P} \cup \{\langle \pi, e' \rangle\}}$$

The second rule describes the *spawning* of a new process:

$$\frac{\pi \notin \mathrm{dom}(\mathcal{P}) \quad \pi' \notin \mathrm{dom}(\mathcal{P}) \quad \pi \neq \pi'}{\mathcal{C}, \mathcal{K}, \mathcal{P} \cup \{\langle \pi, E[\textbf{spawn}\, v] \rangle\} \Rightarrow \mathcal{C}, \mathcal{K}, \mathcal{P} \cup \{\langle \pi, E[\,()\,] \rangle, \langle \pi', v\ () \rangle\}}$$

The third rule describes communication and synchronization:

$$\frac{\mathcal{C}, \mathcal{P} \mapsto (\mathcal{P}', \mathcal{P}'')/\mathcal{A} \quad \mathcal{C}' = \mathcal{C} \pm \{\mathcal{A} \mapsto \textbf{true}\}}{\mathcal{C}, \mathcal{K}, \mathcal{P} \Rightarrow \mathcal{C}', \mathcal{K}, (\mathcal{P} \setminus \mathcal{P}') \cup \mathcal{P}''}$$

As will be seen in the rules below, the set $\mathcal{A}$ is the set of NACK conditions of the events *not* selected in this synchronization. The condition state is updated to enable these NACK conditions.

B.3.2 Rendezvous projection

The *rendezvous projection* is used to choose a possible rendezvous from a set of well-formed processes. We define

$$\mathcal{C}, \mathcal{P} \mapsto (\mathcal{P}', \mathcal{P}'')/\mathcal{A}$$

to mean that there is a rendezvous enabled in $\mathcal{P}$ involving $\mathcal{P}' \subseteq \mathcal{P}$, where the rendezvous maps the processes in $\mathcal{P}'$ to $\mathcal{P}''$. We require that $\mathrm{dom}(\mathcal{P}') = \mathrm{dom}(\mathcal{P}'')$. The following rule allows the addition of processes that are not involved in the rendezvous:

$$\frac{\mathcal{C}, \mathcal{P} \mapsto (\mathcal{P}', \mathcal{P}'')/\mathcal{A} \quad \mathcal{P} \subseteq \mathcal{P}'''}{\mathcal{C}, \mathcal{P}''' \mapsto (\mathcal{P}', \mathcal{P}'')/\mathcal{A}}$$

The basic notion of a set of k processes performing a rendezvous is defined by the following rule:

$$\frac{p_1 = \langle \pi_1, E_1[\textbf{sync}\, ev_1] \rangle \quad \cdots \quad p_k = \langle \pi_k, E_k[\textbf{sync}\, ev_k] \rangle \quad \mathcal{C} \vdash (ev_1, \ldots, ev_k) \leadsto_k (e_1, \ldots, e_k)/\mathcal{A}}{\mathcal{C}, \{p_1, \ldots, p_k\} \mapsto (\{p_1, \ldots, p_k\}, \{\langle \pi_1, E_1[e_1] \rangle, \ldots, \langle \pi_k, E_k[e_k] \rangle\})/\mathcal{A}}$$

B.3.3 Event matching

The actual rules used to specify the event matching depend on the rendezvous primitives provided by the language. Intuitively, the judgement

$$\mathcal{C} \vdash (ev_1, \ldots, ev_k) \rightsquigarrow_k (e_1, \ldots, e_k)/\mathcal{A}$$

means that the event values ev_i match yielding the corresponding results e_i with the additional result of a set of NACK conditions $\mathcal{A}$. For **CML**, which provides two-way rendezvous, we get the following rule:

$$\overline{\mathcal{C} \vdash (\kappa!v, \kappa?) \rightsquigarrow_2 (\,(\,), v)/\emptyset}$$

One-way synchronization on conditions (which includes `alwaysEvt`) is defined by

$$\frac{\mathcal{C}(\gamma) = \mathbf{true}}{\mathcal{C} \vdash \gamma \rightsquigarrow_1 (\,)\,/\emptyset}$$

The semantics of the event combinators are defined by the following rules (for k-way matching):

$$\frac{\mathcal{C} \vdash (ev_1, \ldots, ev_k) \rightsquigarrow_k (e_1, \ldots, e_k)/\mathcal{A}}{\mathcal{C} \vdash (ev_1 \oplus ev', \ldots, ev_k) \rightsquigarrow_k (e_1, \ldots, e_k)/\mathcal{A} \cup \mathrm{nack}(ev')}$$

$$\frac{\mathcal{C} \vdash (ev_1, \ldots, ev_k) \rightsquigarrow_k (e_1, \ldots, e_k)/\mathcal{A}}{\mathcal{C} \vdash (ev' \oplus ev_1, \ldots, ev_k) \rightsquigarrow_k (e_1, \ldots, e_k)/\mathcal{A} \cup \mathrm{nack}(ev')}$$

$$\frac{\mathcal{C} \vdash (ev_1, \ldots, ev_k) \rightsquigarrow_k (e_1, \ldots, e_k)/\mathcal{A}}{\mathcal{C} \vdash (ev_1 \Rightarrow f, \ldots, ev_k) \rightsquigarrow_k ((f\ e_1), \ldots, e_k)/\mathcal{A}}$$

$$\frac{\mathcal{C} \vdash (ev_1, \ldots, ev_k) \rightsquigarrow_k (e_1, \ldots, e_k)/\mathcal{A}}{\mathcal{C} \vdash (ev_1 \mid \gamma, \ldots, ev_k) \rightsquigarrow_k (e_1, \ldots, e_k)/\mathcal{A}}$$

$$\frac{\mathcal{C} \vdash (ev_1, ev_2, \ldots, ev_k) \rightsquigarrow_k (e_1, e_2, \ldots, e_k)/\mathcal{A} \quad \{i_j \mid 1 \le i_j \le k\}}{\mathcal{C} \vdash (ev_{i_1}, \ldots, ev_{i_k}) \rightsquigarrow_k (e_{i_1}, \ldots, e_{i_k})/\mathcal{A}}$$

where the *NACK conditions* of an event are defined as

$$
\begin{aligned}
\mathrm{nack}(ev_1 \oplus ev_2) &= \mathrm{nack}(ev_1) \cup \mathrm{nack}(ev_2) \\
\mathrm{nack}(ev \Rightarrow v) &= \mathrm{nack}(ev) \\
\mathrm{nack}(ev \mid \gamma) &= \mathrm{nack}(ev) \cup \{\gamma\} \\
\mathrm{nack}(ev) &= \emptyset \quad \textit{otherwise}
\end{aligned}
$$

Note that abort events are introduced by the choice combinator — if the match involves one branch, the abort conditions of the other branch are enabled.

B.3.4 Sequential evaluation

The sequential evaluation relation is defined by six rules, which are given in terms of evaluation contexts. The first three of these are the standard rules for call-by-value λ-calculus evaluation:

$$\mathcal{C}, \mathcal{K}, E[b\ v] \hookrightarrow \mathcal{C}, \mathcal{K}, E[\delta(b, v)]$$
$$\mathcal{C}, \mathcal{K}, E[(\mathbf{fn}\ x => e)\ v] \hookrightarrow \mathcal{C}, \mathcal{K}, E[e[x \mapsto v]]$$
$$\mathcal{C}, \mathcal{K}, E[\mathbf{let}\ x = v\ \mathbf{in}\ e] \hookrightarrow \mathcal{C}, \mathcal{K}, E[e[x \mapsto v]]$$

We have special evaluation rules for `alwaysEvt` and channel creation:

$$\mathcal{C}, \mathcal{K}, E[\texttt{alwaysEvt}\ v] \hookrightarrow \mathcal{C} \pm \{\gamma \mapsto \mathbf{true}\}, \mathcal{K}, E[\gamma \Rightarrow (\mathbf{fn}\ () => v)]$$
$$\mathcal{C}, \mathcal{K}, E[\texttt{channel}\ ()] \hookrightarrow \mathcal{C}, \mathcal{K} \cup \{\kappa\}, E[\kappa]$$

where $(\gamma \notin \mathrm{dom}(\mathcal{C}))$ and $(\kappa \notin \mathcal{K})$. The last rule describes the effect of applying `sync` to a guarded event function:

$$\mathcal{C}, \mathcal{K}, E[\mathbf{sync}\ (\mathbf{N}\ v)] \hookrightarrow \mathcal{C} \pm \{\gamma \mapsto \mathbf{false}\}, \mathcal{K}, E[\mathbf{sync}\ (v\ \gamma)] \quad (\gamma \notin \mathrm{dom}(\mathcal{C}))$$

The meaning of function constants is given by the partial function

$$\delta : \mathrm{FCONST} \times \mathrm{VAL} \to \mathrm{VAL}$$

Since a value can have free condition and channel names, we require that the application of δ not introduce any new condition or channel names (this requirement is necessary to preserve well-formed configurations under sequential evaluation). For the standard built-in function constants, the meaning of δ is the expected one; for example,

$$\delta(+, (1, 1)) \equiv_{def} 2$$
$$\delta(\texttt{fst}, (v_1, v_2)) \equiv_{def} v_1$$
$$\delta(\texttt{snd}, (v_1, v_2)) \equiv_{def} v_2$$

There is a technical issue with respect to type soundness and the definition of δ. In the static semantics described below, we place the restriction that $\delta(f, v)$ should be defined for any well-typed application of f to v. If we extended Mini-**CML** with an exception mechanism, then this restriction is not required (*e.g.*, division by zero raises an exception).

The δ function also defines the translation from the surface syntax of Mini-**CML** events to the internal representation. For the base-event constructors, the rules for this are as follows:

$$\delta(\texttt{neverEvt}, ()) \equiv_{def} \Lambda$$
$$\delta(\texttt{recvEvt}, \kappa) \equiv_{def} \kappa?$$
$$\delta(\texttt{sendEvt}, (\kappa, v)) \equiv_{def} \kappa!v$$

Recall that `guard` and `withNack` delay the evaluation of their argument to synchro-nization time, and that the nack event passed to the argument of `withNack` is unique to the synchronization. These functions introduce guarded event functions

$$\delta(\texttt{guard}, v) \equiv_{def} \mathbf{N}(\textbf{fn } a \texttt{=>} v\texttt{ ( )})$$
$$\delta(\texttt{withNack}, v) \equiv_{def} \mathbf{N}(\textbf{fn } a \texttt{=>} (v\ a\ |\ a))$$

where a is a fresh variable. In the case of `guard`, the abort event (bound to a) is ignored by the guarded function, while in the case of `withNack`, the abort event is passed to the guarded function and also used in the abort wrapper. Note that the application of v to a requires evaluation on the left-hand side of the abort wrapper.

Preserving the delay semantics of guarded functions creates some complications in the definition of the `wrap` and `choose` functions. For `wrap` we have the following rules:

$$\delta(\texttt{wrap}, (\mathbf{N}v_1, v_2)) \equiv_{def} \mathbf{N}(\textbf{fn } a \texttt{=>} \texttt{wrap }(v_1\ a, v_2))$$
$$\delta(\texttt{wrap}, (ev, v)) \equiv_{def} ev \Rightarrow v$$

where we assume a is a fresh variable.

The situation is even more complicated in the case of the `choose` function, since guarded functions can appear in either (or both) branches, and we may have both a regular guard and nack guard in the same choice:

$$\delta(\texttt{choose}, (\mathbf{N}v_1, \mathbf{N}v_2)) \equiv_{def} \mathbf{N}(\textbf{fn } a_1 \texttt{=>} \mathbf{N}(\textbf{fn } a_2 \texttt{=>} \texttt{choose }(v_1\ a_1, v_2\ a_2)))$$
$$\delta(\texttt{choose}, (\mathbf{N}v, ev)) \equiv_{def} \mathbf{N}(\textbf{fn } a \texttt{=>} \texttt{choose }(v\ a, ev))$$
$$\delta(\texttt{choose}, (ev, \mathbf{N}v)) \equiv_{def} \mathbf{N}(\textbf{fn } a \texttt{=>} \texttt{choose }(ev, v\ a))$$
$$\delta(\texttt{choose}, (ev_1, ev_2)) \equiv_{def} (ev_1 \oplus ev_2)$$

where we assume a, a_1, and a_2 are fresh variables.

B.4 Execution traces

Unlike in the sequential semantics of **SML**, a **CML** program can have many (often in-finitely many) different evaluations. Furthermore, there are many interesting programs that do not terminate. Thus some new terminology and notation for describing evaluation sequences is required. This is used to describe some reasonable fairness constraints on implementations and to state type soundness results for Mini-**CML**.

Definition B.1 A *trace* T is a (possibly infinite) sequence of well-formed configurations

$$T = \langle\!\langle \mathcal{C}_0, \mathcal{K}_0, \mathcal{P}_0;\ \mathcal{C}_1, \mathcal{K}_1, \mathcal{P}_1;\ \dots \rangle\!\rangle$$

such that $\mathcal{C}_i, \mathcal{K}_i, \mathcal{P}_i \Rightarrow \mathcal{C}_{i+1}, \mathcal{K}_{i+1}, \mathcal{P}_{i+1}$ (for $i < n$, if T is finite with length n). The *head* of T is $\mathcal{C}_0, \mathcal{K}_0, \mathcal{P}_0$.

Note that if a configuration C_0, K_0, P_0 is well-formed, then any sequence of evaluation steps starting with C_0, K_0, P_0 is a trace.

The possible states of a process with respect to a configuration are given by the following definition.

Definition B.2 Let C, K, P be a well-formed configuration and let $\langle \pi, e \rangle \in P$. The *state* of π in P is either *zombie*, *blocked*, *stuck*, or *ready*, depending on the form of e:

- if $e = [v]$, then π is a *zombie*,

- if $e = E[\textbf{sync } ev]$ and there does not exist a set of processes

$$\{\langle \pi_i, E_i[\textbf{sync } ev_i] \rangle \mid 1 \leq i \leq k\} \subseteq P \setminus \{\langle \pi, e \rangle\}$$

  such that $C \vdash (ev, ev_1, \ldots, ev_k) \leadsto_{k+1} (e', e_1, \ldots, e_k)/A$, then π is *blocked*.

- if there is no sequential configuration C, K, e', such that $C, K, e \hookrightarrow C, K, e'$, then π is *stuck*.

- otherwise, π is *ready*.

We define the set of ready processes in C, K, P by

$$\text{Rdy}(C, K, P) = \{\pi \mid \pi \text{ is ready in } C, K, P\}$$

A configuration C, K, P is *terminal* if $\text{Rdy}(P) = \emptyset$. A terminal configuration with blocked processes is said to be *deadlocked*.

Definition B.3 A trace is a *computation* if it is maximal; *i.e.*, if it is infinite or if it is finite and ends in a terminal configuration. If e is a program, then we define the computations of e to be

$$\text{Comp}(e) = \{T \mid T \text{ is a computation with head } \emptyset, \emptyset, \{\langle \pi_0, e \rangle\}. \}$$

We follow the convention of using π_0 as the process identifier of the initial process in a computation of a program.

Definition B.4 The *set of processes of a trace* T is defined as

$$\text{Procs}(T) = \{\pi \mid \exists C_i, K_i, P_i \in T \text{ with } \pi \in \text{dom}(P_i)\}$$

Since a given program can evaluate in different ways, the sequential notions of convergence and divergence are inadequate. Instead, we define convergence and divergence relative to a particular computation of a program.

Definition B.5 A process $\pi \in \mathrm{Procs}(T)$ *converges* to a value v in T, written $\pi \Downarrow_T v$, if $\mathcal{C}, \mathcal{K}, \mathcal{P} \cup \{\langle \pi, v \rangle\} \in T$. We say that π *diverges* in T, written $\pi \Uparrow_T$, if for every $\mathcal{C}, \mathcal{K}, \mathcal{P} \in T$, with $\pi \in \mathrm{dom}(\mathcal{P})$, π is ready or blocked in $\mathcal{P}$.

Divergence includes deadlocked processes and terminating processes that are not evaluated often enough to reach termination, as well as those with infinite loops. It does not include stuck processes.

B.4.1 Fairness

The semantics presented above admits unfair traces, and thus is not adequate as a specification of **CML** implementations. It is necessary to distinguish the acceptable traces. Informally, we require that ready processes make progress and that synchronization on a given channel or condition not be starved.

A couple of definitions are required before formalizing the notions of fairness. We have already defined the notion of a process being ready in a configuration; a similar definition is required for channels and conditions.

Definition B.6 The *synchronization objects* of an event value ev are defined as

$$
\begin{aligned}
\mathrm{SyncObj}(\kappa!v) &= \{\kappa\} \\
\mathrm{SyncObj}(\kappa?) &= \{\kappa\} \\
\mathrm{SyncObj}(\gamma) &= \{\gamma\} \\
\mathrm{SyncObj}(\Lambda) &= \emptyset \\
\mathrm{SyncObj}(ev_1 \oplus ev_2) &= \mathrm{SyncObj}(ev_1) \cup \mathrm{SyncObj}(ev_2) \\
\mathrm{SyncObj}(ev \Rightarrow v) &= \mathrm{SyncObj}(ev) \\
\mathrm{SyncObj}(ev \mid \gamma) &= \mathrm{SyncObj}(ev)
\end{aligned}
$$

We say that a synchronization object ψ is *used* in a synchronization if it is the synchronization object of the chosen base event for some process involved in the synchronization.

Definition B.7 A synchronization object ψ is *enabled* in a configuration $\mathcal{C}, \mathcal{K}, \mathcal{P}$ if there are k processes $\langle \pi_i, E_i[\mathbf{sync}\ ev_i]\rangle \in \mathcal{P}$ for $1 \leq i \leq k$, such that $\psi \in \mathrm{SyncObj}(ev_1)$ and

$$\mathcal{C} \vdash (ev_1, \ldots, ev_k) \rightsquigarrow_k (e_1, \ldots, e_k)/\mathcal{A}$$

The acceptable computations of a program are defined in terms of fairness restrictions.

Definition B.8 A computation T is *acceptable* if it ends in a terminal configuration, or if T satisfies the following fairness constraints:

(1) Any process that is ready infinitely often is selected infinitely often.

(2) Any synchronization object that is enabled infinitely often is used infinitely often.

An implementation of **CML** should prohibit the possibility of unacceptable computations. In practice this requires that an implementation satisfy some stronger property on finite traces.

B.5   Static semantics

It is well known that references (*i.e.*, updatable memory cells) can cause type soundness problems for polymorphic languages like **SML**. Furthermore, it is known that references can be coded using channels and processes, so the question of type soundness of a polymorphic concurrent language like **CML** deserves examination. In this section, we present a type system for Mini-**CML** programs, and state soundness results about the system.

The presentation uses standard notation. Let $\iota \in \text{TYCON} = \{\text{int}, \text{bool}, \ldots\}$ designate the *type constants*, and $\alpha \in \text{TYVAR}$ designate type variables. Then, the set of types, $\tau \in \text{TY}$, is defined by

$$
\begin{array}{llll}
\tau & ::= & \iota & \text{type constants} \\
& | & \alpha & \text{type variables} \\
& | & (\tau_1 \rightarrow \tau_2) & \text{function types} \\
& | & (\tau_1 \times \tau_2) & \text{pair types} \\
& | & \tau\ \text{chan} & \text{channel types} \\
& | & \tau\ \text{event} & \text{event types}
\end{array}
$$

and the set of type schemes, $\sigma \in \text{TYSCHEME}$, is defined by

$$
\begin{array}{lll}
\sigma & ::= & \tau \\
& | & \forall \alpha.\sigma
\end{array}
$$

We write $\forall \alpha_1 \cdots \alpha_n.\tau$ for the type scheme $\sigma = \forall \alpha_1 \cdots \forall \alpha_n.\tau$. The type variables $\alpha_1, \ldots, \alpha_n$ are said to be *bound* in σ. A type variable that occurs in τ and is not bound is said to be *free* in σ. We write $\text{FTV}(\sigma)$ for the free type variables of σ. If $\text{FTV}(\tau) = \emptyset$, then τ is said to be a *monotype*.

Type environments assign type schemes to variables in terms. Since we are interested in assigning types to intermediate stages of evaluation, channel names also need to be assigned types. Therefore, a *typing environment* is a pair of finite maps: a *variable typing* and a *channel typing*:

$$
\begin{array}{rcl}
\text{VT} & \in & \text{VARTY} = \text{VAR} \xrightarrow{\text{fin}} \text{TYSCHEME} \\
\text{CT} & \in & \text{CHANTY} = \text{CH} \xrightarrow{\text{fin}} \text{TY} \\
\text{TE} = (\text{VT}, \text{CT}) & \in & \text{TYENV} = (\text{VARTY} \times \text{CHANTY})
\end{array}
$$

We use $\mathrm{FTV}(\mathrm{VT})$ and $\mathrm{FTV}(\mathrm{CT})$ to denote the sets of free type variables of variable and channel typings, and

$$\mathrm{FTV}(\mathrm{TE}) = \mathrm{FTV}(\mathrm{VT}) \cup \mathrm{FTV}(\mathrm{CT})$$

where $\mathrm{TE} = (\mathrm{VT}, \mathrm{CT})$. Note that there are no bound type variables in a channel typing. The following shorthand is useful for type environment modification:

$$\mathrm{TE} \pm \{x \mapsto \sigma\} \quad \equiv_{def} \quad (\mathrm{VT} \pm \{x \mapsto \sigma\}, \mathrm{CT})$$

where $x \in \mathrm{VAR}$, $\kappa \in \mathrm{CH}$, and $\mathrm{TE} = (\mathrm{VT}, \mathrm{CT})$.

A *substitution* is a map from type variables to types. A substitution S can be naturally extended to map types to types as follows:

$$
\begin{aligned}
S\iota &= \iota \\
S\alpha &= S(\alpha) \\
S(\tau_1 \to \tau_2) &= (S\tau_1 \to S\tau_2) \\
S(\tau_1 \times \tau_2) &= (S\tau_1 \times S\tau_2) \\
S\tau \text{ chan} &= (S\tau) \text{ chan} \\
S\tau \text{ event} &= (S\tau) \text{ event}
\end{aligned}
$$

Application of a substitution to a type scheme respects bound variables and avoids capture. It is defined as

$$S(\forall \alpha_1 \cdots \alpha_n.\tau) = \forall \alpha_1' \ldots \alpha_n'.S(\tau[\alpha_i \mapsto \alpha_i'])$$

where $\alpha_i' \notin \mathrm{dom}(S) \cup \mathrm{FTV}(\mathrm{rng}(S))$. Application of a substitution S to a type environment TE is defined as $S(\mathrm{TE}) = S \circ \mathrm{TE}$. A type τ' is an *instance* of a type scheme $\sigma = \forall \alpha_1 \cdots \alpha_n.\tau$, written $\sigma \succ \tau'$, if there exists a finite substitution, S, with $\mathrm{dom}(S) = \{\alpha_1, \ldots \alpha_n\}$ and $S\tau = \tau'$. If $\sigma \succ \tau'$, then we say that σ is a *generalization* of τ'.

Lastly, the *closure* of a type τ with respect to a type environment TE is defined as $\mathrm{CLOS}_{\mathrm{TE}}(\tau) = \forall \alpha_1 \cdots \alpha_n.\tau$, where

$$\{\alpha_1, \ldots, \alpha_n\} = \mathrm{FTV}(\tau) \setminus \mathrm{FTV}(\mathrm{TE})$$

B.5.1 Expression typing rules

To associate types with the constants, we assume the existence of a function

$$\mathrm{TypeOf} : \mathrm{CONST} \to \mathrm{TYSCHEME}$$

For the concurrency related constants, it assigns the following type schemes:

$$
\begin{array}{lcl}
\texttt{channel} & : & \forall\alpha.(\text{unit} \rightarrow \alpha\ \text{chan}) \\
\texttt{neverEvt} & : & \forall\alpha.(\text{unit} \rightarrow \alpha\ \text{event}) \\
\texttt{alwaysEvt} & : & \forall\alpha.(\alpha \rightarrow \alpha\ \text{event}) \\
\texttt{recvEvt} & : & \forall\alpha.(\alpha\ \text{chan} \rightarrow \alpha\ \text{event}) \\
\texttt{sendEvt} & : & \forall\alpha.((\alpha\ \text{chan} \times \alpha) \rightarrow \text{unit event}) \\
\texttt{wrap} & : & \forall\alpha_1\alpha_2.((\alpha_1\ \text{event} \times (\alpha_1 \rightarrow \alpha_2)) \rightarrow \alpha_2\ \text{event}) \\
\texttt{choose} & : & \forall\alpha.((\alpha\ \text{event} \times \alpha\ \text{event}) \rightarrow \alpha\ \text{event}) \\
\texttt{guard} & : & \forall\alpha.((\text{unit} \rightarrow \alpha\ \text{event}) \rightarrow \alpha\ \text{event}) \\
\texttt{withNack} & : & \forall\alpha.((\text{unit event} \rightarrow \alpha\ \text{event}) \rightarrow \alpha\ \text{event})
\end{array}
$$

We also assume that there are no event-valued constants. More formally, we require that there does not exist any b such that $\text{TypeOf}(b) = \tau$ event, for some type τ.

The typing rules for Mini-**CML** are divided into two groups. The rules for the surface language are given in Figure B.1. There are two rules for `let`: the rule (τ-**let-val**) applies in the non-expansive case (in the syntax of Mini-**CML**, this is when the bound expression is in VAL); the rule (τ-**let**) applies when the expression is expansive (not a value). There are also rules for typing channel names, and pair expressions. In addition to these core typing rules, there are rules for the other syntactic forms (see Figure B.2). Given the appropriate environment, these rules can be derived from rule (τ-**app**) (rule (τ-**const**) in the case of Λ). It is useful, however, to include them explicitly. As before, it is worth noting that the syntactic form of a term uniquely determines which typing rule applies.

In order that the typing of constants be sensible, we impose a typability restriction on the definitions of δ and TypeOf. If $\text{TypeOf}(b) \succ (\tau' \rightarrow \tau)$ and $\text{TE} \vdash v : \tau'$, then $\delta(b, v)$ is defined and $\text{TE} \vdash \delta(b, v) : \tau$. It is worth noting that the δ rules we defined for the concurrency constants respect this restriction.

B.5.2 Process typings

A *process typing* is a finite map from process identifiers to types:

$$
\text{PT} \in \text{PROCTY} = \text{PROCID} \xrightarrow{\text{fin}} \text{TY}
$$

Typing judgements are extended to process configurations by the following definition.

Definition B.9 A well-formed configuration $\mathcal{C}, \mathcal{K}, \mathcal{P}$ has type PT under a channel typing CT, written

$$
\text{CT} \vdash \mathcal{C}, \mathcal{K}, \mathcal{P} : \text{PT}
$$

if the following hold:

$$\frac{\mathrm{TypeOf}(b) \succ \tau}{\mathrm{TE} \vdash b : \tau} \qquad (\tau\text{-}\mathbf{const})$$

$$\frac{x \in \mathrm{dom}(\mathrm{VT}) \quad \mathrm{VT}(x) \succ \tau}{(\mathrm{VT}, \mathrm{CT}) \vdash x : \tau} \qquad (\tau\text{-}\mathbf{var})$$

$$\frac{\mathrm{TE} \vdash e_1 : (\tau' \to \tau) \quad \mathrm{TE} \vdash e_2 : \tau'}{\mathrm{TE} \vdash (e_1 \ e_2) : \tau} \qquad (\tau\text{-}\mathbf{app})$$

$$\frac{\mathrm{TE} \pm \{x \mapsto \tau\} \vdash e : \tau'}{\mathrm{TE} \vdash \mathbf{fn} \ x \mathbf{=>} e : (\tau \to \tau')} \qquad (\tau\text{-}\mathbf{abs})$$

$$\frac{\mathrm{TE} \vdash e_1 : \tau_1 \quad \mathrm{TE} \vdash e_2 : \tau_2}{\mathrm{TE} \vdash (e_1, e_2) : (\tau_1 \times \tau_2)} \qquad (\tau\text{-}\mathbf{pair})$$

$$\frac{\mathrm{TE} \vdash v : \tau' \quad \mathrm{TE} \pm \{x \mapsto \mathrm{CLOS}_{\mathrm{TE}}(\tau')\} \vdash e : \tau}{\mathrm{TE} \vdash \mathbf{let} \ x \mathbf{=} v \ \mathbf{in} \ e : \tau} \qquad (\tau\text{-}\mathbf{let\text{-}val})$$

$$\frac{\mathrm{TE} \vdash e_1 : \tau' \quad \mathrm{TE} \pm \{x \mapsto \tau'\} \vdash e_2 : \tau}{\mathrm{TE} \vdash \mathbf{let} \ x \mathbf{=} e_1 \ \mathbf{in} \ e_2 : \tau} \qquad (\tau\text{-}\mathbf{let})$$

$$\frac{\mathrm{TE} \vdash e : (\mathrm{unit} \to \tau)}{\mathrm{TE} \vdash \mathbf{spawn} \ e : \mathrm{unit}} \qquad (\tau\text{-}\mathbf{spawn})$$

$$\frac{\mathrm{TE} \vdash e : \tau \ \mathrm{event}}{\mathrm{TE} \vdash \mathbf{sync} \ e : \tau} \qquad (\tau\text{-}\mathbf{sync})$$

Figure B.1: Type inference rules for the surface language

- $\mathcal{K} \subseteq \mathrm{dom}(\mathrm{CT})$,

- $\mathrm{dom}(\mathcal{P}) \subseteq \mathrm{dom}(\mathrm{PT})$, and

- for every $\langle \pi, e \rangle \in \mathcal{P}$, $(\{\}, \mathrm{CT}) \vdash e : \mathrm{PT}(\pi)$.

For **CML**, where spawn requires a (unit $\to$ unit) argument, the process typing is $\mathrm{PT}(\pi) = \mathrm{unit}$ for all $\pi \in \mathrm{dom}(\mathcal{P})$.

$$\frac{\text{CT}(\kappa) = \tau}{(\text{VT}, \text{CT}) \vdash \kappa : \tau} \qquad (\tau\text{-}\mathbf{chvar})$$

$$\frac{\text{TE} \vdash \kappa : \tau \text{ chan}}{\text{TE} \vdash \kappa? : \tau \text{ event}} \qquad (\tau\text{-}\mathbf{input})$$

$$\frac{\text{TE} \vdash \kappa : \tau \text{ chan} \quad \text{TE} \vdash v : \tau}{\text{TE} \vdash \kappa!v : \text{unit event}} \qquad (\tau\text{-}\mathbf{output})$$

$$\frac{\text{TE} \vdash ev : \tau' \text{ event} \quad \text{TE} \vdash e : (\tau' \to \tau)}{\text{TE} \vdash ev \Rightarrow e : \tau \text{ event}} \qquad (\tau\text{-}\mathbf{wrap})$$

$$\frac{\text{TE} \vdash e : \tau \text{ event}}{\text{TE} \vdash \mathbf{N} e : \tau \text{ event}} \qquad (\tau\text{-}\mathbf{nack})$$

$$\frac{\text{TE} \vdash ev_1 : \tau \text{ event} \quad \text{TE} \vdash ev_2 : \tau \text{ event}}{\text{TE} \vdash (ev_1 \oplus ev_2) : \tau \text{ event}} \qquad (\tau\text{-}\mathbf{choice})$$

$$\frac{\text{TE} \vdash e : \tau \text{ event}}{\text{TE} \vdash e \mid \gamma : \tau \text{ event}} \qquad (\tau\text{-}\mathbf{abort})$$

$$\frac{\forall \alpha . \alpha \text{ event} \succ \tau}{\text{TE} \vdash \Lambda : \tau} \qquad (\tau\text{-}\mathbf{never})$$

$$\frac{}{\text{TE} \vdash \gamma : \text{unit}} \qquad (\tau\text{-}\mathbf{condition})$$

Figure B.2: Other type inference rules for Mini-**CML**

B.5.3 Type soundness

This section presents a statement of the soundness of the above type system with respect to the dynamic semantics of Section B.3. To prove these results, we first show that evaluation preserves types (also called *subject reduction*), then we characterize run-time type errors (called "*stuck states*") and show that stuck states are untypable. This allows us to conclude that well-typed programs cannot go wrong.

The first step in this process is to show that the sequential evaluation relation preserves the types of expressions.

Theorem B.1 (Sequential type preservation) For any type environment TE, expression e_1 and type τ, such that $\text{TE} \vdash e_1 : \tau$, if $e_1 \hookrightarrow e_2$ then $\text{TE} \vdash e_2 : \tau$.

This result is then extended to concurrent evaluation and process typings.

Theorem B.2 (Concurrent type preservation) If a configuration $\mathcal{C}, \mathcal{K}, \mathcal{P}$ is well-formed with

$$\mathcal{C}, \mathcal{K}, \mathcal{P} \Rightarrow \mathcal{C}', \mathcal{K}', \mathcal{P}'$$

and, for some channel typing CT,

$$\mathrm{CT} \vdash \mathcal{C}, \mathcal{K}, \mathcal{P} : \mathrm{PT}$$

then there is a channel typing CT' and a process typing PT', such that the following hold:

- $\mathrm{CT} \subseteq \mathrm{CT}'$,

- $\mathrm{PT} \subseteq \mathrm{PT}'$, and

- $\mathrm{CT}' \vdash \mathcal{C}', \mathcal{K}', \mathcal{P}' : \mathrm{PT}'$.

- $\mathrm{CT}' \vdash \mathcal{C}, \mathcal{K}, \mathcal{P} : \mathrm{PT}'$.

With these results, it is fairly easy to show soundness results:

Theorem B.3 (Syntactic soundness) Let e be a program, with $\vdash e : \tau$. Then, for any $T \in \mathrm{Comp}(e)$, $\pi \in \mathrm{Procs}(T)$, with $\mathcal{C}_i, \mathcal{K}_i, \mathcal{P}_i$ the first occurrence of π in T, there exists a CT and PT, such that $\mathrm{CT} \vdash \mathcal{C}_i, \mathcal{K}_i, \mathcal{P}_i : \mathrm{PT}$, and either

- $\pi \Uparrow_T$ or

- $\pi \Downarrow_T v$ and there exists an extension CT' of CT with $(\{\}, \mathrm{CT}') \vdash v : \mathrm{PT}(\pi)$.

To state more traditional soundness results, we need to define a notion of evaluation that distinguishes those processes that have run-time type errors.

Definition B.10 For a computation T, we define the *evaluation* of a process π in T by the following partial function:

$$\mathrm{eval}_T(\pi) = \begin{cases} \mathbf{WRONG} & \textit{if } \pi \textit{ is stuck in some configuration in } T \\ v & \textit{if } \pi \Downarrow_T v \end{cases}$$

Theorem B.4 (Soundness) If e is a program with $\vdash e : \tau$, then for any computation $T \in \mathrm{Comp}(e)$ and any process ID $\pi \in \mathrm{Procs}(T)$, the following hold:

(Strong soundness) If $\mathrm{eval}_T(\pi) = v$, and $\mathcal{C}_i, \mathcal{K}_i, \mathcal{P}_i$ is the first occurrence of π in T, then for any CT and PT, such that $\mathrm{CT} \vdash \mathcal{C}_i, \mathcal{K}_i, \mathcal{P}_i : \mathrm{PT}$ and $\mathrm{PT}(\pi_0) = \tau$, there is an extension CT' of CT, such that $(\{\}, \mathrm{CT}') \vdash v : \mathrm{PT}(\pi)$.

(Weak soundness) $\mathrm{eval}_T(\pi) \neq \mathbf{WRONG}$

Notes

The semantics presented here serves two purposes: most important, it provides a reference to guide the implementation of **CML**, and it provides a base to prove the type soundness of the primitives.[3] There are other semantics treatments of **CML** (or at least subsets of **CML**). Mosses and Musicante have defined an *action semantics* for **CML** [MM94], and Ferreira, Hennessy and Jeffrey have explored the semantics of **CML** from a traditional process cacluli point of view [FHJ96]. This latter work is probably the right basis for developing tools for reasoning about **CML** programs.

This appendix is a revised version of the semantics for λ_{cv} that is presented in the author's Ph.D. dissertation [Rep92]. The language λ_{cv} is similar in scope to Mini-**CML**, except that it reflects the design of **CML** circa 1991. The most significant difference is that λ_{cv} uses *imperative types* to avoid problems with polymorphic typing of channels. The other main difference is that the wrapAbort combinator of λ_{cv} was replaced by withNack in Mini-**CML**. The theorems of Section B.5.3 are proved using the "syntactic" approach of Wright and Felleisen [WF91]; the author's dissertation includes the proofs for the λ_{cv} version of the semantics [Rep92]. There is also a discussion of extending λ_{cv} with various features, such as references, exceptions, and the joinEvt event constructor (which was called threadWait).

Kwiatkowska has written a nice survey of fairness issues [Kwi89]. In her taxonomy, the first restriction of Definition B.8 is *strong process fairness* and the second is *strong event fairness*.

---

[3] With the adoption of the value restriction in **SML**'97, the type soundness of **CML** is less in question.

Bibliography

[ASS85] Abelson, H., G. Sussman, and J. Sussman. *Structure and Interpretation of Computer Programs.* The MIT Press, Cambridge, MA, 1985.

[AB86] Abramsky, S. and R. Bornat. Pascal-m: A language for loosely coupled distributed systems. In Y. Paker and J.-P. Verjus (eds.), *Distributed Computing Systems,* pp. 163–189. Academic Press, New York, NY, 1986.

[Agh86] Agha, G. *Actors: A Model of Concurrent Computation in Distributed Systems.* The MIT Press, Cambridge, MA, 1986.

[And91] Andrews, G. R. *Concurrent Programming: Principles and Practice.* Benjamin/Cummings, Redwood City, CA, 1991.

[AO93] Andrews, G. R. and R. A. Olsson. *The SR Programming Language: Concurrency in Practice.* Benjamin/Cummings, Redwood City, CA, 1993.

[AOCE88] Andrews, G. R., R. A. Olsson, M. Coffin, and I. Elshoff. An overview of the SR language and implementation. *ACM Transactions on Programming Languages and Systems,* **10**(7), January 1988, pp. 51–86.

[AS83] Andrews., G. R. and F. B. Schneider. Concepts and notations for concurrent programming. *ACM Computing Surveys,* **15**(1), March 1983, pp. 3–43.

[AJ89] Appel, A. W. and T. Jim. Continuation-passing, closure-passing style. In *Conference Record of the 16th Annual ACM Symposium on Principles of Programming Languages,* January 1989, pp. 293–302.

[AM87] Appel, A. W. and D. B. MacQueen. A Standard ML compiler. In *Functional Programming Languages and Computer Architecture,* vol. 274 of *Lecture Notes in Computer Science.* Springer-Verlag, New York, NY, September 1987, pp. 301–324.

[AM91] Appel, A. W. and D. B. MacQueen. Standard ML of New Jersey. In *Programming Language Implementation and Logic Programming,* vol. 528 of *Lecture Notes in Computer Science.* Springer-Verlag, New York, NY, August 1991, pp. 1–26.

[App92] Appel, A. W. *Compiling with Continuations.* Cambridge University Press, Cambridge, England, 1992.

[AVWW96] Armstrong, J., R. Virding, C. Wikström, and M. Williams. *Concurrent Programming in ERLANG.* Prentice Hall, Englewood Cliffs, NJ, 2nd edition, 1996.

[AG98] Arnold, K. and J. Gosling. *The Java Programming Language.* Addison-Wesley, Reading, MA, 2nd edition, 1998.

[ANP89] Arvind, R. S. Nikhil, and K. K. Pingali. I-structures: Data structures for parallel computing. *ACM Transactions on Programming Languages and Systems,* **11**(4), October 1989, pp. 598–632.

[Bag89] Bagrodia, R. Synchronization of asynchronous processes in CSP. *ACM Transactions on*

Programming Languages and Systems, **11**(4), October 1989, pp. 585–597.

[BST89] Bal, H. E., J. G. Steiner, and A. S. Tanenbaum. Programming languages for distributed computing systems. *ACM Computing Surveys*, **21**(3), September 1989, pp. 261–322.

[BNA91] Barth, P., R. S. Nikhil, and Arvind. M-structures: Extending a parallel, non-strict, functional language with state. In *Functional Programming Languages and Computer Architecture*, vol. 523 of *Lecture Notes in Computer Science*. Springer-Verlag, New York, NY, August 1991, pp. 538–568.

[BMT92] Berry, D., R. Milner, and D. N. Turner. A semantics for ML concurrency primitives. In *Conference Record of the 19th Annual ACM Symposium on Principles of Programming Languages*, January 1992, pp. 119–129.

[BCJ+90] Birman, K. P., R. Cooper, T. A. Joseph, K. Marzullo, M. Makpangou, K. Kane, F. Schmuck, and M. Wood. *The ISIS system manual, version 2.0*. Department of Computer Science, Cornell University, Ithaca, NY, March 1990.

[BJ87] Birman, K. P. and T. A. Joseph. Reliable communication in the presence of failures. *ACM Transactions on Computer Systems*, **5**(1), February 1987, pp. 47–76.

[Bv93] Birman, K. P. and R. van Renesse (eds.). *Reliable Distributed Computing with the Isis Toolkit*. IEEE Computer Society Press, Los Alamitos, CA, 1993.

[Bir91] Birrell, A. D. An introduction to programming with threads. In G. Nelson (ed.), *Systems Programming with Modula-3*, chapter 4, pp. 88–118. Prentice Hall, Englewood Cliffs, NJ, 1991. Also available as *DEC SRC Research Report 35*.

[BCGL87] Bjornson, R., N. Carriero, D. Gelernter, and J. Leichter. Linda, the portable parallel. *Technical Report YALEU/DCS/TR-520*, Department of Computer Science, Yale University, New Haven, CT, February 1987.

[Bor86] Bornat, R. A protocol for generalized occam. *Software – Practice and Experience*, **16**(9), September 1986, pp. 783–799.

[BLL92] Bricker, A., M. Litzkow, and M. Livny. Condor technical report. *Technical Report CS-TR-92-1069*, Computer Sciences Department, University of Wisconsin at Madison, Madison, WI, January 1992.

[Bri77] Brinch Hansen, P. *The Architecture of Concurrent Programs*. Prentice Hall, Englewood Cliffs, NJ, 1977.

[Bri89] Brinch Hansen, P. The Joyce language report. *Software – Practice and Experience*, **19**(6), June 1989, pp. 553–578.

[BD80] Bryant, R. and J. B. Dennis. Concurrent programming. In *Operating Systems Engineering; Proceedings of the 14th IBM Computer Science Symposium*, vol. 143 of *Lecture Notes in Computer Science*. Springer-Verlag, New York, NY, October 1980, pp. 426–451.

[BS83] Buckley, G. N. and A. Silberschatz. An effective implementation for the generalized input-output construct of CSP. *ACM Transactions on Programming Languages and Systems*, **5**(2), April 1983, pp. 223–235.

[Bur88] Burns, A. *Programming in occam 2*. Addison-Wesley, Reading, MA, 1988.

[CP85] Cardelli, L. and R. Pike. Squeak: A language for communicating with mice. In *SIGGRAPH '85*, July 1985, pp. 199–204.

[Car84] Cardelli, L. An implementation model of rendezvous communication. In *Seminar on Concurrency*, vol. 197 of *Lecture Notes in Computer Science*. Springer-Verlag, New York, NY, July 1984, pp. 449–457.

[Car86] Cardelli, L. Amber. In *Combinators and Functional Programming Languages*, vol. 242 of *Lecture Notes in Computer Science*. Springer-Verlag, New York, NY, July 1986, pp. 21–47.

[CG89a] Carriero, N. and D. Gelernter. How to write parallel programs: A guide to the perplexed. *ACM Computing Surveys*, **21**(3), September 1989, pp. 323–357.

[CG89b] Carriero, N. and D. Gelernter. Linda in context. *Communications of the ACM*, **32**(4), April 1989, pp. 444–458.

[CG90] Carriero, N. and D. Gelernter. *How to Write Parallel Programs: A First Course*. The MIT Press, Cambridge, MA, 1990.

[CL98] Chan, P. and R. Lee. *The Java Class Libraries*, vol. 2. Addison-Wesley, Reading, MA, 2nd edition, 1998.

[CM88] Chandy, K. M. and J. Misra. *Parallel Program Design: A Foundation*. Addison-Wesley, Reading, MA, 1988.

[Cha87] Charlesworth, A. The multiway rendezvous. *ACM Transactions on Programming Languages and Systems*, **9**(2), July 1987, pp. 350–366.

[CD88] Cooper, E. C. and R. P. Draves. C threads. *Technical Report CMU-CS-88-54*, School of Computer Science, Carnegie Mellon University, February 1988.

[CHL91] Cooper, E. C., R. Harper, and P. Lee. The Fox project: Advanced development of system software. *Technical Report CMU-CS-91-178*, School of Computer Science, Carnegie Mellon University, August 1991.

[CM90] Cooper, E. C. and J. G. Morrisett. Adding threads to Standard ML. *Technical Report CMU-CS-90-186*, School of Computer Science, Carnegie Mellon University, December 1990.

[CK92] Cooper, R. and C. D. Krumvieda. Distributed programming with asynchronous ordered channels in Distributed ML. In *Proceedings of the 1992 ACM SIGPLAN Workshop on ML and its Applications*, June 1992, pp. 134–148.

[Čub94a] Čubrić, M. *The Bevaviour of Dataflow Networks with Finite Buffers*. Ph.D. dissertation, Department of Computer Science, Concordia University, Montréal, Canada, 1994.

[Čub94b] Čubrić, M. Dataflow language embedded in CML. *ACAPS Technical Memo 83*, McGill University, School of Computer Science, Montréal, Canada, February 1994.

[DoD83] *Reference Manual for the Ada Programming Language*, January 1983.

[DHM91] Duba, B., R. Harper, and D. MacQueen. Type-checking first-class continuations. In *Conference Record of the 18th Annual ACM Symposium on Principles of Programming Languages*, January 1991, pp. 163–173.

[DH89] Dybvig, R. K. and R. Hieb. Engines from continuations. *Computing Languages*, **14**(2), 1989, pp. 109–123.

[EFK89] Evangelist, M., N. Francez, and S. Katz. Multiparty interactions for interprocess communication and synchronization. *IEEE Transactions on Software Engineering*, **15**(11), November 1989, pp. 1417–1426.

[Fel79] Feldman, S. I. Make — a program for maintaining computer programs. *Software – Practice and Experience*, **9**(4), April 1979, pp. 255–265.

[Fel87] Felleisen, M. Reflections on Landin's J-operator: A partly historical note. *Computer Languages*, **12**(3/4), 1987, pp. 197–207.

[FHJ96] Ferreira, W., M. Hennessy, and A. Jeffrey. A theory of weak bisimulation for core CML. In *Proceedings of the 1996 ACM SIGPLAN International Conference on Functional Programming*, May 1996, pp. 201–212.

[FO93] Forsling, M. and M. Ohlsson. Robust control logic environment using Concurrent ML. Master's dissertation, Royal Institute of Technology, Stockholm, Sweden, February 1993.

[Fow90] Fowler, G. S. A case for make. *Software – Practice and Experience*, **20**(S1), June 1990, pp. 35–46.

[Fow93] Fowler, G. S. The shell as a service. In *Cincinnati USENIX Conference Proceedings*. USENIX Association, June 1993, pp. 267–277.

[Fra86] Francez, N. *Fairness*. Springer-Verlag, New York, NY, 1986.

[FHT86] Francez, N., B. Hailpern, and G. Taubenfeld. Script: A communication abstraction mechanism and its verification. *Science of Computer Programming*, **6**, 1986, pp. 35–88.

[GHJV95] Gamma, E., R. Helm, R. Johnson, and J. Vlissides. *Design Patterns*. Addison-Wesley, Reading, MA, 1995.

[GR91] Gansner, E. R. and J. H. Reppy. eXene. In *Proceedings of the 1991 CMU Workshop on*

Standard ML, Carnegie Mellon University, September 1991.

[GR92] Gansner, E. R. and J. H. Reppy. A foundation for user interface construction. In B. A. Myers (ed.), *Languages for Developing User Interfaces*, pp. 239–260. Jones & Bartlett, Boston, MA, 1992.

[GR93] Gansner, E. R. and J. H. Reppy. *A Multi-threaded Higher-order User Interface Toolkit*, vol. 1 of *Software Trends*, pp. 61–80. John Wiley & Sons, New York, NY, 1993.

[GR04] Gansner, E. R. and J. H. Reppy (eds.). *The Standard ML Basis Library*. Cambridge University Press, Cambridge, England, 2004.

[GNN97] Gasser, K. L. S., F. Nielson, and H. R. Nielson. Systematic realisation of control flow analyses for CML. In *Proceedings of the 1997 ACM SIGPLAN International Conference on Functional Programming*, June 1997, pp. 38–51.

[GM88] Gehani, N. H. and A. D. McGettrick (eds.). *Concurrent Programming*. Addison-Wesley, Reading, MA, 1988.

[GR86] Gehani, N. H. and W. D. Roome. Concurrent C. *Software – Practice and Experience*, **16**(9), September 1986, pp. 821–844.

[Gel85] Gelernter, D. Generative communication in Linda. *ACM Transactions on Programming Languages and Systems*, **7**(1), January 1985, pp. 80–112.

[GB82] Gelernter, D. and A. J. Bernstein. Distributed communication via global buffer. In *ACM SIGACT-SIGOPS Symposium on Principles of Distributed Computing*, August 1982, pp. 10–18.

[GMP89] Giacalone, A., P. Mishra, and S. Prasad. Facile: A symmetric integration of concurrent and functional programming. In *TAPSOFT'89 (vol. 2)*, vol. 352 of *Lecture Notes in Computer Science*. Springer-Verlag, New York, NY, March 1989, pp. 184–209.

[Gor79] Gordon, M. J. C. *The Denotational Description of Programming Languages*. Springer-Verlag, New York, NY, 1979.

[Haa90] Haahr, D. Montage: Breaking windows into small pieces. In *USENIX Summer Conference*, June 1990, pp. 289–297.

[Hal93] Halbwachs, N. *Synchronous Programming of Reactive Systems*. Kluwer Academic Publishers, Boston, MA, 1993.

[HTA+93] Hall, M., M. Towfiq, G. Arnold, D. Treadwell, and H. Sanders. *Windows Sockets: An Open Interface for Network Programming under Microsoft Windows (Version 1.1)*, January 1993.

[HM90] Halpern, J. Y. and Y. Moses. Knowledge and common knowledge in a distributed environment. *Journal of the ACM*, **37**(3), July 1990, pp. 549–587. An earlier version appeared in the *Proceedings of the 3rd ACM Conference on Principles of Distributed Computing*.

[Hal85] Halstead, Jr., R. H. Multilisp: A language for concurrent symbolic computation. *ACM Transactions on Programming Languages and Systems*, **7**(4), October 1985, pp. 501–538.

[Har86] Harper, R. Introduction to Standard ML. *Technical Report ECS-LFCS-86-14*, Laboratory for Foundations of Computer Science, Department of Computer Science, University of Edinburgh, August 1986.

[Har93] Harrison, R. *Abstract Data Types in Standard ML*. John Wiley & Sons, New York, NY, 1993.

[HJT+93] Hauser, C., C. Jacobi, M. Theimer, B. Welch, and M. Weiser. Using threads in interactive systems: A case study. In *Proceedings of the 14th ACM Symposium on Operating System Principles*, December 1993, pp. 94–105.

[HFW84] Haynes, C. T., D. P. Friedman, and M. Wand. Continuations and coroutines. In *Conference Record of the 1984 ACM Symposium on Lisp and Functional Programming*, July 1984, pp. 293–298.

[Hen88] Hennessy, M. *Algebraic Theory of Processes*. The MIT Press, Cambridge, MA, 1988.

[Hoa74] Hoare, C. A. R. Monitors: An operating system concept. *Communications of the ACM*,

17(10), October 1974, pp. 549–557.

[Hoa78] Hoare, C. A. R. Communicating sequential processes. *Communications of the ACM*, 21(8), August 1978, pp. 666–677.

[Hoa85] Hoare, C. A. R. *Communicating Sequential Processes*. Prentice Hall, Englewood Cliffs, NJ, 1985.

[Hol83a] Holmström, S. PFL: A functional language for parallel programming. In *Declarative Programming Workshop*, April 1983, pp. 114–139.

[Hol83b] Holt, R. C. *Concurrent Euclid, the UNIX System, and Tunis*. Addison-Wesley, Reading, MA, 1983.

[Hud89] Hudak, P. Conception, evolution, and application of functional programming languages. *ACM Computing Surveys*, 21(3), September 1989, pp. 359–411.

[HS88] Hudak, P. and R. S. Sundaresh. On the expressiveness of purely functional I/O systems. *Technical Report YALEU/DCS/RR-665*, Department of Computer Science, Yale University, New Haven, CT, 1988.

[INM84] INMOS Limited. *Occam Programming Manual*. Prentice Hall, Englewood Cliffs, NJ, 1984.

[KM77] Kahn, G. and D. B. MacQueen. Coroutines and networks of parallel processes. In *Information Processing 77*, August 1977, pp. 993–998.

[Kna92] Knabe, F. A distributed protocol for channel-based communication with choice. *Technical Report ECRC-92-16*, European Computer-industry Research Center, October 1992.

[KH88] Kranz, D. A. and R. H. Halstead, Jr. Mul-T: A high-performance parallel Lisp. In *Proceedings of the SIGPLAN'89 Conference on Programming Language Design and Implementation*, June 1988, pp. 81–90.

[KR95] Krishnamurthy, B. and D. S. Rosenblum. Yeast: A general purpose event-action system. *IEEE Transactions on Software Engineering*, 20(9), October 1995, pp. 845–857.

[Kru91] Krumvieda, C. D. DML: Packaging high-level distributed abstractions in SML. In *Proceedings of the 1991 CMU Workshop on Standard ML*, September 1991.

[Kru92] Krumvieda, C. D. Expressing fault-tolerant and consistency-preserving programs in Distributed ML. In *Proceedings of the 1992 ACM SIGPLAN Workshop on ML and its Applications*, June 1992, pp. 157–162.

[Kru93] Krumvieda, C. D. *Distributed ML: Abstractions for Efficient and Fault-Tolerant Programming*. Ph.D. dissertation, Department of Computer Science, Cornell University, Ithaca, NY, August 1993. Available as Technical Report TR 93-1376.

[Kwi89] Kwiatkowska, M. Z. Survey of fairness notions. *Information and Software Technology*, 31(7), September 1989, pp. 371–386.

[LR80] Lampson, B. W. and D. D. Redell. Experience with processes and monitors in Mesa. *Communications of the ACM*, 23(2), February 1980, pp. 105–116.

[Lan65] Landin, P. J. A correspondence between Algol 60 and Church's lambda notation: Part I. *Communications of the ACM*, 8(2), February 1965, pp. 89–101.

[LHG86] Liskov, B., M. Herlihy, and L. Gilbert. Limitations of synchronous communication with static process structure in langauges for distributed programming. In *Conference Record of the 13th Annual ACM Symposium on Principles of Programming Languages*, January 1986, pp. 150–159.

[LS83] Liskov, B. and R. Scheifler. Guardians and actions: Linguistic support for robust, distributed programs. *ACM Transactions on Programming Languages and Systems*, 5(3), July 1983, pp. 381–404.

[MN91] Manasse, M. S. and G. Nelson. Trestle reference manual. *Technical Report 68*, Digital System Research Center, Palo Alto, CA, December 1991.

[MP92] Manna, Z. and A. Pnueli. *The Temporal Logic of Reactive and Concurrent Systems (Specification)*, vol. 1. Springer-Verlag, New York, NY, 1992.

[McI90] McIlroy, M. D. Squinting at power series. *Software – Practice and Experience*, **20**(7), July 1990, pp. 661–683.

[Mil90] Milewski, J. Functional data structures as updatable objects. *IEEE Transactions on Software Engineering*, **16**(12), December 1990, pp. 1427–1432.

[MT91] Milner, R. and M. Tofte. *Commentary on Standard ML*. The MIT Press, Cambridge, MA, 1991.

[MTH90] Milner, R., M. Tofte, and R. Harper. *The Definition of Standard ML*. The MIT Press, Cambridge, MA, 1990.

[Mil89] Milner, R. *Communication and Concurrency*. Prentice Hall, Englewood Cliffs, NJ, 1989.

[MPW89a] Milner, R., J. Parrow, and D. Walker. A calculus of mobile processes, Part I. *Technical Report ECS-LFCS-89-85*, Laboratory for Foundations of Computer Science, Department of Computer Science, University of Edinburgh, June 1989.

[MPW89b] Milner, R., J. Parrow, and D. Walker. A calculus of mobile processes, Part II. *Technical Report ECS-LFCS-89-86*, Laboratory for Foundations of Computer Science, Department of Computer Science, University of Edinburgh, June 1989.

[MTHM97] Milner, R., M. Tofte, R. Harper, and D. MacQueen. *The Definition of Standard ML — Revised 1997*. The MIT Press, Cambridge, MA, 1997.

[MMS79] Mitchell, J. G., W. Maybury, and R. Sweet. *Mesa Language Manual (Version 5.0)*. Xerox PARC, April 1979.

[MKH91] Mohr, E., D. A. Kranz, and R. H. Halstead, Jr. Lazy task creation: A technique for increasing the granularity of parallel programs. *IEEE Transactions on Parallel and Distributed Systems*, **2**(3), July 1991, pp. 264–280. A longer version is available as DEC CRL report 90/7, November 1990.

[MT93] Morrisett, J. G. and A. Tolmach. Procs and locks: A portable multiprocessing platform for Standard ML of New Jersey. In *Proceedings of the 4th ACM SIGPLAN Symposium on Principles & Practice of Parallel Programming*, April 1993, pp. 198–207. An earlier version is available as CMU report CMU-CS-92-155.

[MM94] Mosses, P. D. and M. Musicante. An action semantics for ML concurrency primitives. In *FME'94*, October 1994.

[Mye86] Myers, B. A. A complete and efficient implementation of covered windows. *IEEE Computer*, **19**(9), September 1986, pp. 57–67.

[Nel91] Nelson, G. (ed.). *Systems Programming with Modula-3*. Prentice Hall, Englewood Cliffs, NJ, 1991.

[NN93] Nielson, F. and H. R. Nielson. From CML to process algebras. In *CONCUR'93 — 4th International Conference on Concurrency Theory*, vol. 715 of *Lecture Notes in Computer Science*. Springer-Verlag, New York, NY, August 1993, pp. 493–508.

[NN94] Nielson, H. R. and F. Nielson. Higher-order concurrent programs with finite communication topology. In *Conference Record of the 21st Annual ACM Symposium on Principles of Programming Languages*, January 1994, pp. 84–97.

[Nik91] Nikhil, R. S. *ID Language Reference Manual*. Laboratory for Computer Science, MIT, Cambridge, MA, July 1991.

[Oka98] Okasaki, C. *Purely Functional Data Structures*. Cambridge University Press, Cambridge, England, 1998.

[OT91] Oram, A. and S. Talbott. *Managing Projects with make*. O'Reilly & Associates, Sebastopol, CA, 2nd edition, 1991.

[PR97] Panangaden, P. and J. H. Reppy. The essence of Concurrent ML. In F. Nielson (ed.), *ML with Concurrency*, chapter 1. Springer-Verlag, New York, NY, 1997.

[PT92] Panangaden, P. and K. Taylor. Concurrent common knowledge: Defining agreement for asynchronous systems. *Distributed Computing*, 1992, pp. 73–93.

[Pau96] Paulson, L. C. *ML for the Working Programmer*. Cambridge University Press, Cambridge,

England, 2nd edition, 1996.

[Pel92] Pellerin, C. The concurrent constraint programming language taskell. Master's dissertation, School of Computer Science, McGill University, Montréal, Québec, Canada, January 1992.

[PF95] Peyton Jones, S. and S. Finne. Composing Haggis. In *Proceedings of the Fifth Eurographics Workshop on Programming Paradigms in Graphics*, September 1995.

[PGF96] Peyton Jones, S., A. Gordon, and S. Finne. Concurrent haskell. In *Conference Record of the 23rd Annual ACM Symposium on Principles of Programming Languages*, January 1996, pp. 295–308.

[PT97] Pierce, B. C. and D. N. Turner. Pict: A programming language based on the pi-calculus. *Technical Report CSCI 476*, Computer Science Department, Indiana University, Bloomington, IN, 1997.

[Pik83] Pike, R. Graphics in overlapping bitmap layers. *ACM Transactions on Graphics*, **2**(2), April 1983, pp. 135–160.

[Pik89a] Pike, R. A concurrent window system. *Computing Systems*, **2**(2), 1989, pp. 133–153.

[Pik89b] Pike, R. Newsqueak: A language for communicating with mice. *Technical Report 143*, AT&T Bell Laboratories, April 1989.

[Pik90] Pike, R. The implementation of Newsqueak. *Software – Practice and Experience*, **20**(7), July 1990, pp. 649–659.

[Pik94] Pike, R. Acme: A user interface for programmers. In *Proceedings of the Winter 1994 USENIX Conference*, January 1994, pp. 223–234.

[PvE93] Plasmeijer, R. and M. van Eekelen. *Functional Programming and Parallel Graph Rewriting*. Addison-Wesley, Reading, MA, 1993.

[Puc98] Pucella, R. Reactive programming in Standard ML. In *Proceedings of the 1998 International Conference on Computer Languages*, May 1998, pp. 48–57.

[Ram90] Ramsey, N. Concurrent programming in ML. *Technical Report CS-TR-262-90*, Department of Computer Science, Princeton University, April 1990.

[Rea89] Reade, C. *Elements of Functional Programming*. Addison-Wesley, Reading, MA, 1989.

[RC86] Rees, J. and W. Clinger (eds.). The revised[3] report on the algorithmic language Scheme. *SIGPLAN Notices*, **21**(12), December 1986, pp. 37–43.

[Rep88] Reppy, J. H. Synchronous operations as first-class values. In *Proceedings of the SIGPLAN'88 Conference on Programming Language Design and Implementation*, June 1988, pp. 250–259.

[Rep89] Reppy, J. H. First-class synchronous operations in Standard ML. *Technical Report TR 89-1068*, Department of Computer Science, Cornell University, Ithaca, NY, December 1989.

[Rep90] Reppy, J. H. Asynchronous signals in Standard ML. *Technical Report TR 90-1144*, Department of Computer Science, Cornell University, Ithaca, NY, August 1990.

[Rep91a] Reppy, J. H. CML: A higher-order concurrent language. In *Proceedings of the SIGPLAN'91 Conference on Programming Language Design and Implementation*, June 1991, pp. 293–305.

[Rep91b] Reppy, J. H. An operational semantics of first-class synchronous operations. *Technical Report TR 91-1232*, Department of Computer Science, Cornell University, Ithaca, NY, August 1991.

[Rep92] Reppy, J. H. *Higher-order Concurrency*. Ph.D. dissertation, Department of Computer Science, Cornell University, Ithaca, NY, January 1992. Available as Technical Report TR 92-1285.

[RG86] Reppy, J. H. and E. R. Gansner. A foundation for programming environments. In *Proceedings of the ACM SIGSOFT/SIGPLAN Software Engineering Symposium on Practical Software Development Environments*, December 1986, pp. 218–227.

[Rey93] Reynolds, J. C. The discoveries of continuations. *Lisp and Symbolic Computation*, **6**(3/4),

November 1993, pp. 233–247.

[RLW85] Rovner, P., R. Levin, and J. Wick. On extending Modula-2 for building large, integrated systems. *Technical Report 3*, Digital System Research Center, Palo Alto, CA, January 1985.

[STW93] Schmidtmann, C., M. Tao, and S. Watt. Design and implementation of a multi-threaded Xlib. In *Proceedings of the 1993 Winter USENIX Conference*, January 1993, pp. 193–203.

[Sha94] Shao, Z. *Compiling Standard ML for Efficient Execution on Modern Machines*. Ph.D. dissertation, Department of Computer Science, Princeton University, Princeton, NJ, November 1994.

[SA94] Shao, Z. and A. W. Appel. Space-efficient closure representations. In *Conference record of the 1994 ACM Conference on Lisp and Functional Programming*, June 1994, pp. 150–161.

[Sha89] Shapiro, E. The family of concurrent logic programming languages. *ACM Computing Surveys*, **21**(3), September 1989, pp. 413–510.

[Shi97] Shivers, O. Continuations and threads: Expressing machine concurrency directly in advanced languages. In *Proceedings of the Second ACM SIGPLAN Workshop on Continuations*, January 1997.

[SC91] Siegel, E. H. and E. C. Cooper. Implementing distributed Linda in Standard ML. *Technical Report CMU-CS-91-151*, School of Computer Science, Carnegie Mellon University, October 1991.

[Sta92] Stansifer, R. *ML Primer*. Prentice Hall, Englewood Cliffs, NJ, 1992.

[Ste90] Stevens, W. R. *UNIX Network Programming*. Prentice Hall, Englewood Cliffs, NJ, 1990.

[TMC^{+}96] Tarditi, D., G. Morrisett, P. Cheng, C. Stone, R. Harper, and P. Lee. TIL: A type-directed optimizing compiler for ML. In *Proceedings of the SIGPLAN'96 Conference on Programming Language Design and Implementation*, May 1996, pp. 181–192.

[Tof89] Tofte, M. Four lectures on standard ml. *Technical Report ECS-LFCS-89-73*, Laboratory for Foundations of Computer Science, Department of Computer Science, University of Edinburgh, March 1989.

[Ull98] Ullman, J. D. *Elements of ML Programming*. Prentice Hall, Englewood Cliffs, NJ, ML97 edition, 1998.

[UNI90] UNIX System Laboratories, Inc., Englewood Cliffs, NJ. *UNIX System V Release 4 — Programmer's Reference Manual*, 1990.

[Wan80] Wand, M. Continuation-based multiprocessing. In *Conference Record of the 1980 Lisp Conference*, August 1980, pp. 19–28.

[WS83] Wegner, P. and S. A. Smolka. Processes, tasks and monitors: A comparative study of concurrent programming primitives. *IEEE Transactions on Software Engineering*, **9**(4), July 1983, pp. 446–462.

[WF91] Wright, A. and M. Felleisen. A syntactic approach to type soundness. *Technical Report TR91-160*, Department of Computer Science, Rice University, April 1991.

Index

Printed in the United States
By Bookmasters